D1447431

The Rise and Fall of a Frontier Entrepreneur

For Gail
Best Wishes!

Drawing of Benjamin Rathbun (n.d.),
the only visual representation of Rathbun known to exist.
Artist unknown.

The Rise and Fall
of a Frontier Entrepreneur

Benjamin Rathbun, "Master Builder and Architect"

✸

Roger Whitman

Edited by

SCOTT EBERLE *and* DAVID A. GERBER

Syracuse University Press
and
Buffalo and Erie County Historical Society

Copyright © 1996 by Syracuse University Press
Syracuse, New York 13244-5160

All Rights Reserved

First Edition 1996

96 97 98 99 00 01   6 5 4 3 2 1

This book is published with the assistance of a grant from the Terence L. Mills Trust.

The paper used in this publication meets the minimum requirements of American National Standard for Information Sciences—Permanence of Paper for Printed Library Materials, ANSI Z39.48-1984.♾™

Library of Congress Cataloging-in-Publication Data

Whitman, Roger, 1905–1954.
   The rise and fall of a frontier entrepreneur : Benjamin Rathbun, "Master Builder and Architect" / Roger Whitman ; edited by Scott Eberle and David A. Gerber.—1st ed.
     p. cm.
   Includes bibliographical references and index.
   ISBN 0-8156-2694-0 (alk. paper).—ISBN 0-8156-0337-1 (pbk. : alk. paper)
   1. Rathbun, Benjamin, d. 1887. 2. Buffalo (N.Y.)—Biography.
3. Businessmen—New York (State)—Buffalo—Biography.
4. Entrepreneurship—New York (State)—Buffalo—History—19th century. I. Eberle, Scott G., 1952– . II. Gerber, David A., 1944– . III. Title.
F129.B853R389 1996
338′.04′092—dc20
[B]   95-45203

Manufactured in the United States of America

Contents

Illustrations

Benjamin Rathbun   *frontispiece*

DAVID A. GERBER is professor of history at the State University of New York at Buffalo, where he has taught since 1971. His work in American history has included writings on race, ethnicity, religion, disability, and gender. His book *The Making of an American Pluralism: Buffalo, New York, 1825–1869* was the winner of the Herbert Gutman Award for outstanding books in American social history.

SCOTT G. EBERLE, vice president for research and interpretation at the Strong Museum in Rochester, New York, is also the institution's chief historian. His many exhibit projects include *Yesterday's Tomorrow: Buffalo's Pan American Exposition, Small Wonders: A Fantastic Voyage into the Miniature World,* and *Say Ahh: Examining America's Health,* as well as a collaborative exhibit with the Children's Television Workshop. He is coauthor of *Second Looks: A Pictorial History of Buffalo and Erie County.*

Preface

DAVID A. GERBER

During the summer of 1984, while doing research in the Archives at the Buffalo and Erie County Historical Society, I found an entry in the card catalog that struck me as curious. Amid the items that one would have expected to find there—inventories of correspondence—there was noted an unpublished, book-length typescript, which had been given over along with the rights to its publication to the society by its author, a journalist. Bearing the vague title *A Queen's Epic: Benjamin Rathbun and His Times,* referring perhaps to Buffalo's early, unofficial designation as the Queen City of the Great Lakes, the work had languished, for the most part unconsulted and unread, for more than four decades. So I was told by the archival assistant who brought it to me, and who, I think not unintentionally, sought to add the pleasures of discovery to my gathering sense of curiosity by suggesting I would be one of the very few people who knew of its existence.

As I began to read Roger Whitman's carefully typed work of 325 legal-size pages, it struck me at first that it was a small gem, representative of a largely forgotten type of history—nonscholarly in its lack of concern with the historical literature produced by academic professionals, moralistic in tone and purpose, and literary in style. This was historical literature associated most often with leisured men and women of letters who were intelligent chroniclers of significant lives. As an example of this genre, I found Whitman's work at first predictably true to form. It went off in several directions at once, and not always successfully, and it sometimes became immersed in details, without giving the reader the benefit of an explanation as to why most of the detail or any of the directions were significant. Yet it was deeply researched in the right sort of primary sources, well versed in the technical matters vital to the success of its argument (in this case, the intricacies of early nineteenth-century American finance and land development), and as compassionate in its judgments about the people who were its subject as it was astute in attempting to understand the psychological, cultural, and situational sources of their behavior.

As I read further, I gave up the condescending idea that what was before me was nothing more than a quaint "small gem," and concluded that, though the work was often rough, I was in the grip of a first-class historian, whose talents deserved some wider recognition. Slowly the idea emerged in my mind over the next several years, as I worked at completing my own manuscript on antebellum Buffalo, that Whitman's unheralded, lovingly done book should finally see the light of day. Scott Eberle, a friend and coauthor of a book on the history of Buffalo, was then on the staff of the Buffalo and Erie County Historical Society. He read Whitman's work, and shared my enthusiasm as well as my criticisms. Our collaboration was born out of a shared sense that both Whitman and readers of history alike had been done a disservice by the fact that, as a consequence of circumstances beyond anyone's control, this work had never seen the light of day. William Siener, the director of the Buffalo and Erie County Historical Society, has shared this sense with us, and has consistently encouraged us in our labors. Our judgment was also based on confidence in the honesty and integrity of Whitman and the work he produced. Both of us have been immersed in some of the same sources and secondary historical literature as Whitman, and neither of us has ever had any reason to doubt the validity of his scholarship.[1]

1. Although reconstructing Whitman's research would be a protracted process, necessarily incomplete after so many years, and of doubtful assistance ultimately in testing his trustworthiness and his skill as a scholar, it is nonetheless the case that what familiarity we do have with the scope and scale of Whitman's archival, governmental, and secondary sources does go far in establishing reasons for our confidence in him. Such a familiarity is possible to the extent that an extensive collection of Whitman's research notes, bibliographies, newspaper clippings, and letters to relevant archives and governmental agencies are to be found in the Roger Whitman Collection (#B80–10) at the Buffalo and Erie County Historical Society, Nottingham Court, Buffalo, New York 14216. The collection consists of three boxes of materials, two of which comprise files concerning this manuscript, and in particular documenting the history of the Rathbun family in the various locations in Connecticut, New York, and Ohio where it resided, Benjamin Rathbun's business dealings and interests (mercantile, hotel, real

I may only guess at the reasons Roger Whitman did so much research, produced a polished draft of a book, had two copies neatly bound, hired a literary agent, and then abandoned the project short of publication. We do not know much about Roger Whitman, and our attempts to find out more have not been successful. Whatever answers there are to the puzzle of his authorship of this work have to be inferred from the outlines of the sketchy biographic profile we do possess.[2]

Roger Whitman was born in New York City in 1905, but came with his family to live in Niagara Falls, New York, when he was seven. Educated in the local public schools, Whitman then attended the University of Rochester. Soon after graduating in 1928, he began a long association with the *Niagara Falls Gazette,* one of the principal daily newspapers of the small city twenty miles north of Buffalo that is known for its location along the great cataract of the Niagara River. The city is less commonly associated with the gigantic food processing and petrochemical complexes that established themselves at the turn of the century to take advantage of abundant, newly developed hydroelectric power. In the thirteen years Whitman spent at the *Gazette* he served the paper in many different ways, principally reporting and editing. Working on general city news, especially about the diverse and highly developed local economy, he made many contacts in the city and developed a specialty in industrial, commercial, and real estate news that would serve him well in his efforts to write the history of Benjamin Rathbun's protean career as storekeeper, hotel proprietor, building contractor, manufacturer, and land developer in Buffalo and Niagara Falls.

During these years in Niagara Falls Whitman began his dogged pursuit of the elusive character and crowded career of Benjamin Rathbun, to whom he might have been attracted if for no other reason than that he once briefly owned Niagara Falls and many of the

---

estate, and banking), and Benjamin Rathbun's legal problems and trial. There is also much biographic information on Rathbun's Buffalo contemporaries. Unfortunately what the collection lacks is any information that may help us document Roger Whitman's life, beyond, that is, his scholarly concerns. The reader is also invited to consult Whitman's bibliography on pages 225–28.

2. The biographic record consists unfortunately of nothing more than two clippings in the files of the Buffalo and Erie County Historical Society, both of them from the Niagara Falls, New York, *Gazette,* one of them dated April 28, 1942, the other, an obituary from sometime in 1954. All efforts to communicate with surviving relatives of Roger Whitman have proven unavailing.

scenic vistas from which it could best be viewed on the American
side of the international border formed by the Niagara River. One
imagines Whitman inspired perhaps by some bit of oral tradition he
heard by chance from old hands at the *Gazette* about a great tycoon of
a distant time who ended up a jailbird, after having been found guilty
of a number of particularly clumsy forgeries of the signatures of
some of the most prominent local men of the era. It was the sort of
story, of great, lost status and wealth that had powerful resonances
for an alert mind during the Great Depression of the 1930s, when
many entrepreneurial fortunes and reputations were lost. One sees
Whitman, merely at first out of curiosity, consulting what few published sources were available to him, and coming to wonder why so
little had been written about the fallen Rathbun, who came to call
himself in the years just before his fall by the grandiose designation,
"Master Builder and Contractor," (and, sometimes, "Master Builder
and Architect") and was widely revered as such by his contemporaries, in the case of some of them even beyond the time he entered the
gates of Auburn Prison. Probably at that point Whitman became lost
in his subject. Now we may imagine him writing letters to libraries, in
Connecticut, in New York City and upstate New York, and in Toledo,
to track down Rathbun and his family, and spending Saturdays and a
chance weekday opportunity, when on assignment at Buffalo, at the
historical society. He might have haunted the Niagara Falls Public
Library, where he would probably have become well known to the
staff as a busy man of somewhat eccentric interests who made singular
demands on their time.

Just when it was that Whitman finished his research and began to
write his history we cannot know. What seems clear, however, is that
he was well into his research in late April 1942, when he accepted a
position as an information specialist in the wartime Office of Solid
Fuels Coordination, where his talents in gathering facts and putting
them into simple declarative prose could be of use in the marshaling,
distributing, and conservation of coal and other natural resources
vital to the war effort. A draft of the book was finished in the years
just after the war, complete with index, and an agent employed to
find Whitman a publisher. We know only that the book was never
published, and that Whitman presented two copies of the typescript
to the historical society, which eventually obtained the rights to the
work. After the war, Whitman did not return to Niagara Falls or to
journalism, and he moved far, both professionally and geographi-
cally, from the world in which he had once pursued his historical

interests. Much of the last decade of his life was spent working in the New York City headquarters of the Union Carbide Corporation, whose substantial manufacturing presence in Niagara Falls may well have presented Whitman years before with the opportunity to form the contacts that later led to employment. Whitman died an untimely death at forty-nine, in 1954, at Manhasset, Long Island, his postwar home.

Many years now separate Whitman's life and those of the two editors, who were children when he died. He left no clues behind that would help us establish in what form he would have liked this work published. We have not had the benefit of preliminary drafts of Whitman's work that would help us chart his intellectual development, let alone any statements about the origins of his interest in Rathbun or the assumptions that guided his research strategy. We do not know how final a draft Whitman believed he had produced. Without the author's guidance, we have proceeded on our own, walking the ever-so-thin line between loyalty to an author whose intentions and methods we could never truly know and the desire to perfect his work and make it interesting to both professional and lay historians many years after his death.

As our change of the title indicates, we have interpreted our editorial privilege liberally, but we think not irresponsibly. Whitman's original manuscript, which may still be consulted at the Buffalo and Erie County Historical Society, was far too laden with both undigested genealogical and commercial detail and gossip about the extraordinary and ordinary people with whom Rathbun interacted. The unanalyzed material weighted down the manuscript, hiding Whitman's substantial and humane intelligence and discouraging a careful reading. In the interests of narrative continuity and systematic analysis of the major theme, we deleted much less-than-relevant detail. In doing so, in effect, we decisively tipped the balance in the manuscript toward Rathbun, and especially toward the story of his spectacular rise and his even more spectacular fall, and away from "his times," which was the catchall formulation Whitman used to conceptualize the extensive passages that detailed social networks and social circles, personal biographic profiles, landownership patterns, and business deals he seems to have relished describing, even though they were often tangential to where he appeared to desire to end up some pages later.

Furthermore, Whitman did not create footnotes for his manuscript. Preferring an accepted convention of popular history, he instead chose a detailed narrative bibliography. To re-create all his research to produce citations for significant facts and suggestions in the text would have been cumbersome and protracted, so we have decided to present this work as Whitman had it. We have also taken the opportunity, in an occasional note, to explain further, to correct, or to update some fact or suggestion Whitman makes that invites comment. Finally, we have corrected awkward formulations and stylistic infelicities and we have often added the rhetorical signposts and flags that are needed to establish narrative continuity where the author neglected to be as authoritative or confident a guide as he might have been.

The book, however, remains largely Roger Whitman's. The introduction that follows is ours, but its purpose, to place in context why this particularly American narrative of the rise and fall of an ambitious but morally flawed striver continues to be of relevance to us, carries an implicit endorsement of Roger Whitman's genius in seeing the necessity of telling the story of Benjamin Rathbun.

Author's Preface

ROGER WHITMAN

Time has turned the austere flesh and blood of Benjamin Rathbun into a figure of American folklore. The man who, in his heyday, was the greatest businessman west of the Atlantic seaboard has been transformed from "the Girard of the West"[1] into a character vaguely recalled as "The great speculator" or occasionally, "The builder of Buffalo."

Neither sobriquet more than suggests his strange and important part in the financial and speculative orgy of the Jacksonian period, or his crimes, so daring and stupendous that they were unique. They give no hint of that life, which, with its overtones of fate and doom, unfolded like a classical tragedy upon the colorful stage of early western New York State.

A conspiracy of silence, in which Rathbun himself concurred, obscured his role and buried his achievements. The disastrous depression of 1837, to which he contributed a full share, prejudiced judgments enough to make people forget that in his prime Rathbun's name was synonymous with Buffalo, then the greatest port in inland America.

His revolutionary ideas of integrating and consolidating business and his understanding of the value of advertising and publicity made him an anachronism in his day. But whether his career and fate

---

1. Referring to Stephen Girard, the legendary nineteenth-century Philadelphia entrepreneur.

might have been different in a period of more stable financing is an
unanswerable question.

❧

The author is indebted to the untiring encouragement and assistance of his wife, Elizabeth W. Whitman, who herself cheerfully did a
substantial share of the research required in the assembly of this
material. He is grateful also to Mrs. Claude A. Robinson, of Richfield
(Monticello), New York, for the loan of the original records of the
Richfield Baptist Church; to Robert W. Bingham, director, and Miss
Alice J. Pickup, librarian, of the Buffalo Historical Society for suggestions and for help in utilizing the records in that society's possession,
and to Warden J. F. Foster, of Auburn Prison, for finding the original
Rathbun commitment record.

Benjamin Rathbun in His Time and Our Own

SCOTT EBERLE *and* DAVID A. GERBER

Just eight weeks before his death in 1887, in his eighty-second year, Benjamin Rathbun had the opportunity to reflect on the meanings of his life. An acquaintance from the distant past had written Rathbun to solicit memories of the old northwestern frontier, the settlement of which between 1817 and 1840 coincided with the rapid rise and catastrophic fall of Rathbun's own fortunes. However, Rathbun did not elect to take advantage of the occasion. Instead he settled upon a response that offered little foundation, on the face of it, for the inspiration of a future biographer. "I have lived," said Rathbun evasively, "in a very eventful period." Rathbun might have recounted the stories that made his life so remarkable and laden with meaning, but he chose instead formulaic memories from his boyhood of George Washington's death and of his later experiences of early steamboat travel on the Great Lakes.[1]

The evasion, though, was characteristic of Benjamin Rathbun. A studied opacity was the habit of a lifetime.

Fifty years earlier, riding the crest of a giant wave of regional economic growth, Rathbun had called himself the "Master Builder and Architect." The title was grandiose but undeniably well earned—descriptive but unrevealing. Self-promotion was not self-revelation.

---

1. The quotations and factual details in this introduction that are taken from Roger Whitman's text are not footnoted. Noted instead will be the points made in historical and other literature that contextualize, amplify, and reinforce Whitman's own findings and his text.

Rathbun, the highly public figure, deliberately exposed little to the scrutiny of his peers.

From his headquarters at Buffalo, Rathbun joined and encouraged the wild financial and real estate speculation of the 1830s. His contribution was tangible as well. As the "Master Builder and Architect" of many construction projects during the boom, Rathbun had commanded a massive labor force. Where only a few years before log cabins had stood, he had built large commercial, governmental, and private residential structures that set new standards for style and luxury. He had opened well-stocked retail stores and large and, for the day, elegant hotels. He had run stagecoach lines across New York State, and operated Buffalo's first streetcar system. He had acquired the ownership of banks, and established extensive links to the nation's principal financial institutions. For a brief time, too, for all practical purposes, he had under his personal control the American Falls at the great cataracts of the Niagara River, not to mention the destiny of the nearby industrial and tourism city he planned to develop singlehandedly. These protean activities reveal a passion to grow ever more powerful, to shape the present and to control the future.

Rathbun's passion for power and control, however, was made all the more desperate by his inability to raise the capital he needed to sustain and expand his operations. The nation's primitive financial system was not equal to the challenge of Rathbun's vision—or of his cunning. After exhausting all the legal, if crude and ineffective, methods it established for facilitating credit, as his indebtedness grew, Rathbun chose forgery as a device for making his own capital. He stood accused of forging the names of some of Buffalo's most prominent men on his promissory notes. Though a jury and a great many of his contemporaries believed him guilty, there would still be a division of opinion about his culpability even as his obituaries were being printed. In death, as in life, Rathbun attracted much suspicion and much devotion, the devotion perhaps a source of some solace to him as he languished in Auburn State Prison, doing five years at hard labor while in the prime of life.

When Rathbun's enormous regional transportation, real estate, and construction empire collapsed under the accumulated weight of debts, and law enforcement agents initiated the process that sent him to Auburn, the shock waves rocked markets far beyond Buffalo. Wall Street financial houses and a number of banks throughout the North had extensive dealings with Rathbun and with the capitalists whose fortunes were tied directly to him. Rathbun's inability to repay large loans contributed mightily to the sudden and sharp contraction that became known as the Panic of 1837. The long depression that followed was only just receding six years later when Rathbun left prison. His property under the control of others, and his very freedom in jeopardy, Rathbun found himself at the center of the worst financial crisis the young nation had yet to experience. In the minds of many of his contemporaries, Rathbun soon became a symbol, for the better but more often for the worse, of the unsettling social and economic forces unleashed by the capitalist commercial revolution of the early nineteenth century. After the shame and dehumanization of prison, four more decades of life lay before him.

After the remarkable events in Buffalo, and his imprisonment at Auburn, Rathbun had one more brief incarnation as the keeper of a fashionable hotel in New York City. Family tragedy, however, added to more business reversals to fill these years with a sense of protracted calamity. Too weary, or still too guarded, Benjamin Rathbun chose to say nothing more revealing to the voice from the distant past than "I have lived in a very eventful period."

Luckily, Roger Whitman did not accept Rathbun's evasion. Instead, he sought to explain why Rathbun could rise so far out of obscurity and how he could do it so fast. He also detailed Rathbun's meteoric fall from prominence, wealth, and power back into anonymity, insolvency, and disgrace. For Whitman the explanations are mostly general economic ones that highlight the inadequacy of the financial structures of the era, but economic explanations, as Whitman understood, can take us only so far. Hundreds of thousands of men played for high stakes within this structure, but few as effectively and none more catastrophically than Benjamin Rathbun. Whitman embarked, therefore, on an effort, largely implicit and hence not completely satisfactory, to come to terms with Rathbun's character, which mediated the general social influences that worked on him. Psychological explanation threads its way through the narrative. Whitman offers us tantalizing suggestions about the evolution of Benjamin Rathbun from his childhood on a marginal farm in the poor, hilly country of Windham County in northeastern Connecticut to Master Builder and Architect.[2]

To assist the reader, in this introduction we briefly offer three

2. Whitman did not develop the Connecticut context of Benjamin Rathbun's background. The general context may be traced in: Ellen D. Larned, *History of Windham County*, 2 vols. (Worcester, Mass.: the author, 1874–80); Allen B. Lincoln, ed., *A Modern History of Windham, Connecticut: A Windham County Treasure Book*, 2 vols. (Chicago: S. J. Clarke Publishing Company, 1920); Lois Kimball Mathews Rosenberry, *Migrations from*

frames of reference that contextualize Roger Whitman's book: the historiographical, the historical, and the literary.

✐✑◉❙

The period of American history in which Benjamin Rathbun rose to prominence and fell suddenly into disgrace has long had a fascination for social commentators and historians. Between the end of the War of 1812 and the mid-1840s, the United States began to assume the characteristics by which it has been known for most of its history: a highly economically developed, urban, and industrial society, characterized in daily life in the experience of ordinary people by great opportunity alongside broad and abiding inequality. The escalation of social, economic, and cultural change was played out in intense political conflict that gave rise to the first modern political party system in our history. The first mass parties, the Whigs and the Democrats, offered varying symbolic and programmatic responses to the problems caused by intense and rapid change.

Althought most would agree on the general picture, from the beginning of analysis of the era there has been disagreement on the precise significance and meanings of its central trends. Beginning with the extended and astute commentary of the French nobleman Alexis de Tocqueville, nineteenth-century observers fastened on the growth of legal and political rights among the broad masses of white men as the central development of the age. Tocqueville's analysis, from within the very center of the period, was based on a nine-month visit to the United States from May 1831 to February 1832, during which he observed the rise of what he took very likely to be America's central contributions to civilization: mass democracy, which was achieved through the enfranchisement of the masses of white men, and the sovereignty of the people over the government. Tocqueville approved of these trends, which he found to be rooted in the Protestant Reformation and in Puritan society in New England. His approval, however, was mostly relative to the situation in the static, reactionary European regimes of his day. At a deeper level, he feared the cultural implications of mass democracy, which he associated with

---

Connecticut Prior to 1800 (New Haven: Yale Univ. Press, 1934); and Percy Wells Bidwell, "Rural Economy in New England at the Beginning of the Nineteenth Century," *Transactions of the Connecticut Academy of Arts and Sciences*, 20 (Apr. 1916), 338, 352.

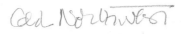
the tyranny of the majority over the individual and with soulless conformity to the values and habits associated with the frantic pursuit of money making. Tocqueville would have found Benjamin Rathbun a representative product of this emergent American civilization—and a warning to it.[3]

Later in the century Frederick Jackson Turner, America's first eminent professional student of its own history, also embraced the Tocquevillian idea of the "Age of the Common Man." However, in two path-breaking early works, a landmark essay, "The Significance of the Frontier in American History" (1893) and a book, *The Rise of the New West* (1906), Turner vigorously parted company with the French observer when it came to finding causes and weighing the significance of developments. For Tocqueville democracy was ultimately constitutional and legal arrangements; for Turner it was an attitude and an ethos, which was not descended from the Puritan-inspired New England town meeting, let alone from Europe. Rather it was rooted in the experience of the European white man's pursuit of free, fertile land and individual self-determination on successive North American frontiers over three centuries. The settlement of the post-War of 1812 frontier was the most dynamic of all, especially in the Old Northwest. Freed finally of the restraints posed by British threats to American security, lacking the obstacle that southern slavery placed in the way of free competition, and containing in its prairie lands some of the world's most fertile soil, the Old Northwest seemed to Turner to breed the very essence of American equalitarianism and democracy.

No more fitting symbol of the spirit of this Age of the Common Man existed for Turner than Andrew Jackson and the rise of the new Democratic party around Jackson's personality, politics, and leadership. Turner associated some of the most significant reforms of the era—for example, the extension of the vote, the abolition of imprisonment for debt, and the liberalization of legislative apportionment —with the ethos of western frontier democracy. Turner admired the Jacksonian political movement, which he saw engaged in a fierce,

3. Alexis de Tocqueville, *Democracy in America*, 2 vols., J. P. Mayer and Max Lerner, eds., George Lawrence, trans. (Garden City, N.Y.: Doubleday, 1966). The influence of Tocqueville is traced in Yehashua Arieli, *Individualism and Nationality in American Ideology* (Cambridge, Mass.: Harvard Univ. Press, 1964). For the contemporary context of Tocqueville's work, see, George W. Pierson, *Tocqueville and Beaumont in America* (New York: Oxford Univ. Press, 1938).

sectional struggle with the conservative, capital-rich East. For Turner a dramatic aspect of this struggle was Jackson's attack on the federally chartered Bank of the United States at Philadelphia, a bastion of eastern interests, and its aristocratic president, Nicholas Biddle, for the tight-money policies that hindered rapid western development. Jackson refused to recharter the bank in 1832. In doing so, he helped loosen national financial restraints, which would be significant in Rathbun's own story.[4]

In the first half of the twentieth century Turner's sectional interpretation of the era would be subject to a withering attack by a small army of historians, who examined his central contentions in microscopic detail. These attacks denied the significance Turner wished to attach to the frontier experience. The frontier was not necessarily a leveling experience, said Turner's critics, because to begin with not everyone had the resources to pursue its bounties. Nor were the Jacksonians simply the western frontier democrats Turner wished to make of them. The Democratic party's constituency proved, on close inspection, a complex coalition of workers, farmers, entrepreneurs, and slaveholders. They were further divided by region as well as by social class and religion. The reforms of the era turned out to have a more complex social and regional provenance than Turner had conceived.[5]

Turner's late-nineteenth-century, postfrontier understanding of the central forces of the era give way to a conceptualization more plausible to those seeking the origins of the urban-industrial society of the early twentieth century. The growth of mass production industries gave rise to bitter, divisive class struggle and occasional armed class warfare, to new radical political formations, such as the Socialist and Communist parties, and to new social movements, such as industrial unions. Millions of previously unorganized mass production

4. Accessible editions of Frederick Jackson Turner's relevant works are: *Rise of the New West, 1819–1829*, 1906 ed. (New York: Harper and Row, 1968); and *The Significance of the Frontier in American History*, Harold Simonson, ed. (New York: Continuum, 1990), which contains the original essay, prepared as a public address and not published in book form until 1920, and other supplementary papers. An astute evaluation of Turner is Richard Hofstadter, *The Progressive Historians: Turner, Beard, Parrington* (New York: Alfred A. Knopf, Inc., 1968), pp. 47–164.

5. Convenient summaries of the voluminous historical literature critical of Turner's "frontier thesis" are: George W. Pierson, "American Historians and the Frontier Thesis in 1941," *Wisconsin Magazine of History*, 26 (Autumn 1942), 36–60, and 26 (Winter 1942), 170–85. Also see Patricia Nelson Limerick, *The Legacy of Conquest: The Unbroken Past of the American West* (New York: Norton, 1987) for a recent post-Turner synthesis.

workers struggled with America's largest corporations. During the Great Depression of the 1930s, these class-conscious unions entered into a social democratic alliance with other radicalized forces, such as significant sectors of American farming, within a reconstituted Democratic party. Under the leadership of Franklin Delano Roosevelt, the Democrats united country and city and the major sections of the country in a new reform coalition.

From the perspective of the era of industrialization, class antagonism, not Turner's sectional conflict, now appeared to move American history. Read back into the early nineteenth century, class antagonism offered a more plausible explanation for the conflict and turmoil that Turner had observed. Those who became known as "progressive historians" proceeded to rewrite the history of the Age of the Common Man. Beginning most prominently with Charles A. Beard, and culminating most extensively with Arthur Schlesinger, Jr.'s *The Age of Jackson* (1945), they wrote ordinary farmers and workers into the Jacksonian narrative at the expense of western frontiersmen. For Schlesinger, the Jacksonian Democratic party drew its energy and direction from a national democratic uprising of these two groups. In coalition farmers and workers struggled against a reactionary national business class that attempted to monopolize power and wealth through control of politics and such financial institutions as the Bank of the United States. Schlesinger's work obviously bore the stamp of his social democratic allegiance to Roosevelt and the New Deal Democratic party. It was no less than an effort to endow that party with a timeless role in defending the interests of the ordinary citizen.[6]

Schlesinger's interpretation, however, proved no less incontestable than Turner's. Most important, it turned out on close inspection that there were ample numbers of entrepreneurial men-on-the-make among the Jacksonians, just as there were among the Whigs, and that much of Jacksonian-era radicalism and the assault itself on the Bank of the United States were orchestrated by businessmen, not by a movement from the bottom of society by workers and farmers. The historical literature of the immediate postwar period that was generated by the critique of Schlesinger suggested that far from there having been a united business class, deep divisions had existed among capitalists and businessmen and those aspiring to achieve their status. A further suggestion seemed inescapable: acquisitiveness and entre-

6. Charles A. Beard, *The Rise of American Civilization*, vol. 1 (New York: MacMillan, 1929); Arthur Schlesinger, Jr., *The Age of Jackson* (Boston: Little, Brown, 1945).

preneurial energy had pervaded American society, crossing the boundaries of political party, region, and social class, and providing the bases of a cultural consensus on the level of values and aspirations that united Americans. Or, so perhaps it was logical to conclude in the political and cultural climate of the United States between 1945 and the mid-1960s, when the influence, authority, and power of American business and finance were at their zenith at home and abroad. It was not difficult to believe that America was and always had been a market-driven business civilization, to the evident satisfaction of its aspiring and prosperous citizens.[7]

However, the debate does not end with the critique of Schlesinger —nor is it possible to imagine it will ever end, given the centrality of the period for understanding the birth of modern America. A recent synthesis of the Jacksonian era, Charles Sellers's *The Market Revolution: Jacksonian America, 1815–1846* (1991), has advanced another, and very different, interpretation of the dynamics of the period. The product of almost three decades of research by one of the most eminent American historians of nineteenth-century politics, this work directly challenges the view that there was a broad consensus within American society on the embrace of capitalism. In fact, Sellers turns that view on its head in advancing the argument that capitalism was imposed on an unwilling, indeed hostile, majority. Sellers's book was conceived amid the intense political conflicts of, and the dramatic revival of radicalism during, the 1960s, which fundamentally redirected the author's conception of America away from the view of a consensually based business civilization that had dominated the historiography of his early years as a scholar. In the 1960s Sellers came to view America as a deeply flawed democracy, conflict-ridden, elite-dominated, and based more on coercion and manipulation than the popular will.[8]

7. Charles Sellers, "Andrew Jackson and the Historians," *Mississippi Valley Historical Review* 44 (March 1958), 615–34; Marvin Myers, *The Jacksonian Persuasion: Politics and Belief* (Stanford: Stanford Univ. Press, 1957); Edward Pessen, *Jacksonian America: Society, Personality, and Politics* (Homewood, Ill. Dorsey Press, 1969). On the "consensus" historiography of the American past in the immediate postwar period, see John Higham, "The Cult of American Consensus: Homogenizing Our History," *Commentary* 17 (Feb. 1959), 93–100, and idem, "Beyond Consensus: The Historian as Moral Critic," *American Historical Review* 67 (Apr. 1962), 609–25.

8. Charles Sellers, *The Market Revolution: Jacksonian America, 1815–1846* (New York: Oxford Univ. Press, 1991, pbk. 1994). For an extended discussion of Sellers's work, see "Forum," *Journal of Policy History* 6, no. 2 (1994), 232–81, in which appear William E. Gienapp, "The Myth of Class in Jacksonian America," 232–59, and idem, "A Historical History," 277–81; Iver Bernstein, "Moral Perspective and the Cycles of

It is worthwhile to review Sellers's understanding of the age, because we find surprisingly significant reflections of his arguments prefigured in Roger Whitman's smaller, localized study.

Sellers proceeds from some basic understandings about the era's dynamics that have long been shared by its interpreters. From the American Revolution to the end of the War of 1812, the infant American republic was a provincial society of vast distances, poor transportation, weak internal markets, and intense localism. After the War of 1812, however, the federal and state governments subsidized improvements in transportation to ensure national security, facilitate the settlement of new western territories, stimulate national cohesiveness, and increase commerce. A result was a rapid expansion in the scope and scale of markets that Sellers appropriately calls a "revolution." This revolution helped give rise to developments that further accelerated its enormous potential to change the world: innovations in business organization intended to enhance the competitive position of firms; laws intended to encourage investment by protecting profit and limiting liability; and efforts to discipline labor to modern production methods and industrial work rhythms to increase productivity, while limiting the growth of wages.[9]

For all the power of these forces liberating entrepreneurial energy, Sellers does not believe that they represented the will of the majority. Rather, combining Turnerian and progressive formulations with recent understanding of social class formation, Sellers locates their origins in the older, eastern seaboard states among an emergent urban, bourgeois class of capitalists and businessmen and their employees and agents. The lives and beliefs of this class and those identifying with it revolved around the values of free competition and individual acquisition appropriate to a market-driven economy. Away from the eastern seaboard, Sellers contends, as the market worked its

Jacksonian History," 260–71; and Herbert Hovencamp, "Comment on Charles Sellers's *The Market Revolution* and William Gienapp's 'The Myth of Class in Jacksonian America'," 272–76.

9. George Rogers Taylor, *The Transportation Revolution, 1815–1860* (New York: Rhinehart, 1951); Carter Goodrich, *Government Promotion of American Canals and Railroads, 1800–1890* (Westport, Conn.: Greenwood Press, 1974); Glenn Porter and Harold C. Livesay, *Merchants and Manufacturers: Studies in the Changing Structure of Nineteenth Century Marketing* (Baltimore: Johns Hopkins Univ. Press, 1971); Thomas C. Cochran, *Frontiers of Change: Early Industrialization in America* (New York: Oxford Univ. Press, 1981); Susan Previant Lee and Peter Passell, *A New Economic View of American History* (New York: W. W. Norton, 1979); Morton Horowitz, *The Transformation of American Law, 1780–1860* (Cambridge: Harvard Univ. Press, 1977).

way inland via the new canals and railways, it encountered a very different, premodern and precapitalist America of subsistence farmers, artisans practicing traditional crafts, and laborers working according to preindustrial rhythms. Their values, says Sellers, were the "enduring human values of family, trust, cooperation, love, and equality."[10] In *The Market Revolution* the central conflict of this time of transformation was between cultural values shaped by the contending social forces of traditionalism and modernization. As Sellers traces the political struggle of the age, Whigs emerge as the servants of capital. Democrats were progressives whose chief flaw lay in their compromise with slavery. Lines of tension between modernity and tradition also appear in a broad range of other institutions and human activities outside politics—from poor relief to sexual relations. In the end, however, in Sellers's telling, the enormous power of capitalism to remake the world in its own image, though holding out the possibility of improvements in the quality of life to the majority, triumphs over the traditionalism of the majority. If Sellers's account at times lacks nuance, romanticizing tradition and demonizing capitalist modernity and the capitalist marketplace, no one has described more dramatically or comprehensively the powerful, ramifying forces liberated by the market revolution nor fathomed how fundamental was their assault on the world inherited from the eighteenth century.

ᘔ☙◖

Where may we locate Roger Whitman among these conflicting interpretations? Where do we find Benjamin Rathbun within this epoch of transformation?

Unlike most historians of the Jacksonian era, Whitman is not much interested in how the era's central forces are reflected in politics

---

10. Sellers, *The Market Revolution*, 6. Some additional works on cultural values, change, and conflict that highlight the modern-premodern dichotomy with reference largely to the first half of the nineteenth century are: James Henretta, "Families and Farms: *Mentalité* in Pre-Industrial America," *William and Mary Quarterly* 25 (Jan. 1978), 3–32; Allan Kulikoff, "The Transition to Capitalism in Rural America," *William and Mary Quarterly* 46 (Jan. 1989), 120–44; Sean Wilentz, *Chants Democratic: New York City and the Rise of the American Working Class, 1788–1850* (New York: Oxford Univ. Press, 1986); Paul E. Johnson, *A Shopkeeper's Millennium: Society and Revivals in Rochester, New York, 1815–1837* (New York: Hill and Wang, 1978); Stuart M. Blumin, *The Emergence of the Middle Class: Social Experience in the American City, 1760–1900* (New York: Cambridge Univ. Press, 1080).

and ideology. In common with Sellers, however, he is very much concerned with the relationship between the market revolution and the fundamental cultural values by which people attempt to give life coherence and stability. This interest, itself perhaps conditioned by pessimistic ruminations on the nature of business civilization from within the depths of the Great Depression, may well have been what quickened Whitman's fascination in postfrontier Buffalo and in the story of Benjamin Rathbun, whose entrepreneurial career personified the emergence of capitalism out of the traditionalist, communal world of the late eighteenth century.

No place seems better than early-nineteenth-century Buffalo, amid this market revolution, to launch such an inquiry into the relationship between economic activity and cultural values. Buffalo stood at the very center of the developments in transportation that were forming a dynamic, national market in the United States. Buffalo's location at the terminus of the Erie Canal and the head of the continuously navigable portion of the Great Lakes enabled it to profit mightily from the expansion of trade. The new capitalist economy, however, was also structurally weak, and Buffalo would lose greatly in all its reversals. Under the impact of the market revolution, Buffalo was for a time the world's busiest grain port. Before the Civil War, Buffalo's economy floated on a sea of grain. Grain produced in the newly settled states of the Old Northwest flowed to Buffalo in many thousands of boatloads. There it was brokered and bought, and transshipped down the Erie Canal to markets in the East. Later, Buffalo's grain became the cheap bread that fed hungry masses in Europe's teeming cities.[11]

The consequences of the 1825 completion of the Erie Canal for Buffalo, which would quickly become known as "the great natural gateway between East and West," were immediate and dramatic. Vessels arriving in Buffalo's harbor increased from 418 in 1826 to 3,955 in 1837. Canal clearances in that same period increased from 1,100 yearly to 4,755. In the first years of the Canal's existence much of this commerce was intrastate connecting the prosperous and productive areas of New York State. However, interstate commerce grew along-

11. Most of the description of Buffalo during the era of its commercial preeminence follows closely the discussion in David A. Gerber, *The Making of an American Pluralism: Buffalo, New York, 1825–1860* (Urbana and Chicago: Univ. of Illinois Press, 1989), 3–39. Other accessible sources are also cited, particularly where they pertain to national, regional, and sectional developments that impacted on Buffalo.

side that within the state, and in doing so sent powerful multiplier effects throughout the entire sectional economy. The Canal's first significant interstate function in this development was to bring west-bound migrants to Buffalo, from which they began journeys to the new states of Ohio, Michigan, and Indiana. Along with them came eastern and European finished goods, 36,000 tons of which were transhipped at Buffalo in 1836 alone. These products assisted western settlers in building homes, making farms, and setting up workshops for themselves.

As western settlers prospered they sent produce, provisions, and (above all else) grain back east. By 1836, Ohio's grain crop exceeded New York State's. New feeder canals tapped the grain-producing hinterlands of these three states and routed crops to Lake Erie ports and hence to Buffalo and the Erie Canal. In 1838, Buffalo's flour and bulk wheat receipts exceeded those of New Orleans, previously the nation's premier western port. As contemporaries themselves recognized, this development marked a historic turning point in the internal affairs of the young nation. Before the Erie Canal opened, northern trade had followed the Ohio River to the Mississippi and then to the ports on the Gulf of Mexico and the Atlantic. The trip from Buffalo to the eastern seaboard, via the Erie Canal and the Hudson River, was shorter, cheaper, and safer. When the Illinois-Michigan Canal opened, it linked Buffalo to the fertile Illinois prairies and secured even more advantage for the northern route. What contemporaries could not appreciate was the role this reorientation of trade would ultimately play in separating the economies, and hence the political interests, of North and South, and in so doing helping accelerate the process by which, over the issue of the expansion of slavery, southern secession and Civil War ultimately would take place.[12]

Nor were contemporaries then in a position to imagine how brief the era of Buffalo's commercial supremacy would be. There was little competition from other routes to the seaboard, such as the one across Pennsylvania, because they were invariably longer, costlier, and usu-

---

12. Gerber, *The Making of an American Pluralism*, 4–6; no author, "The Great Lakes—Their Cities and Trade," *DeBow's Review* 40, New Series 1 (1853), 381–82 (quote); John G. Clark, *The Grain Trade of the Old Northwest* (Urbana: Univ. of Illinois Press, 1966); Ronald E. Shaw, *Erie Water West: A History of the Erie Canal, 1792–1854* (Lexington: Univ. of Kentucky Press, 1966); Taylor, *The Transportation Revolution, 1815–1960*, 162–63.

ally more dangerous. Before the 1850s, no one envisioned the new technology of the railroad ever supplanting the Erie Canal. Indeed most of Buffalo's entrepreneurs and political leaders believed that railroads would be the servants of canals rather than their masters, which was the case by 1860. With millions of dollars of trade and hundreds of thousands of bushels of wheat transshipped to Buffalo by the mid-1830s, it was not implausible to adopt the optimistic view of the city's competitive position and of its future articulated by the editor of the 1836 *Buffalo City Directory*. Buffalo, he said, "has no rival —it can have none—it is the medium through which all others, both East and West, must draw their wealth and resources; and so, far from feeling distrust and jealousy at the prosperity of our neighboring cities, we look upon them as the most efficient auxiliaries of our own. The cities west of us may improve in wealth and importance, but they are our tributaries, their growth, our growth, their greatness, our greatness . . . thus rendering Buffalo that which it may ever claim to be—the GREAT NATIONAL EXCHANGE." Such a state of mind hardly prepared people for the dramatic decline of prosperity that accompanied the Panic of 1837 and the long depression of 1837–43. It did even less to prepare them for the time, in the future, when the even faster and more efficient railroads, capable of sustaining commerce through the rigors of a North American winter, supplanted the waterborne commerce on which Buffalo's dominance depended. As the demographic center of the country moved westward and as railroads spanned vast distances, a new transportation hub, Chicago, would inherit Buffalo's commercial hegemony. On the eve of the Civil War, Buffalo's elite, which had shown little enthusiasm for large investments in industrialization, were left desperately seeking to create an industrial strategy to sustain the city's prosperity.[13]

During the season of its predominance, however, even amid the periodic downturns in the business cycle, Buffalo symbolized for contemporaries the fruits of the market revolution. Its population rose from about 2,500 in 1825 to 8,668 in 1830, and thereafter doubled or nearly doubled every decade, reaching 81,129 by 1860, when it became the nation's tenth largest city. Its boundaries expanded to

13. Gerber, *The Making of an American Pluralism*, 7–10; Directory for the City of Buffalo (Buffalo: n.p., 1836), 8; Clark, *The Grain Trade of the Old Northwest*, 250–83; David M. Ellis, "The Rivalry Between the New York Central and the Erie Canal," *New York History* 29 (July 1948), 268–88; *Buffalo Commercial Advertiser*, Mar. 24, 1860.

encompass its once powerful rival, the village of Black Rock, which had waged a spirited campaign to be the terminus of the Erie Canal. Irish and German immigrants flocked to the city's burgeoning job markets, and filled the neighborhoods emerging out of the marshy, flatlands being annexed to the south and east of the central business district.[14] The first decade of this remarkable growth forms the chronological heart of Whitman's narrative. Whitman vividly captures the buoyant optimism, soaring ambition, foolhardy speculation, and ordinary greed that took root as Buffalo opened to its new possibilities.

Foolhardy speculations and ordinary greed link Roger Whitman to the study of conflicting cultural values during the era, and mark a place for this book as a contribution to the study of the era's central dynamics. Analysis of the habits and values that accompany the boomtown's lust for moneymaking forms the core of Whitman's analysis of Rathbun and his entrepreneurial cohort. The portrait Whitman paints is hardly pretty and rarely fond, but it seems accurate. In its development of the central character, Benjamin Rathbun, it acknowledges complexity and does not want for compassion.

It is difficult to imagine men who more completely personify the culture of the emergent class of postfrontier capitalists than Rathbun and his peers, who seem consumed by the passionate, indeed compulsive, pursuit of wealth and the power to command wealth. In Whitman's telling, this has its positive and negative sides, though these are not always easy to sort out. These men are, as he portrays them, not particularly public minded. To be sure, they hold elective office, but politics and ideology do not seem to overly concern them. The civic projects these men plan are so vast and expensive that they seem less like practical endeavors at improvement than projections of a very large collective ego. Towering war monuments and an instant university, conceived on the models of the English-speaking world's great academic institutions, preoccupy them. Meanwhile the unpaved streets are veritable seas of mud, and there are no sidewalks. There is little evidence of charity among them, though they are quite capable of individual acts of benevolence. ("I have looked in vain for the record of a single charitable association," said the Buffalonian em-

---

14. Gerber, *The Making of an American Pluralism*, 12–21, 47–52, 113–16, 121–235; Laurence A. Glasco, *Ethnicity and Social Structure: Irish, Germans, and Native-Born of Buffalo, New York, 1850–1860* (New York: Arno Press, 1980).

ployed in 1882 to write an anniversary history of the town, as it had been when incorporated fifty years before.)[15]

Above all, it seems to Whitman's mind, is the lack of a deeper human solidarity among them. In the struggle of his life, Rathbun is deserted by his brother Lyman, who flees to Texas where he remains until he dies (never seeing his wife again), and by his most trusted employee, his nephew Rathbun Allen, who flees to New Orleans. Both of them seek to avoid prosecution, and seem content to let Benjamin alone take full responsibility for crimes that appear very likely to have been committed jointly. Even more central to Whitman's story is the suggestion that Rathbun's fellows among Buffalo's commercial elite conspired to get rich by taking advantage of his legal and financial problems and psychological vulnerability to gain control and divide up his immensely valuable assets. They knew well that Rathbun had not been above forging their names on his promissory notes, but then these men, as bankers and money brokers, had charged the credit-starved Rathbun such exorbitant rates of interest that he grew deeply and soon desperately in debt. Evermore intricately together they wove a web of mutual exploitation and greed by which, in the end, they succeeded in trapping not only each other but also, because of their enormous economic power, the ordinary people whose security as citizens and workers depended on them.

Yet in Whitman's story the employees and wage-earners, possess the redeeming, traditional virtues of loyalty, solidarity, and generosity that Sellers argues had been challenged by the new values associated with the capitalist marketplace. There is Henry Hawkins, the brave and elegant former slave, who challenges his master's right to own him, negotiates his emancipation, and buys the freedom of his family out of his wages. Hawkins, who served as maître d'hôtel at the Eagle Tavern, Rathbun's first successful venture in Buffalo, remained Rathbun's trusted employee and loyal friend through good times and bad. He is one of the very few associates from the old days of prosperity who remain faithful to Rathbun in the years after his prison term. Other steady supporters among the artisans worked for Rathbun. Their names are conspicuous among those who help put up bail money when Rathbun and his relatives are taken to jail. Their devotion, surpassed only by the devotion of Alice Rathbun,

15. City of Buffalo, *Semi-Centennial of the City of Buffalo* (Buffalo: n.p., 1882), 39. The author of the statement is not identified.

Benjamin's wife, stands in sharp contrast to the greed of most of Buffalo's entrepreneurs. The smaller canvas painted by Roger Whitman, who was doubtless, during the Great Depression, influenced by the popular criticism of the business system he heard around him and, as a reporter, by his own observations of that system in crisis, could well form a scene in the broad-scale mural painted by Charles Sellers, whose work shows the influences of the radicalism of a later day.

⅌

In the center of Whitman's canvas is the enigmatic Benjamin Rathbun, who emerges both as a historical figure and as a character out of a modern myth. This classic story of ambition gone bad forms the underside of the self-made man narrative. It is not only an American story. As we shall see, Europeans, such as the Norwegian dramatist Henrik Ibsen, have appreciated its narrative power just as much as Americans. However, it has had great attractions for Americans, for the quest for opportunity and the price paid in pursuing it have had special meanings in a society in which inherited wealth and social status have been widely believed to be less a barrier to individual achievement.[16]

The narrative of ambition gone bad is articulated less frequently, publicly, and officially than our comforting rags-to-riches narratives, for it is not a representation of ourselves that does much to create collective pride. Yet it is much more compelling in its multiple powers over our imaginations, and so it enjoys an important place in the popular culture. We are intrigued at the thought of the terrors, the rot, and the self-deception that may lie beneath the glittering surfaces that are the public image of the rich, famous, and powerful. We wonder how close those we imagine to be emboldened by greed, pride, or ruthless ambition come to the very brink of self-destruction, even at the height of their eminence. These imaginings have attractive functions besides their inherent interest as drama. They under-

---

16. The principal studies of the narrative of success, and of its underside, which is always at the least implicit in such discussions, are: John G. Cawelti, *The Apostles of the Self-Made Man* (Chicago: Univ. of Chicago Press, 1965); Irvin G. Wylie, *The Self-Made Man in America: The Myth of Rags to Riches* (New York: Free Press, 1966); Richard M. Huber, *The American Idea of Success* (New York: McGraw-Hill, 1971).

score the importance of straight-and-narrow path morality, and provide us, should we be tempted to stray from that path in the service of our own ambitions, with reasons not to do so. They offer compensations for our own lack of success by providing us with explanations why others do so much better than we do—they lie and cheat.

Rathbun's story contains all the symmetry of the ambition-gone-bad narrative, for simultaneously he embodies the American success ethic and he is an icon of fraud and failure. Knowing of the fraud and failure, we can never see the success ethic in the same way. We are impelled to read all of the story of Rathbun's long climb out of obscurity with the expectation that we will find the clues that explain his sudden and complete fall from prominence.

The familiar elements of the rags-to-riches story and its underside are certainly plentiful in the Rathbun biography, as Whitman presents it. Though he certainly did not wear "rags," and indeed the family prided itself on dressing better than its neighbors, Rathbun's Connecticut origins were humble. When he went west to seek his fortune on successive frontiers, he was armed with little more than was tangible than connections to prosperous relatives who had no special obligations to help him. More significant, it would seem, were Benjamin's own cunning, his ability to impress people and gain their trust, and the thin residue of his family's Calvinistic religious culture, which placed a value on worldly achievements as one possible sign of divine favor. Rathbun overcame hardship, and though rumors would remain, he remade his reputation after an early, highly questionable business failure, from which he had fled to the remote frontier. He pioneered synergistic ways of coordinating large-scale business ventures that were strikingly ahead of his time, but led him into debt and ultimately crime. He grew enormously successful, and became a spokesman for the American bourgeois ethic of individual upward social mobility through hard work, deferred gratification, religious piety, and constant attention to even the most remote details in business. Should anyone forget just what secular altar Rathbun worshiped at, he named his omnibus coaches for the expressive symbols of the class that commanded the market revolution. "Enterprise," "Experiment," and "Encouragement" sped up and down the primitive highways of New York State, their names prominently painted on each coach near the signatured logo of their owner. Yet we cannot help wondering just what it was, if anything, Rathbun *really* believed in. Was he merely a cynical opportunist? Or was he an ordinary man caught up in forces of his own creation that proved ultimately beyond his control?

Roger Whitman appreciates the great suffering caused by Rathbun's crimes, but he never falters in his compassion. He seems to see Rathbun as the sort of tragic, protean bourgeois figure of the type Ibsen created in drama after drama, only to destroy. In plays such as *The Master Builder* (1892), eerily close to Rathbun's preferred professional designation,[17] Ibsen conceived of powerful men bent on controlling the present and achieving a sort of immortality by putting their heroic stamp on the future. Yet their reaching always exceeds their grasp, for they are impaired at the start by a flaw deeply buried in their character and personal history. Whether it is some shameful deed in the distant past, some self-deceptive understanding of their own motives, some foolish, thoughtless pride, or more likely a lethal combination of all three, in the end they are brought down from the heights they seek to occupy and forced to reside in the community of ordinary human beings. With all of their flaws, we nonetheless feel pity for these tragic figures, if only because the self-understanding they finally achieve comes at such bitter and painful cost. In Rathbun,

17. In keeping with our (Ibsenian) conception of Rathbun's character, we have seen Rathbun's professional title as evidence of his tendencies toward a singular combination of formality and self-promotion. Prof. Kathleen Kutolowski (personal communications, February 26, 28, 1995) has suggested another explanation: "Master builder and architect" was a coded Masonic reference, rich in the symbolism of the order, that identified Rathbun for business and social purposes to other members of the secret society. The suggestion has proven tantalizing but unsubstantiable. Rathbun did come from a Connecticut town (Ashford) and county (Windham) that had a strong Masonic presence in the late eighteenth and early nineteenth century; see Dorothy Ann Lipson, *Freemasonry in Federalist Connecticut* (Princeton: Princeton Univ. Press, 1977), 138, 158, 159–62, 203–4, 351–53. Whitman establishes active participation in the order among Rathbun's friends and relatives, as does the roster of the Grand Lodge of New York (personal communication, William D. Moore, director, Chancellor Robert R. Livingston Masonic Library of the Free and Accepted Masons of New York Grand Lodge, March 2, 1995). Yet it has proven impossible to document Rathbun's membership, though it is not at all implausible that a man of Rathbun's ambitions would want his status confirmed by membership in the order, which attracted a particularly prestigious cohort of men at the time. At the same time, the Masons were controversial, as Whitman documents, and Rathbun sought, above all else, to avoid controversy, particularly when he was an innkeeper drawing his clientele from all sectors of society and political opinion. Masonry also took time, and Rathbun, with his complete immersion in business, may not have been willing to give up his time to something for which there was no immediate return. Under any circumstance, it is not clear what we learn about Rathbun, if we could confirm that he was a Mason. The picture Whitman creates would stay the same.

however, we are deprived of evidence of an eventual reconciliation with the self. However, as tragedies accumulate—disgrace, imprisonment, insolvency, violence, his son's insanity, his nephew's suicide— we cannot help feeling he is being punished way out of proportion to his crimes.

Yet if the Rathbuns among us are a problem for themselves, we must not forget the extent to which they remain a problem for us. In an economy with inconsistent and often absent public oversight and a culture that encourages individual initiative and imparts social status to material success, all that seems to preserve the possibility of moral order is the hope that people are what they appear to be—that they can be taken at their word and can be judged by their appearance. It is certain, though, that nothing is easier for the clever and cunning than to develop the *look* of respectability and speak the right lines in social situations that matter.

This was a dilemma that caused much anxiety in Rathbun's own time. A rapidly expanding economy with almost no regulation created tremendous opportunity to use all sorts of tricks and poses to gain opportunity and get rich. Perhaps even more important was the setting of this new economy, America's "infant capitals and embryo cities," as one European traveler described the nation's cities.[18] In these new societies of strangers, in which population might double annually, people washed up from all points of the compass. Some, it is true, followed migration chains that ran from the village they had left to a relative or friend in the city. There were many, however, whose origins were obscure and who became what they strategically represented themselves as being, and ultimately what others took them to be. Rathbun was hardly alone in his ability to mobilize—in dress, public demeanor, formal religious devotion, and speech—the symbols of respectability to create a self-representation that led others to respect and trust him. In this way he largely succeeded in overcoming the rumors about his past, and perhaps also ultimately managed to convince himself that he really was the model of decorum and success he wished others to believe him to be.[19]

18. Tyrone Power, *Impressions of America During the Years 1833, 1834, and 1835,* vol. 1 (London: R. Bentley, 1836), 388–89.

19. Karen Halttunen, *Confidence Men and Painted Women: A Study of Middle Class Culture in America* (New Haven: Yale Univ. Press, 1982); John F. Kasson, *Rudeness and Civility: Manners in Nineteenth Century Urban America* (New York: Hill and Wang, 1990), esp. 70–111.

In the end, however, there seems only Rathbun's gravity, isolation, and self-deception, and his utter ruin, which he accepts with a strange, near-complete resignation, as if he were relieved that at last he had the opportunity to be free of his ambition.

If there is any image that seems to convey the feeling of what it must have been like to be this troubled American man on the make, it is the striking picture that Whitman gives us out of the period just before the fall of Rathbun's empire. Rathbun is in a desperate rush, driven to distraction by the demands of his many projects and of his increasingly suspicious creditors. Riding in a cold coach over tortuous, deeply rutted roads late into the night, he is chilled to the bone, yet trying to write a letter as the coach bumps its way along. The letter is intended as a word of encouragement to his agent, with whom he has schemed to come up with ways to gain time amid mounting debts. Yet the encouragement soon wanes and what is left comes close to despair. "You must," Rathbun writes, "struggle along the best way you can. . . . For one month [it will be] hard every day. It's all hard. Our whole life is hard. Hope we shall have an easier time in the next. There is no back[ing] out of it now. We must go straight through."

The Rise and Fall of a Frontier Entrepreneur

1

Shadows of the Future

In 1790, with the wind of a cold December 1 whistling south from Massachusetts and stirring the snow already on the ground, twenty-year-old Patience Jones Rathbun bore her first child, a son, named Benjamin. The event occurred in the small home near Westford hamlet in northeastern Connecticut where she and her young husband, Moses, had begun housekeeping after they were married ten and one-half months before.

Moses was good looking, impulsive, and intensely ambitious. He was canny in the way of those dependent for a livelihood on the stony soil of hilly Windham County. Moses wanted to please his father, a minister, on whose farm he worked.

The grandfather, sixty-one-year-old Rev. John Rathbun, was an imposing figure in Westford. He owned one of the largest farms and was also pastor of the Baptist Church, which he had founded and had now led for nine years.

There were many earlier, New England Rathbuns (or Rathbone, as the name had been originally). The first immigrant, Richard, had come to Ipswich, Massachusetts, a century and a half before. Piety ran as deep in the family as its American roots. The great-great-grandmother, Mary Weightman Rathbone, was a daughter of the first Baptist minister in Connecticut and a descendant of the last man in England burned at the stake for his religious dissent.

Benjamin spent his early years close to the stern, practical Calvinism of his grandfather. He was surrounded, molded, and hemmed in by scriptural admonition. Somewhere in the Bible, he soon discovered, was a phrase appropriate to any problem, and knowing where that phrase was usually brought victory in arguments with neighbors.

1

Toward his mother Benjamin felt deep affection, but busy with a growing family and a multitude of household chores, Patience could spend little time training her eldest son. Moreover, even though always ready to do what his own father wanted, in his own home Moses dominated his family and he considered the training of his sons his prerogative. Moses instilled in the growing boy the conviction that the way to get ahead in the world was not by physical labor, but by intelligence—and cunning.

Besides his parents and grandparents, many other relatives were at hand, too, for most of the Reverend Rathbun's children had married and remained in Windham County. These early relationships within a large extended family taught the boy the virtue of strong family loyalty.

Neighbors found that Moses had a keen and agile mind and much personal attractiveness. Yet he was ambitious and possessed an evident desire to get far ahead of his neighbors. Moses was convinced that a storekeeper could get ahead fast. His eldest brother, John, had become such a successful trader that within a few years he left for New York City to begin a grocery business with $30,000 capital.

Moses did not drink, smoke, play cards, or dance, in agreement with other Baptists he knew. Yet in an un-Baptist fashion, he insisted that his children always wear clothing that the local farmers reserved for Sunday best. It was probably from his father that Benjamin acquired an interest in using dress to create a personal image that he never lost.

Benjamin was exposed to other influences in those days that helped shape his character. These influences included very probably a few years of basic schooling as well as associations in school and out with other boys. Great ambitions were common in the fiercely democratic Connecticut of the young Republic. Dreaming of becoming governor or president, or at least affluent, was a commonplace fantasy. Young Benjamin also probably listened to the continual discussions of the neighbors and relatives in Windham County who were moving to newly opened lands to the West. Reports came back from migrants, most of whom had gone into New York State, of the fertile, easily tilled, and cheap land in the Mohawk and adjacent valleys of central New York. Opportunities lay ahead. The new settlements lacked general stores, taverns, and inns.

Moses was excited by these reports, but did not wish Benjamin to leave. After his wife's death in 1804, however, the aging patriarch, the Reverend Rathbun, decided that he would sell his farm, give up the ministry, and make his home with his eldest son, John, whose store in New York City had made him wealthy. The Connecticut Rathbun clan was breaking up. Moses and his family moved to New York State in August 1807 to join Moses' brother, David Rathbun, who was then at "Beardsley's settlement" in Otsego County.

Benjamin, meanwhile, prepared for a mercantile career. In 1807, now a handsome young man, courteous, respectful, and vigorous, he went to New York to visit his rich Uncle John, probably to get a job. His uncle had an extensive wholesale business, which supplied retailers all over the new nation. Some of his customers were members of the large extended Rathbone clan, and business and family would be intimately interconnected in both Uncle John's and Benjamin's generations. Like many of the "self-made" men of his time, Benjamin's success was founded firmly on a foundation of family support.

Uncle John must have felt comfortable in sending Benjamin to one link in this family commercial network: the Oxford, New York, Rathbones, who also ran a general store. Benjamin made the nearly two-hundred-mile trip that same fall up the rudimentary tracks that ran northwest toward the back country from the settled lower reaches of the Hudson.

At the age of eighteen in the spring of 1808, Benjamin started a mercantile career as a clerk in a new branch store the Oxford, New York, Rathbone brothers set up in Lisle Township, on the Tioughnioga River, a few miles within the northern part of what is now Broome County. Writing years later of his own youth, Thurlow Weed[1] recalled that the new Rathbone store created great excitement in the neighborhood and that the isolated farmers and their wives got up expeditions, ostensibly to buy supplies, but just as often to learn what was going on in the world. Not the least of the store's attractions, Weed said, was the young Benjamin, whose "fine person and fashionable style of dress were the subject of remark and admiration among his wondering rural customers." Benjamin remained through 1808 and part of 1809 with his cousins.

While Benjamin was beginning his commercial apprenticeship, learning the rudiments of frontier trading and accumulating a little

1. Thurlow Weed (1797–1882), a New York State editor and politician who for many years was the close friend and adviser of William Henry Seward, the important antislavery New York politician who would eventually be a United States senator and Lincoln's secretary of state.

money, Moses was buying land for a homestead for his family. He now had five children besides Benjamin, and was residing at Monticello, the new local name for the hamlet that had originally been named after Obadiah Beardsley, its first settler. Early in 1808, he added a farm of sixty-seven acres. Moses planned to build a general store, near the center of the settlement and next to a tavern, at the spot where rude trails into the country branched off the turnpike to the north and south. Besides the advantages of a promising location, Moses now had personal ties in the district. He was familiar with many of the families, fellow Connecticut migrants, already settled in the area. Yet more of them were already on their way.

Benjamin felt that he had learned enough by the fall of 1809 to leave service with his Rathbone cousins and rejoin his family. He doubtless had managed to save some money and he was assured of a job with his father. Moses was doing very well. He had built up his stock and his store was rapidly outdistancing in popularity his only competitor.

When he rejoined his family, Benjamin was of marriageable age. His inherited good looks, his fastidious dress and speech, his invariable courtesy and gentlemanly demeanor, and his ill-concealed desire to better himself made him a good "catch" in the eyes of the country belles. Benjamin's choice was Alice Loomis, younger of the two daughters of Capt. Thaddeus Loomis and his wife, Thankful Meachum Loomis. Like the Rathbuns, the Loomises had come from Connecticut and from religiously inclined people. They were descendants of an immigrant who settled, like the first Rathbun, at Ipswich, Massachusetts, in the early seventeenth century. The Loomises were among the earliest settlers around Monticello, in Otsego County, coming there shortly after the close of the Revolution, in which Captain Thaddeus had served briefly. Captain Thaddeus was elected a county supervisor to represent the town at the second such election. It is unlikely that Benjamin and Alice were engaged long. Benjamin was too impatient for that, and local customs did not favor long engagements, particularly when the families of the couple had no objections to the marriage. They were married on December 15, 1811, when he was twenty-one and she was not yet nineteen years old. The marriage was performed by the Episcopal minister whose church the Loomises attended and which Benjamin had recently joined.

His son's apostasy irritated Moses, who had been engaged for some time in organizing a Baptist Church, but Moses was too practical a businessman to let his business partnership with his hardworking son be permanently damaged by differences in religion. He may well have found a scriptural passage appropriate to the situation. He and Benjamin together were making an outstanding success of the store.

Benjamin and Alice set up housekeeping in the settlement, and in the first few years of their marriage had a son, whom they named Thaddeus Loomis Rathbun. They wanted more children, but Loomis, as they called him, remained an only child.

In the next few years, Benjamin rapidly amassed money, buying and selling land, building a new general store, and adding a shoe-maker's shop to which the farmers came from miles around to have their boots made and repaired. Moses was closely associated with Benjamin in these transactions, though now as the subordinate rather than as the major partner. Benjamin had matured rapidly; his mind was full of plans and schemes. Moses more and more followed where Benjamin led. To raise money for one of their joint projects, Moses mortgaged some of his property to his twin brother, Aaron, who was then living in Saratoga County.

Much of the detail of what the Rathbuns did at Monticello has been obscured by time. References to their experiences, made a quarter of a century later, indicate that Benjamin and Moses opened, probably in connection with the store, a kind of "exchange office" where the paper bank issues of the time were exchanged with bills, and notes were discounted, much on the order of a bank. These small operations, set up with little capital, were mushrooming throughout the United States because of the chaotic currency situation. Small state-chartered banks printed paper money in huge issues. This swelled the stream of credit flowing from the newly established Second Bank of the United States.[2] The Rathbuns apparently expanded their operations by issuing notes that passed as currency and served as the basis of the credit that they used to buy and sell land.

Outside his business, Moses' chief interest was in the affairs of the

2. The First Bank of the United States was established in 1791 during the Washington administration despite a sharp split in the cabinet between Jefferson, who opposed it, and Hamilton, who was its principal advocate and architect. Its charter was not renewed, however, in 1811 because of partisan wrangling in Congress, discontent with the fact that British capitalists owned two-thirds of the bank stock, and the growth of sentiment among American capitalists and politicians for state banks. The Second Bank of the United States was established by Congress in 1816, largely as an answer to the disruption of the currency created by the War of 1812. Headquartered at Philadelphia, with eventually twenty-five branches around the nation, it proved to be as controversial a financial institution as has existed in American history. Its tight-money policies under director Nicholas Biddle, identification with conservative interests, and weakening of state and local banks led to the failure of its rechartering efforts in 1832.

Baptist Church in which, because he was the most literate member of the congregation, he served as clerk. All the records of the church up to 1815 are in his script. A "close-communion Baptist Church," as Moses euphemistically described it, the congregation spent much time making sure that fellow members kept on straight and narrow paths. Deviation resulted in the offending brother or sister being brought before a covenant meeting to explain the lapse. If the explanation were insufficient, especially in the cases of less consequential members of the group, he or she was excommunicated instantly.

To facilitate their borrowing operations, Moses, Patience, and the youngest children moved in 1815 to Hartwick Township, just to the south, where Moses had access to an entirely new group of farmers. Benjamin took care of the greatly augmented business in Monticello.

Benjamin had had an idea for a long time, and late in 1815 or early in 1816 he put it into effect. He erected on his land on the north side of the highway east of the intersection of the roads the second tavern in Monticello's history. The tavern's style was typical of the time: three stories high, of wooden clapboards, with a long, covered front porch and steep stairs, where wagons and stages could pull up to discharge their passengers without forcing them to step into the mud. Built on the site of the first school in the township, it utilized some of the material from that earlier, now disused, building. The tavern was so well built that it lasted until 1922.

The design of the tavern at Monticello was entirely Benjamin's and marked the beginning of his career as an architect and contractor. He wove into its construction his ideas of what travelers would like and what features might also be useful to the resident community. Though primitive by later standards, it was one of the first inns for the succor of stagecoach passengers that was constructed west of Albany. It incorporated some innovations that would be utilized by other builders along the main lines of travel in coming decades. Fifty feet long and twenty-five feet deep, its first floor included a large sitting room-dining room, a parlor for ladies, and a bar for men. The second floor held sleeping rooms. In a pinch the large meeting room on the third floor could be used as a men's dormitory.

Stages jerked and rolled tediously on the busy but poorly maintained Great Western Turnpike. They needed such a stopping point. Jacob Brewster's, diagonally across the road, was thoroughly unsatisfactory. Brewster was one of the "big" men of Monticello. He owned much land, a sawmill, and a blacksmith shop. But, as church records reveal, Brewster was also a drunken, blaspheming, and lecherous rascal who kept such an inhospitable house that travelers disliked stopping there. His moral career is testimony to the raw life of the frontier settlement.

Benjamin was an important member of the Baptist Church and often named to committees that were sent to bring erring brothers and sisters back on the path of righteousness. Brewster was formally charged by James N. Graves, the church's presiding deacon, with "disorderly walk," and specifically, in the singular spelling of the church record, with "intemperance and imoral Conduct towards Sertain littel girls & lude Conduct and Conversation with other women than his wife."

The church was consumed by the testimony; several special meetings examined Brewster's case in every detail. In summary, the record states: "That Jacob Brewster has been guilty of intoxication, of liued conduct with women, by offering a half a dollar [to one] to put his hand into the bosom and a dollar for the privilige of putting his hand into the bed, to another, and said [for saying that] there was no hurt to be with other women than his wife. It likewise appears that he had been guiltey of leued conduct with certain little girls, by putting his hand under their cloths, and putting their hands into his britches; this was done two days successively, and lastly that he showed his privates to some young women intentionally."

The hand of fellowship was thereupon withdrawn from Brewster, though in a year, needing his tavern for business meetings of the church, he was readmitted to the Christian company. The pages of the record containing the testimony against him were sealed shut against prying eyes with dabs of sealing wax.

Rathbun's tavern was a sharp contrast in every way to Brewster's, just as Rathbun himself was different from the scandalous, roistering Brewster. Boasting of the best service and accommodations in the area, it was clean, up to date, and respectable. It was "really a model and the admiration of travelers," one of his friends of later years wrote. "It was much in advance, in appearance and in general accommodations, over the other public houses of the country.

Benjamin obtained agreements that made his tavern the stopping point for most of the regular stagecoach operations, and he soon secured the bulk of the respectable bar trade for many miles around. Successful stage houses along the main arteries of travel were frequently the road to instant wealth, and Benjamin could certainly hope for prosperity in the situation.

Rathbun's experience in this tavern, his contacts with stagecoach operators, and his mercantile, land, and "banking" business gave him a grounding in practical finance, as it was practiced in the Western settlements at that time, that he never forgot. These years taught him something about risk, too.

There were rumors many years later to what happened to the Rathbun enterprises in 1817, although all detail of what occurred has been lost. Benjamin and Moses must have far overextended their credit and they went bankrupt suddenly. Their failure, to look at it charitably, may have been due to the financial contraction that began that year. Waves of bankruptcies left fortunes wrecked in their wake and caused suffering throughout the West. Failure in itself was not particularly uncommon nor was it necessarily permanently harmful to the reputations of the persons concerned, although it was still possible under certain circumstances to go to jail for unpaid debts. Nevertheless, at least to escape the wrath of their neighbors—and perhaps to avoid prosecution—the Rathbuns and their families felt it necessary to flee.

No indictments were forthcoming, but the memory of this failure lingered. Many years afterward, enemies in Buffalo charged that the Rathbuns' failure was a result of forgery, and that $12,000 was involved. In Monticello, where their rise had been spectacular, they certainly left behind embittered neighbors and the wreckage of high hopes. The tavern, the popular spot for communal socializing that Benjamin had built so well, outlasted nearly every other contemporary structure in that area of Otsego County and indeed almost outlived the hamlet of Monticello. The Rathbuns survived as a family, too, even though Alice's relatives urged her to leave one so "bankrupt in property and character."

Moses and Patience, together with their unmarried children and their married daughters and families, hurriedly left Otsego and moved 160 miles westward to Batavia. The Holland Land Company, which owned most of the state west of the Genesee River, had headquarters there.[3] Many Rathbun relatives had already settled nearby. Benjamin may have taken his wife and son to Batavia. If he did, it

---

3. Organized by a group of Dutch capitalists, the Holland Land Company had purchased most of western New York State from Philadelphia politician and land speculator Robert Morris. The purchase, completed during 1792–93, helped greatly to advance the settlement of the region, which was surveyed under the direction of the company and opened to migrants in 1796. In actuality, only after 1800 did the first sizeable parties of settlers begin to appear in western New York.

was not for long. Rathbun's sights were set beyond Batavia—and, if rumor were true, he had good reason to want to be outside the state.

Benjamin took his little family by stage forty miles farther westward to Buffalo, the last way station on the route to the Far West— the lower Great Lakes country. From there, by sailing vessel, they went to the Maumee in Ohio. This was the name by which the whole valley of the Miami, including the site of the present Toledo, was then known.

Rathbun could not have known much about the Ohio country: few did at that time. Land speculators were just discovering and publicizing its great promise through newspapers and posters in eastern cities. Advertisements detailed the great opportunities in the unsettled worlds up the lakes. Rathbun himself was now too experienced to be deceived by the feverish advertising. Good judgment made him one of the first settlers in the already planned area that lay within the boundaries of the city of Toledo.

By a legislative act of 1816, Congress authorized the sale of a military reservation of twelve square miles at the foot of the Maumee River rapids. The Port Lawrence Company bought part of this reservation and began to lay out a village and sell lots—the usual real estate promotion development of the period. Rathbun bought one of the first of these lots, probably planning to erect a store and perhaps a tavern on the site.

Years later, writing to a friend of earlier days, Rathbun sketched the story of his life in Toledo, his memories forming one of the few written accounts historians have of that city's beginnings.

The Rathbuns arrived in the spring of 1818. Not a single house stood on the site of Toledo. The only shelter, Rathbun later wrote, was a crude caging on the flat not far from what was then called Swan Creek, and nearby that was a two-story log warehouse. The Rathbuns shared this warehouse with Maj. Coleman I. Keller, his wife Amelia, and their family. The Kellers are remembered as one of Toledo's founding families.

Financial loss soon added to the discomfort of the primitive conditions, swamps, and heat. The Port Lawrence Company was unable to complete its agreed deferred payments to the federal government for the land. Before the summer was over, it had to turn part of its holdings, including the lot Rathbun had paid for with the little money he had salvaged from his Monticello fiasco, back to the government.

Like Keller, others would eventually profit. But Rathbun, his finances close to exhaustion, could not wait, and moved his family out of the area in August of 1818. They appear to have retreated along Lake Erie to the east, this time to try their luck in the new "City of Sandusky." Speculators were busy there too. An advertisement signed by a Connecticut promoter and published in western New York newspapers, had this to proclaim in heavy black type of the then almost uninhabited "city": "The best harbor on the south shore of Lake Erie; fine country; a fine location exceeded only by New Orleans for trade."

While the Rathbuns were at Sandusky, they were among the handful of spectators who assembled on the shore to see a novel sight —the first visit of the first steamboat on the Great Lakes. This boat, the paddle wheel brig *Walk-in-Water,* built in Buffalo by New York and Albany capitalists, left the Niagara River on its maiden trip on August 25, 1818, and reached Detroit in forty-four hours running time, going at the amazing speed of seven and one-half miles per hour. Belching smoke from the softwood, pine, and hemlock used to fire its boilers, a band playing on its deck as it made stops at Erie, Grand River, Cleveland, and Sandusky, it was the wonder of the age.

This maiden voyage augured well for the prosperity of the then still isolated Lake Erie settlements. But Rathbun's situation was now worse than it had been in Toledo. Sickly and virtually destitute, the Rathbuns were said later to have left Sandusky in the spring of 1819 carrying "the whole wardrobe of the household on their backs."

After the ice was out of the lakes and the boats were running again, Rathbun managed to get his family on board a vessel, backtrack down Lake Erie to Buffalo, and then rejoin his father and mother in Batavia. The danger of prosecution in New York had apparently passed. Perhaps, as was suggested later, kinfolk had "fixed" the complaints in Otsego County.

The return to Batavia was simply an expedient dictated by the necessity of obtaining temporary shelter for his wife and child, and a base from which he could find a place to begin life afresh. Rathbun certainly was too experienced now to settle anywhere except in a place with a definitely assured future. He was going to be certain this time; adversity had convinced him that he could not afford another folly like the Ohio venture.

He apparently stayed in Batavia only long enough to cultivate the friendship of several successful businessmen. Benjamin already had schemes for the future in which men with money would have a part. One of those he became acquainted with was James Brisbane, protegé of the aged Joseph Ellicott, head agent of the Holland Land Company, which years before had opened western New York to settlement. Brisbane, the leading Batavia merchant, was about to give up his store because he had found that he could make money faster by buying and selling choice land. Another was chubby, black-haired David E. Evans, nephew of Ellicott and state senator of Genesee County. He was dabbling in various investments while waiting to inherit his uncle's fortune. Ellicott was letting his nephew and others do more and more of the work as his long reign over western New York's landed interests was inevitably nearing its end. Rathbun liked the genial Evans, though he little guessed how disastrous the acquaintance would prove to be. Although these contacts would be useful in the immediate future, it is improbable that Rathbun obtained any substantial financial aid in Batavia. Without resources, Rathbun left Batavia armed only with his own self-assurance and the conviction that he could out-argue most of his associates. He headed west again.

Hardly stopping at Buffalo, which he knew from his previous observations had a reasonably assured future as a transportation center, he went northward by stage to the scenic hamlet of Niagara Falls, then hopefully called "Manchester" after the English industrial city made rich by waterpower.

Rathbun stayed there only a few days, but long enough to conclude that this would be an ideal spot for a tavern. Although the fame of the great cataracts was attracting more visitors every year, there were no public houses worthy of respectable patrons. On the American side a twenty-four-foot square log "tavern and boarding house" kept by Parkhurst Whitney was the principal hotel; on the Canadian side there was a similarly modest place for travelers. Rathbun was sure that with a little money and imagination a man could make a fortune in short order by conducting an attractive, up-to-date tavern.

He canvased the few in Manchester who might have the money to finance his start: Samuel DeVeaux, a shrewd trader and merchant, and Augustus Porter, business administrator of the firm of Porter, Barton and Company, which held a thirteen-year concession from the state to control the portage where goods were freighted overland seven and a half miles around the cataracts. But Rathbun's efforts were in vain. DeVeaux, holding tight to the fortune he was beginning to amass, was interested but flatly refused, and Porter, already committed to help Whitney enlarge his tavern, and embarrassed for cash by the recent suspension of the Bank of Niagara at Buffalo, also declined to help. Never one to cling to a hopeless cause, Rathbun left Niagara and went back to Buffalo.

Rathbun was sure from what he had seen and heard that there

would be no mistake in settling in Buffalo. He thus felt secure in acting on an opportunity about which he had known for some time.

An advertisement had been running intermittently since April in the *Niagara Journal:* "For sale or to let that large and commodious Brick House situated near the center of the village of Buffalo and lately occupied by Mr. Gaius Kibbe as a tavern. E. F. Norton."

Rathbun went to Norton, a struggling lawyer turning his hand to anything that promised a profit, and effected an agreement with him to lease the tavern and its furniture. Undoubtedly the terms were modest; Rathbun had no money. Moreover, the future looked uncertain. The contraction of credit that began after the War of 1812 was continuing. Prices fell to as little as one-third their postwar high points.

In the trough of a depression, Rathbun nonetheless was determined to rebuild his fortune.

2

Buffalo's Eagle Tavern

Kibbe's Tavern, or Norton's Tavern as it had also and briefly been
known, was a flat, square, three-story structure built of the red bricks
burned from the clay common in the area. It faced east on the muddy
and rutted Main Street between Court and Eagle streets. Diagonally
opposite across an unkempt plaza (later the ornate Lafayette Square)
stood the county's unfinished brick courthouse, looking directly down
Court Street toward what was later called Niagara Square. Kibbe's
Tavern was one of the few substantial buildings in the motley config-
uration of houses, stores, stables, pigpens, cow barns, chicken coops,
open sewers, and outhouses that made up the village of Buffalo. It
is difficult to imagine a more primitive town that still laid claim to
civilization. Brooks flowed through and across main streets; gullies
and ravines cut the higher sections; swampy places near the shore
offered hazards to the unwary. Irregular heaps of partly burned logs
and unoccupied lots were continuing reminders that the British had
destroyed all but two buildings when they devastated the entire border land along the Niagara River six years before.

Yet the settlers' shoddy touch could not detract fully from the
village's natural beauty. The site, which Joseph Ellicott had carefully
mapped out partly on a bluff or terrace fifty feet above the junction
of Lake Erie and the Niagara River, and partly on low ground, had a
kind of grandeur. Ellicott's village plan, in fact, had been influenced
by his brother Andrew who, as United States surveyor general, laid
out Washington, D.C. The diagonal, radiating avenues and broad
plazas on the map of Buffalo were reflections of the grandiose plan
for the Federal City on the Potomac.

South of Rathbun's new tavern, at the foot of Main Street, the meandering, silt-filled Buffalo Creek flowed sluggishly into the lake, forming the village's only protected harbor. Passengers and freight had to be lightered to the vessels standing in the lake off the river's mouth.

The tavern was strategically located from the standpoint of traffic. Past it moved stages, horsemen, bullock carts, and the huge, canvas-topped freight wagons pulled by as many as nine horses. Main Street ran north from the tavern, then, curving eastward, became the principal turnpike road to Williamsville hamlet, Batavia, and central New York. The newer Batavia Road (now Broadway Avenue) reached the village at one side of the courthouse and opposite Rathbun's tavern. Court Street provided ready access westward to the Black Rock Road (now Niagara Street), which ran to that downriver port where Porter, Barton and Company's goods, poled upriver from the Niagara Falls region in flatboats, were loaded on lake ships. From the village of Black Rock, just north of Buffalo, the road continued on to the Falls, or if travelers wished to cross the river to Canada, a ferry maintained regular service at the Rock.

Both inside and outside, the tavern was shabby, but Rathbun had no money for renovation. He had to do the refurbishing himself or arrange when he could for artisans to barter their work for tavern services.

With vigor that belied his spare frame, Rathbun threw all his energy into making the tavern a success. His wife, equally strong, did her part in overseeing the housekeeping arrangements. Neither, at any period in their lives, spared effort when it was needed to gain the goals Rathbun had set.

Then and later Rathbun presented an imperturbable and attractive countenance to the public. His calm and confident air helped resolve endless emergencies. What people recalled most about him was his unreadable expression, which concealed the busy, focused mind behind it. Almost devoid of humor, Rathbun never joked and rarely smiled except in greeting. Naturally economical in conversation, he had a ready flow of language when he wanted to convince someone. Adversity had sharpened his natural shrewdness. A calculating imagination kept the end of the game always in sight. He was planning the last move from the very opening gambit. Some intuition made him know what people would like before they knew it themselves. He invested his services with a solicitous quality that convinced his patrons that he was giving them more than they expected. Also,

Rathbun was something of a showman, constantly evolving ideas to keep himself and his tavern in the public eye without seeming to do so.

Pure chance brought him an unexpected windfall of business very shortly after he took over the tavern, and gave him the opportunity to impress more potential patrons. This was one of those rare and gruesome entertainments, a public hanging, held so near the tavern that the writhings of the unfortunate victim could be seen from its upper windows. Nearly everyone in Buffalo that December and many from rural areas assembled to see a soldier swing from the gallows, the second civil execution in the town's history. The tavern bar was crowded that day, countryman and villager uniting in washing down memories of the excitement. Rathbun was everywhere, making these guests at home, trying to impress them enough to encourage their return.

After he took over the establishment, which was popularly known as "Rathbun's Tavern," he gave it a more formal name, "The Eagle Tavern," appropriate because of its proximity to Eagle Street, and a patriotic gesture as well. A little later he erected a golden eagle, with outstretched wings, standing on a gilded glove as a signboard for the prominent space over the center door. (See illustrations 1 and 4).

Rathbun worked hard at being the genial, attentive host. He improved and established definite standards of service; he freshened the sleeping accommodations and made them more comfortable; he added a bit here, a bit there as experience dictated and his pocket-book permitted, to improve the tavern's operation. He was on the job night and day, working, overseeing, lending a hand whenever the work was beyond the capacity of his limited staff. These changes, the new name, and the calm graciousness Rathbun displayed as host rapidly transformed the second-rate Eagle into a first class tavern. It surpassed in a year or two the popularity of Joseph Landon's Stage House, which, until then, had been the best Buffalo had to offer. Thereafter, consciously or unconsciously, Buffalo residents and visitors began to consider the Eagle the best hotel in the settlement, even amid a good growth in lodging houses with taprooms in the next few years. Rathbun deliberately catered in the Eagle to the better class of trade, both local and transient. Reasonably gentlemanly conduct was required of guests, especially in the bar.

In a comparatively short time after he took over the tavern, the depressing effects of the money shortage began to wear off and people spent more freely. Commercial travel, chiefly of eastern manufacturers' agents and fur buyers, had been increasing for years. Agents of John Jacob Astor, who was doing much of his fur buying on the Niagara Frontier at that time, stayed in Buffalo while awaiting the arrival of cargoes or arranging purchases with traders dealing directly with the hunters and Indians who supplied pelts.

Moreover, demands for accommodation for discriminating tourists were also increasing sharply. The fame of Niagara Falls, considered by many the greatest natural spectacle in the Western Hemisphere, had spread everywhere. More and more were making the "fashionable tour": a trip to Niagara Falls, Montreal and Quebec, and Saratoga Springs. Hundreds were coming yearly now by stage from Albany to Buffalo, and then on to the Falls. The well-publicized "tour" usually took them back east by way of Lewiston, the village at the north end of the portage on the lower Niagara below the cataracts, by Lake Ontario steamboat to Sacket's Harbor, and then to Canada. Saratoga was on the last leg homeward to the populous eastern seaboard. As Rathbun improved his tavern, its reputation spread, and soon it was mentioned in the "tour's" guidebooks and by word of mouth among travelers from distant places.

Because Rathbun only rented the building, he was aware that Norton might sell the Eagle at the first opportunity, and he would then lose his hard-won success. Rathbun must have worked hard to find a person willing to buy the building as an investment. Undoubtedly he communicated with his Uncle John in New York, and possibly with John's son, John Rathbone, Jr., who was engaged in high financing operations on various lands in New York State and Ohio and served on the boards of several New York City banks.

Although his New York City relations did not undertake the transaction, they may have helped Rathbun find some potential investors, for early in 1822 Norton sold the tavern for $10,000 to investors from New York City. With them, Rathbun immediately effected a lease to perpetuate his control of the Eagle. Then he dared to begin improving the structure itself.

Leaving the Main Street front unchanged, he added greatly to the building to accommodate its increased patronage. He built an addition, nearly duplicating the dimensions of the original building, behind the old tavern, and he connected to it by a short wing. Then another wing was added to the rear of the new structure. The whole came to comprise a long, rambling building, running more than halfway through the lot toward Pearl Street.

He then got the right to use the property adjoining the tavern on the south. He erected big sheds and barns at the rear forming a large unpaved yard beside the Eagle, which became a stage terminal. This area provided a convenient unloading place for passengers arriving by stagecoach or on horseback. Tight against the south wall of the Eagle and connected to it by an inside door, he built a small boxlike structure, which for all of Buffalo became the "Stage Office." The stage business, the great passenger transportation medium of the time, was one in which Rathbun dabbled to ensure his tavern a steady source of patrons. Bela D. Coe, who was by that time the most significant force in this business in Buffalo, had his own barns adjacent to the Eagle's stage yard.

In the first five years after Rathbun came to Buffalo, the town was incorporated and became the seat of a new county, Erie, carved out of the enormous Niagara County. The population of Buffalo had more than doubled. Business was really beginning to prosper, and more and more buildings were being erected. The additions to the Eagle were keeping pace with the growth and needs of the village.

Rathbun's success revived his self-confidence. His ideas began expanding as his horizons widened. In Buffalo he was dealing with men like himself: men on the make, of equally obscure origins and checkered pasts, who were interested only in the present and the future. They had come west on the gamble that land values would rise and that business opportunities would expand. When Rathbun arrived most of the fewer than one thousand persons in the village were relatively young newcomers with few possessions. Many were adventurers who stopped awhile and then moved on; others, who had planned to stay only long enough to make some money, married and settled permanently, and became the city's founding fathers.

As the tavern and village prospered, Rathbun diversified his business interests. One of his first projects was to erect stores on the vacant lot that adjoined the tavern to the north. The space above the stores would supplement the Eagle's capacity and the stores would bring people near the Eagle and its taproom. New commercial space was sorely needed.

William Kibbe still owned the half acre of good, reasonably level land that Rathbun wanted to use. Kibbe was not attracted to Rathbun's idea of financing a new building and countered with an offer to sell. Having foreseen that possibility, Rathbun had an alternative plan. He approached tall, dignified Philander Bennett and his law partner, Henry White, with a proposal that they buy the lot and put up the money for a building. Bennett was a successful merchant who had recently been admitted to the bar. Rathbun's persuasive arguments, together with the assurance that Bennett and White could have a new and centrally located office, convinced them, and they enlisted the support of two physicians to join in buying the lot on shares and paying for the construction. The additional partners were Dr. Benjamin C. Congdon, who had been a partner of Dr. Cyrenus Chapin in his drugstore and healing business, and Dr. Henry R. Stagg, a young physician who later married a daughter of Samuel Wilkeson, the town's most articulate booster and an early mayor and entrepreneur.

With the assistance of these partners, Rathbun designed and erected a long, two-story building, called the "Eagle Building," on the corner of Court Street. The first floor split into six separate stores. People thought of the "Eagle Block" as Rathbun's even though he did not own the land. Architecture contributed to the impression, for the newer buildings matched the tavern. A railing with heavy posts decorated the flat roof facing Main Street, corresponding to the smaller railing along the roof of the tavern. The second floor connected with the tavern's second floor making additional sleeping quarters. A few front rooms, however, were reserved for offices, and Bennett and White moved into the one nearest the tavern as soon as it was completed. The stores soon were rented.

The tavern, the stage yard, and the stores were now a unit, one of the most imposing structures and by far the largest single establishment in the village.

Some enterprising person started the first Buffalo theater in 1821 in a Main Street building opposite the Eagle, but poor actors and bad scenery kept it from prospering. Rathbun watched this process, doubtless with disappointment, for a successful theater might have brought business to the Eagle. But the failure gave Rathbun an idea. He arranged with traveling acts and menageries to hold their shows in the Eagle's own stage yard. One of these featured an elephant, a lion, a camel, and other exotic novelties. These shows attracted large crowds, which slaked their thirst at the Eagle.

Rathbun's promotions accomplished their purpose. By 1826, the Eagle was host to every community gathering of any consequence. Here the Erie County Medical Society assembled; the sheriff auctioned foreclosed properties; private schools held their graduation exercises; and civic meetings convened.

With its central location and conviviality, the Eagle Tavern soon became the logical place for consummating business deals and talking politics—*the* ideal place to take the political pulse of Buffalo. Bitter political arguments regularly broke out in the taproom. Politics in the 1820s was unsettled. Since the disintegration of the Federalist party, which had had the support of most western New Yorkers, there was only one regional party, the Republican. Voters National were prone to follow personalities more than partisan labels. Henry Clay was a favorite in Buffalo, because the Kentuckian wanted to use federal monies to develop better roads and harbors and improve navigable waters in the interior of the country. But John Quincy Adams also had his supporters, as did the charismatic military hero, Andrew Jackson. Jackson's partisans were an argumentative and assertive group often led by the great hulking braggart, Alanson Palmer, one of the town's truly notable characters and an Eagle habitué. A land speculator who lavishly spent his wife's inheritance, Palmer sported expensive jewelry and colorful clothing, including a silk shirt with a large embroidered image of Jackson himself on the chest. No one could have been more different in personal style from Rathbun, but in the end their individual fates were more similar than not.

Rathbun himself carefully avoided entanglement in a polemics that provided the chief political conversation of the period. It is in a tavern keeper's interest to prolong the conversation, but not to antagonize the guests. So Benjamin worked at providing a comfortable atmosphere, kept his own counsel, and pleaded the press of business when patrons sought his opinions. When he did express himself, Rathbun spoke for both the development of the town and the Niagara Frontier and the prosperity of the major landed interests.

Rathbun seized civic celebrations as opportunities to bring the tavern to public notice all over the western country. Often he accomplished this with the help of cooperative newspaper editors he courted with standing offers of the tavern's hospitality. Fourth of July 1826 marked the fiftieth birthday of the Declaration of Independence. Buffalo's celebrations were anticipated widely, and Benjamin was in the middle of the day's events. The town's parade began and ended at the Eagle Tavern, where a banquet attended by the leading citizens was held. The dinner was "served in the well known style of Mr. Rathbun," wrote the editor of the *Buffalo Patriot,* and a very merry evening was enjoyed by the increasingly inebriated assemblage. Many toasts were offered to all the dignitaries of state and nation as well as to a few local celebrities. A Mr. Bull, perhaps the jeweler whose store was down the street, led the assemblage in emptying its glasses in this choice bit of doggerel addressed to "Our Distinguished Citizen and host, the Keeper of the Eagle Tavern, Benjamin Rathbun, Esq.":

> The Head which so admirable contrives
> The heart which so readily indicates,
> The hand which so rapidly executes,
> Shall never want means to accomplish.

Rathbun must have received this confirmation of his growing reputation as an entrepreneur modestly and graciously. He never displayed any of the exaggerated self-importance of some of his successful contemporaries. He kept his manners and wits about him. Unlike most of his patrons, he never drank. He would lift a glass to his lips when a toast was called, but put it down untouched. This eccentricity in a day of almost universal male tippling may well have added to his stature in the eyes of some of his associates, for it appeared the sign of an unusually firm will.

Rathbun was able to take part in many of these affairs at the Eagle because he had assembled and trained a staff to relieve him of most of the onerous work of the tavern. By February 1820, Rathbun had brought his younger brother, Lyman, then in his twenty-first year, to Buffalo to help him. Lyman, dark-haired, and shorter than Benjamin, had a perpetually flushed face and a share of the family shrewdness. He was hotter tempered, more spontaneous and sociable, and, in the sharpest apparent contrast, a flamboyant dresser.

Lyman was particularly adept at handling calculations, which had always been one of Benjamin's weakest points. Benjamin hated the dull work of adding, subtracting, and totaling; he liked to toy with ideas, convince others that the ideas were sound, and then make the same ideas work. He was glad to entrust much of the tavern's bookkeeping and other financial details to Lyman, while he himself exercised occasional oversight and at times made out the bills. Because they often dealt with Lyman, guests at the tavern assumed, probably erroneously, that Lyman alone handled the money.

A year or two after he took over the Eagle, Benjamin had a stroke of luck in another selection. He gave the job of maître d'hôtel to Henry Hawkins, a twenty-six-year-old former slave, who proudly told his friends that he bore in his veins the blood of Sir Henry Hawkins, the Elizabethan scourge of the Spanish Main. Though unlettered, Hawkins was both courageous and bright. Born into bondage in

Maryland, he accompanied his master on a trip to Canandaigua and then announced his refusal to return to a slave state.

Hawkins had a streak of loyalty, however, that set him apart and probably helped recommend him to Rathbun. The story of his freedom proved this. His master had not wanted to free him, and the master's wife, who was ill, would not go south unless Hawkins drove the family carriage. The master thereupon gave his word to Hawkins that if he would drive them to their destination, he would not compel him to stay. Trusting this assurance of a gentleman, Hawkins made the trip knowing that the master could legally break his word. Upon their arrival, the family bade Hawkins farewell, and he returned to Buffalo a free man.

Rathbun quickly recognized Hawkins's great abilities, and promoted him to steward. Hawkins's skilled hand helped give the Eagle that refined touch that distinguished it from most frontier taverns of the day. As Buffalo's social life began to develop, Rathbun ingratiated himself with affluent and influential women by allowing Hawkins to cater their private parties.

As the years went on, Hawkins married and raised a family in Buffalo. He also expended most of his earnings buying the freedom of his brothers and sisters in Maryland. But to those who knew him, and nearly everyone in Buffalo did, his most outstanding characteristic was his unflagging dedication to Benjamin Rathbun. Nothing that Rathbun did swayed Hawkins's loyalty.

The two men, both born in obscurity, if under radically different circumstances, were quite a team. Working together they transformed the Eagle into a unique institution—a romantic mixture of country inn, old stage house, and metropolitan hotel of the more luxurious type then developing in New York City.

3

The Forests Recede

The emergence of the Eagle Tavern as a famous inn only five years after Rathbun's arrival measured the broader forces of growth and change that were transforming Buffalo. In those five years men made reputations and laid the basis for fortunes. Forces pushing the wilderness back would shape Buffalo's commercial destiny for more than a century ahead.

Dominating attention was the bitter rivalry between Buffalo and Black Rock village, its neighbor to the northwest along Scajacquada Creek, over which one would become the terminus of the Erie Canal. As canal construction advanced slowly westward from the Mohawk Valley roughly paralleling the main turnpikes, rivalry was expressed in a clash of personalities. The rivals were moved less by abstract civic loyalties than by the clear certainty that the outcome would radically affect the future value of property and the volume of their business.

Of course Rathbun became a partisan of Buffalo in this dispute, as did all of the town's prominent men. He had arrived at a crucial time. It was obvious that the town where the canal ended would benefit immensely. The depression had not slowed the westbound stream of immigrants; if anything, the movement had been accelerated as people reached out to improve their individual fortunes. The forests of western New York retreated as settlers hacked out their farms. More important still, a great tide of migrants swept even farther westward, up the lakes and into the Ohio country. It was easy to see that as the thousands of miles of inland shore were settled, more and more goods would be flowing east and west through the transshipment point on the Niagara Frontier.

Rathbun opened the Eagle Tavern's private rooms to the local committees working to effect the canal terminus decision. Even if his circumstances prevented him giving much financial assistance, he was ready, day or night, to do everything he could to help the town where he had cast his lot. As time went on, Rathbun himself raised his voice at these meetings. His schemes for influencing both public opinion and the state legislature soon gave him a standing with the important figures of Buffalo that he could have achieved in no other way. He played an intimate role in developments that were to transform Buffalo beyond the expectations of even its most farsighted citizens.

Chief among those attending the canal lobby meetings were the traders, merchants, and forwarders[1] with the largest pocketbooks. Almost always present was the tall rangy Samuel Wilkeson, whose face and body reminded many of Andrew Jackson. A trader and forwarder, and soon a manufacturer, Wilkeson was one of the growing class that profited by handling the transfer of goods from wagons or boats to upper lake craft. He had an obvious stake in the outcome. So did the vigorous George Coit and his brother-in-law, Charles Townsend. These Connecticut natives had been in Buffalo since before the War of 1812 and, after selling their apothecary, began the town's first major forwarding concern.

Congressman Albert Tracy, with whom Rathbun had struck a close acquaintance, often was present. The two men did not exactly share the same politics. A follower of DeWitt Clinton politically, Tracy was considered a firebrand by some conservatives because he strongly opposed Ellicott using the resources of the Holland Land Company to support Martin Van Buren and his "Albany Regency" in New York State politics. Tracy wrote anonymous articles for the *Niagara Journal* to help stir up sentiment against the Holland Company in particular, and propertied interests generally, an orientation hardly to Rathbun's liking. Indeed, Tracy urged taxation of nonresident property owners and suggested that settlers refuse to pay their debts to the company. But Rathbun probably recognized in Tracy a man of great ability and political authority.

Frequent canal meetings fed the rumors that flew wildly about the city. An apparent victory for Buffalo one day became defeat the next; defeat then once again turned into victory. For a time it seemed

---

1. "Forwarders" were those who dispatched goods and commodities to the East and the West from the crucial Buffalo–Black Rock transshipment point. More generally, the forwarder was a commissioned shipper.

impossible that there would ever be a clear-cut, let alone a favorable, decision from Albany on the momentous issues at stake.

This acrimonious "neighborhood quarrel" was not about whether Black Rock would be on the line of the canal. That was reasonably certain, for it was dictated by that village's location. Rather, the issue was whether the canal should be extended past the Rock to Buffalo village and Lake Erie. The chief financial argument for the extension was that the excavation required for the canal bed would be less costly if it ended at Buffalo, because the level of the lake and Buffalo Creek was higher than the level of the Niagara River at the Rock. The other argument was that Buffalo would be a better port because vessels docking there would not have to ascend the fast-flowing Niagara for about a mile and a half to get to the lake.

Buffalo's location had been recommended by the canal engineers. Yet location and logic were not enough; political considerations entered into every decision.

Politically Black Rock's outstanding advantage lay in the astute, solidly built person of its chief citizen, businessman, lawyer, and land-owner, Maj. Gen. Peter B. Porter, younger brother of Augustus Porter of Niagara. An intelligent, courageous, and crafty man, Porter had never hesitated to use every power in the arsenal to get his way. He had been close to the development of western New York since its early days, helping devise the policies that had built it up. The Porter fortunes grew apace. His political machinery had been a bulwark of a number of gubernatorial administrations.

General Porter had raised himself to national stature in Congress before the War of 1812. During the war, he was a resourceful leader of volunteers on the frontier, though the local campaigns hardly raised the military stature of the young Republic. Porter declined President Madison's offer of appointment as commander in chief of the United States Army. He had fought a bloodless duel in an argument with another general over the fiasco of American arms on the Niagara Frontier. From his postwar listening post, a heavy stone mansion at Black Rock, Porter oversaw his firm's lucrative shipping activities on the Niagara.

The Porter brothers owned land in Buffalo, but it was then of minor commercial importance. Their best lands lay along the Niagara, the choicest lots of the "Mile Strip," the mile-deep shoreline property from Lake Ontario to Lake Erie that the state had sold separately from the rest of western New York.

The outline of the battle between Porter's followers and Buffalo had been laid long before Rathbun arrived. Buffalo leaders did not underestimate Porter; they had clashed with him before.

Personal interest and political principle could not be separated. For six years a member of the state's Canal Commission after its establishment in 1810, Porter had opposed building any canal except from the Hudson to Lake Ontario at the village of Oswego. That route would have ensured the perpetuation of a key role for the Niagara portage and secured for the long-term the carrying business of Porter, which controlled the forwarding business on Lakes Erie and Ontario that connected with that portage. Porter's political ambition brought him into conflict with DeWitt Clinton, also a member of the Canal Commission from its start and a voluble exponent of maximum canal development. In 1817, Clinton defeated Porter for the Republican gubernatorial nomination, largely on the canal issue. Clinton's easy victory at the polls over Daniel D. Tompkins, who had been under Porter's influence, forecast further extension of the canal and the end of the Porters' control of the Niagara portage.

When the legislature finally authorized construction of the canal and work was begun, Porter and other opponents did not give up. In April 1819, however, the commission decided to continue the canal west of Seneca Lake to the Great Lakes. Now Porter expediently changed tactics, and he threw his influence behind the effort to terminate the canal at Black Rock.

The clash united most of those in Buffalo with a stake in the fight. Individually, none of the Buffalo lobbyists had wealth comparable to Porter, and politically they lacked his well-established connections. But collectively, as the shrewd Wilkeson told them, Albany had to reckon with them, for they represented an emerging local elite in a rapidly growing town.

These men of business recognized that the principal weakness of Buffalo's case was that it lacked an adequate harbor. Although they would not admit that Black Rock's exposed, downriver location constituted a harbor, lake boats did dock there. The sight of the *Walk-in-Water*, bypassing Buffalo completely, going downstream at the end of a voyage with its decks crowded, flags flying, and a band playing, was a continuous source of irritation, and it boded ill for the future. Their solace, and chief argument, was to watch the boats coming upstream from the Rock, fighting the fast-flowing current to get to Lake Erie. Except in an unusually favorable gale, sailing craft never made the upriver trip unaided. The *Walk-in-Water,* its puny engine beating the paddles madly against the current, always needed help making the trip.

Assistance to lakebound craft came from the "horn breeze," a sobriquet given the team of as many as fourteen oxen that hauled boats at the end of a six-hundred-foot hawser. The sight of the husky Sheldon Thompson, one of Porter's chief lieutenants, personally directing the "breeze" was a commonplace. Only he could handle the awkward arrangement satisfactorily and to keep the pontoons used to float the hawser from tangling. The thirty-five-year-old, long-nosed and clean-shaven Thompson, a former ocean sailor, had married a daughter of the prolific Benjamin Barton. Barton was a partner in Porter, Barton and Company.

Buffalo had long tried to get action in its behalf. Buffalo sent a committee to Albany in 1816 to petition for harbor improvement financed by the state, but all it obtained was authority for a survey of the creek. William Peacock, an adjutant of Ellicott and husband of one of Ellicott's many nieces, made the study without cost. He found that the creek could be turned into a harbor by erecting piers out to deep water, thus narrowing the channel and keeping out the sand. He estimated the cost at a modest $10,000 to $13,000, depending on whether stone or wood was used. A year later the federal government, which took a military interest in the river because it was an international border, built a thirty-foot lighthouse on the shore near the creek. So far, however, the lighthouse had been more useful to mariners going to Black Rock than for those discharging at Buffalo.

Early in the year in which Rathbun had arrived in Buffalo, a new nine-man civic committee banded together as the Buffalo Harbor Company and again appealed for state aid. Bolstered by Peacock's report, it had met with success, although in an unexpected and none too welcome form. The legislature approved a loan of $12,000 to Buffalo for the work, to be secured by a bond endorsed individually for $24,000 by the company's members. In the light of the depressed local economy this seemed a macabre joke. Members of the committee were failing; the only bank in town was thought likely to fail. Few dared risk their property on such a gamble, even though they might hope that tolls from the harbor would repay the debt.

By December, after months of agonizing argument, only two members of the committee were willing to sign. These were Oliver Forward, the lawyer, and Townsend, the forwarder. Aided by some of the others who were willing to lend moral support, even if they could not or would not risk their capital, Townsend and Forward convinced Wilkeson that he too should join. He had not been on the nine-man committee, and he questioned the wisdom of the arrangement. But he knew that they would not get the canal terminus unless they improved the harbor. By early 1820, with an $8,000 bond from each of the three men on deposit with the state, the money from Albany was finally forthcoming.

The new three-man Buffalo Harbor Company hired an eastern engineer to do the job, but the scale of his plans frightened them immediately. Obviously the $12,000 would be insufficient if he did the work.

Again the Eagle was filled with anxious talk. Could one of the three direct the work? Townsend's invalidism eliminated him, while Forward had to attend the legislative session, and Wilkeson was busy with his trading interests. The impasse was resolved only when Wilkeson proposed to abandon temporarily his own business and take over the job of directing the work. It was not clear what Wilkeson could accomplish, for he had never undertaken any such work before.

What followed, however, was a triumph of common sense. Improving, devising shortcuts, cutting costs, in the first season the thirty-nine-year-old Wilkeson worked knee deep in water alongside his hired laborers. They flung a wooden cribbing filled with stones and brush nine hundred feet into the lake where they planned the harbor entrance. He made a ton-pile driver from the barrel of an old mortar, a relic of the late war. He got stone free from the nearby Canadian shore, somewhat to the resentment of the population of the nearby town of Fort Erie.

A tremendous storm threatened to undo the work, but most of the cribbing held. When work ended for the season in the fall, everything was left in readiness when the lake thawed next spring. The spring freshet in the creek did what Wilkeson had hoped. It scoured a new straight channel through the sand, fifty yards away from the original one and alongside the new cribbing.

Meanwhile, with money threatening to run low, pledges of $1,000 more were made (though only $300 was eventually paid) for further work. In the spring a second pier, a line of double piles, was constructed rapidly. When the men, laboring in water, rebelled against working on rainy days, Wilkeson raised their pay $2 a month. Once when a freshet threatened damage he called for volunteers, and Rathbun, his brother, and many others worked part-time day and at night

by torchlight to strengthen the pier. Wilkeson was able to deepen the
channel with an improvised dredge of sheet iron and timber hung
under a barge and pulled by a horse and winch on land. In just 221
working days the channel was open, and the harbor was complete.

At first Black Rock partisans watched these amateurish proceedings and commented derisively. But soon Porter and Sheldon
Thompson, seeing a harbor emerging, began to seek ways to improve
their own harbor.

About this time, nature played its role in the competitive drama.
A late fall storm cast the *Walk-in-Water* ashore and destroyed the
reputation of Capt. Jedediah Rogers. Because the New York financiers who had built the boat were paying $3,000 a year to Robert
Fulton under his patent, which was then assumed to be valid, they
decided to build a successor immediately. Early in 1822, Noah Brown,
the engineer who had built the *Walk-in-Water*, came to Buffalo to
make arrangements at the Rock for the construction of a new boat.

When they heard that Brown was in town, Wilkeson and Townsend mapped a campaign that caught Porter unaware. By offering
timber at twenty-five percent under Black Rock prices, and by promising to pay $150 a day indemnity for any time after May 1 that
the boat might be prevented from leaving Buffalo harbor after its
launching, Brown was induced to build the craft at Buffalo. This was
certainly a blow to Black Rock's self-confidence.

More civic meetings and appeals raised pledges to make sure that
money would be available to meet the bond. But winter storms filled
the harbor channel with sand for a hundred yards. Again, at
Wilkeson's direction, $1,300 was raised and volunteers cleared the
channel in time to permit the *Superior,* the new boat using the engine
thriftily salvaged from the *Walk-in-Water,* to get to the lake without
payment of any penalty. Buffalo could finally assert that it had a
harbor.

Meanwhile both communities appealed to the legislature. This
time they were treated impartially. Buffalo's $12,000 debt would be
canceled if an eight-foot channel were assured and Black Rock could
have an equal sum to build a dam between two islands in the river to
create a harbor with a higher water level. Thompson, for the Black
Rock Company, built the dam complete with a lock, which permitted
boats to get to the river below.

The launch of the *Superior,* which people considered enormous
because it displaced 346 tons, and the completion of Buffalo harbor
brought the canal issue to a head. Chairman Clinton, David Thomas

(the canal engineer who favored the extension), and members of the Canal Commission spent a week at the Eagle Tavern in June 1822 listening to impassioned arguments. General Porter, supported by Thompson and the loud-voiced lake captains, presented Black Rock's case. The more ponderous Wilkeson, enlivening his facts with a grim humor and assisted by the imposing merchant Reuben B. Heacock, argued for Buffalo. The raucous disputes at these hearings in the small room at the Eagle were mild compared with what was going on outside. Porter and others shuttled back and forth to Albany playing all their political cards. Passions ran high. Articles in the *Buffalo Journal* were particularly intemperate, displaying a vindictiveness that was soon equaled by a new paper at Black Rock. The engineer, Thomas, was rumored to have been speculating in Buffalo lots. The Black Rock Harbor Company published a mass of documents and affidavits belittling Buffalo. It even asserted naively that ending the canal at the Rock was vital to the state, for it would enable land buyers there who had purchased from the state at only one-eighth down, to pay for their properties in full.

Uncertainty disappeared when the Canal Commission let three contracts for excavating the Buffalo extension. The village went wild with enthusiasm and plans were hastily made to celebrate the start of work. A large group assembled early in the morning of August 8, 1822, at the Eagle, fortified themselves against the rigors of summer heat, and paraded, dusty and perspiring after their early libations, down Main Street to the point where the canal was to enter the Little Buffalo Creek, a branch of the larger stream. There the Reverend Miles P. Squire, the Presbyterian minister, offered prayer for the success of the project. Six old residents appointed for the honor doffed their coats and turned the first sod. Then the rest of the paraders joined the digging.

Some further work was done on both the canal extension and on the Black Rock pier in the following fall and winter, but a rude awakening was ahead for the people of Buffalo. In June 1823, the Canal Commission met there and, to the dismay of the village, abruptly suspended work on the extension. Porter had triumphed again. Fearing defeat now, the Buffalo group immediately made several offers, but they were not accepted and the commission heaped insult upon injury by appropriating $84,000 for a harbor and canal terminus at Black Rock. Now Buffalo embarked on a campaign of speech making, letter writing, and political logrolling, which proved successful. That fall the commission relet the Buffalo contracts, but without rescinding its Black Rock action. It was the last major decision. Both places got the canal, and Black Rock obtained a harbor. Few, however, now doubted that Buffalo, with its new harbor, would capture most of the canal trade away from its rival.

Construction of the canal brought a flood of moneymaking schemes along the route. Leading Buffalo figures snatched up large parcels of land and laid out villages at the junction of the Niagara and Tonawanda Creek, which served as the canal waterway locally for a full twelve miles. Wilkeson and Dr. Ebenezer Johnson, the early settler who would serve as the town's first mayor, got the contract to dam the Tonawanda near its mouth to raise the creek to lake level.

Improvement of Buffalo's harbor made its business boom, with fortunate results for Rathbun and others in a position to benefit from heavier travel. In 1819, only 96 vessels were reported as arriving at and departing from the port. But the figures increased some twenty percent or more each year. By 1825, some 359 vessels used the port. It was an incredibly valuable trade from the earliest days. One trip of the *Walk-in-Water,* for instance, left for Mackinac in 1820 with goods valued at $100,000 to stock John Jacob Astor's American Fur Company's western trading posts. Return voyages carried furs and other wilderness products of even greater value.

Buffalo felt the influence of the Erie Canal long before the excavation even neared the village. Rathbun's extensions of the Eagle reflected the added business pouring into the town. The flow of immigrants, commercial travelers, and tourists increased, and eastern-made goods became more plentiful at lower prices as barges were able to float further and further west. By 1825, Buffalo's population had risen to twenty-four hundred and its buildings numbered between four hundred and five hundred. Business conditions were constantly improving, particularly in comparison with the depressed years. New construction, additional docking and storage facilities, and a new taste for luxury measured the boom. Money flowed more freely; more was available to chance in new enterprises. Wages, profits, and prices rose. A long-projected fire and marine insurance company was now chartered.

It needs to be noted that these changes reflected an improving national business climate. Paper money circulated more easily, and currency markets achieved stability, because of the efficient operations of the Bank of the United States under its new president, Nicholas Biddle. Canal construction injected money into Buffalo's economy, as did the long-delayed federal payment for local damages suffered in the 1813 invasion.

The long-dormant Bank of Niagara finally showed signs of reviving. Cornelius Van Antwerp, former sheriff of Albany County, decided to put money into Buffalo, and bought the bank's depreciated stock at bargain prices. He installed William Williams, who had been a teller in the old bank, as cashier. The bank's revival, however, did not end the scandals that had attended the earlier days of this ill-fated local institution. The respectable Oliver Forward and several others who had been associated with it were indicted for "conspiracy to defraud the public and the bank" as a result of a series of "infamous transactions." Apparently nothing came of the charges, and it is not unlikely that an envious and vindictive General Porter had a hand in the indictments. Even amid the area's new found prosperity, a cloud of scandal and greed would hang over the reputations of its economic leaders.

While Buffalo eagerly awaited completion of the canal, two events occurred to keep the Rathbun family in the public eye and to bring money into the Eagle's till. The great summer and fall of 1825 made Buffalo residents feel that their town had come of age.

The first of these was the anxiously awaited visit of the aged Marquis de Lafayette, then on his triumphal return with his son to the country he had helped free. Already exhausted by dinners, long rides, poor accommodations and a near-drowning accident when a boat overturned, the marquis and his party were met at Dunkirk, down the Lake Erie shore some forty miles, by the Buffalo reception committee. They led him to the comparative comfort of the steam brig *Superior,* which had been polished to a shine, for the ride to Buffalo.

The gregarious Lyman Rathbun had organized a militia rifle company, part of the 47th Infantry Brigade, which he dressed in particularly resplendent uniforms and drilled to perfection. Captain Rathbun and his "Frontier Guards" were selected as Lafayette's guard of honor when the *Superior* docked at the Buffalo wharf, its flags streaming and a band playing. Met by Buffalo's leading citizens, including Benjamin Rathbun himself, the noted visitor listened to a lengthy oration by Oliver Forward, now the area's representative in the New York State Senate. Moved by the occasion, Forward astonished his fellows by his oratorical prowess. For a generation, they could recall the grandiloquent cadences and the moving similes and metaphors of that address, even though its content had long been forgotten.

Among those on hand to shake hands with the nation's honored guest was the aged Red Jacket, famed chief of the Senecas, one of the few western New Yorkers the marquis was supposed to have once known. When the two shook hands, Red Jacket was wearing the great military medal embossed with his own figure, which had been presented to him by President Washington.

Surrounded by Captain Rathbun's militia and followed by citizens on foot, Lafayette's carriage made its way up Main Street to the Eagle Tavern. Here Benjamin Rathbun had erected a large tent. Gawking crowds jammed outside. Later in the day, Lafayette was driven to Niagara to view the great Falls, which had first been described to the European world by a fellow Frenchman, Father Louis Hennepin.

Only ten days after Lafayette's visit, another event excited Buffalo. It was a public hanging, this time a triple one. The felons were the three Thayer brothers—Nelson, twenty-five, Israel, twenty-three, and Isaac, twenty-one years—who had murdered an English-born lake sailor named John Love in a cabin in the nearby hamlet of North Boston. Nelson and Israel were swaggering toughs who liked to shock the staid and pious. They had named their horses God Almighty and Jesus Christ, to blaspheme the more readily. The facts were clearly against them, and they had been convicted at a trial that aroused such interest that the proceedings and the men's confessions had been published and were widely circulated in pamphlet form.

Fifteen or twenty thousand persons, the greatest throng ever seen on the Niagara Frontier, assembled on June 17 for the gruesome finale. The men were taken from the prison in the late morning, marched to the front of the courthouse by Sheriff Wray F. Littleton, Jr., his heavy sword of office rattling by his side, and surrounded by the militia, including Capt. Lyman Rathbun and his company. Dignitaries, including Benjamin Rathbun, had places of honor in the Eagle's windows overlooking the scene. A band was on hand, and unconsciously the three brothers, clad in white caps and shrouds, kept time to the dirge as they marched through Court Street to the three gibbets. Behind the condemned followed a wagon bearing three empty caskets.

Their father, Israel, Sr., whose trial as an accessory had been deferred, was released on bail on the morning of the execution to permit him to view the morbid spectacle from the courthouse steps, a privilege he exercised. Later, either because vengeance had been satisfied or the evidence was weak, he was acquitted.

The men climbed to the gallows where they sat on the platform, the dangling ropes in front, while Methodist preacher Gleason Fillmore read the full narrative of their confessions. This, he explained later, was at the prisoners' request. The newspapers pretended disgust at the protracted ceremony, but more likely they resented how the elaborately staged event took the edge from the printed revelations.

The Thayer brothers dispatched, attention again shifted to the construction of the canal, which had now reached the Niagara Frontier. Five double masonry locks had to be built into the limestone and slate escarpment, at a point some twenty-five miles away in Niagara County. Done mostly by hand, this was the greatest single task of the canal project. Finally, the locks completed, water was let into the western section. October 26, 1825, was set as the date for the official celebration.

DeWitt Clinton and an entourage of state and local dignitaries assembled in Buffalo to mark the completion of the greatest public works job in the state's history. Most of the visitors stayed at the Eagle.

The celebration started early in the morning with a parade that began at the courthouse and proceeded to the new canal terminus. Major Camp, the contractor, served as marshal. Again the Frontier Guards, with Captain Rathbun at their head, led the line of march to the dockside.

The packet *Seneca Chief,* constructed just for the occasion and made of Lake Erie red cedar, was the first boat to go through the completed canal. After speech making, Governor Clinton and chosen representatives of the larger communities boarded the barge. There the governor ceremoniously took aboard a keg of Lake Erie water, which was to be emptied formally into the salty waters of New York harbor at the journey's end. Wilkeson, Buffalo's acknowledged canal leader, got aboard to make the full journey, and several lesser Buffalo figures were to travel part way. Six handsome gray horses had been chosen to haul the packet to Tonawanda where they would be replaced by fresh animals for the next few miles.

Cannon, left from Commodore Oliver Hazard Perry's victorious Lake Erie fleet in the war, had been set along the entire route of the canal, each within earshot of the next. As the boat got under way, the cannon at the Terrace was fired. The sound was picked up at Tonawanda, a cannon there was fired, and miles beyond, another cannoneer relayed the commemorative shot. The rolling sounds thundered across the state. At New York City the process was repeated in reverse. Three hours and twenty minutes later the gun of the Terrace rumbled the completion of the "cannon telegraph" message: the Atlantic was linked to the lakes.

While Buffalo citizens were turning back to parade toward the courthouse for the rest of the ceremonies, the official packet glided on its way to Black Rock. But en route, the poorly constructed towpath at the side gave way under the weight of the pack animals. The three teams wavered, slipped, and then floundered into the shallow canal, halting the barge and threatening to disrupt the elaborate plans. But the driver never hesitated. He leaped into the canal and forced the horses back up the broken bank, while the official party applauded this demonstration of skill.

In front of Buffalo's courthouse, speaker after speaker launched into optimistic orations projecting a glorious future. When they had tired themselves and their audience, the assembly broke up, all who could be accommodated going to the Eagle. That night the festivities concluded with a grand ball at the Eagle, which "most of the fashion and beauty of the village attended."

The *Seneca Chief* continued its eastward voyage, halting at all major settlements for celebrations and arriving in New York City on November 4. There, a keg of Atlantic Ocean water was loaded aboard and the packet started upstream on the Hudson. It was back in Buffalo, the first round-trip in Erie Canal history, on November 23.

Buffalo had instantly become the major inland port of North America.

4

The Opportunist

Buffalo prospered, and so did its leading men. Rathbun was now not merely a successful hotel keeper, but a leading citizen. He had played his cards carefully; his friendships had brought him close to successful men. His advice in the canal and harbor program, his assistance in every civic activity, his carefully planned charities, all had accomplished their ends. The "coming" men looked on him as one of their own. He was seen to be a shrewd man ready to make the most of every financial opportunity, one who was worth watching and helping because he knew what he was doing.

This was all the more noteworthy in the light of the rumors occasionally still repeated by travelers who knew of his business troubles years before. As time went on, even the most hard-headed seem to have come to feel that these tales did him an injustice and must have perverted the truth. Even Levi Beardsley, an important lawyer and associate from those earlier days, stayed at the Eagle without embarrassment. In his memoirs, written years later, after he had served prestigiously as president of the New York State Senate and judge of the Court of Errors, Beardsley merely recalls that he had a pleasant day with Rathbun while in Buffalo transacting business connected with land he owned locally.

Rathbun's acceptance as a worthy and responsible citizen was also due in part to one of those vague beliefs that prevail in all ages. In those days of small business enterprise, tavern keepers were among the major figures of every community. When they, like other small businessmen, were successful, it was assumed that they would be similarly successful in any field. People were quick to recognize their outstanding qualities and to accept tacitly their leadership.

His apparently exemplary life, too, was an asset. Outside his home and business, his chief concern was the affairs of St. Paul's Episcopal Church, where he was for years a vestryman. One of the three Christian congregations in Buffalo when he arrived, St. Paul's soon moved into its new wooden building, a massive pseudo-Gothic and blue-painted structure, facing Main Street across a broad square. The Methodists already had a small chapel on Franklin Street and a little later the Presbyterians erected their first church near the Episcopal site, which led that area to be called "The Churches." Though St. Paul's had no monopoly on the successful businessmen, the parish had more than a proportionate share of the well-to-do. Rathbun became one of its largest contributors as time passed. Alice became deeply involved in the social-charitable activities of the women of the church. Though never prominent in St. Paul's affairs, Lyman Rathbun contributed regularly when it appealed for money. Henry Hawkins was also baptized and confirmed in St. Paul's, its first black communicant, and shortly afterward he became its sexton, a post he held for many years. Already a recognized part of Buffalo's social life, Hawkins's presence and that of his family now became integral to of St. Paul's Sunday services. The affluent could feel that a friendly and respectful greeting to the aristocratic, stylish Hawkins family at services exemplified of their Christian beliefs.

Benjamin acquired a two-story red brick residence on the east side of Main Street at the corner of North Division Street. The Eagle was only a block and a half away. Here with Alice and their son, Loomis, he might have attempted to relax in a quiet haven away from the pressures that greatly preoccupied him, as he increasingly diversified his endeavors. For this restive man, however, home was something less than a haven, for personal difficulties racked the Rathbun household. Loomis grew into an increasingly troublesome boyhood. Protective of Loomis, Alice revolted against Benjamin's control for the first time in their marriage. Though enrolled in Buffalo's military school, Loomis remained a discipline problem, and would years later be a part of his parents' final tragedy.

Almost as pressing a problem was his father, Moses, upon whom middle age had had a decidedly disturbing effect. Still jaunty, still spouting scriptural quotations, Moses had reached that time of life when the ardors of youth might reasonably be expected to be cooling. Yet his interest in chasing women, especially younger ones, was unabated—and a potential scandal.

There had been some trouble in Batavia; Patience had let her son

Benjamin know that it would be better if he brought them to Buffalo where, she imagined, the presence of his two sons and several daughters might have a moderating influence on Moses' conduct.

A year or two after he went into the Eagle, Benjamin prevailed upon his father to move to Buffalo. Patience was beginning to age. Her health was poor. She had never recovered from the blow that had destroyed the stability of her life in Otsego County. She had grown tired of her husband's hypocrisy and of the gossip, which she seemed unable to escape.

Not long after her arrival in Buffalo on October 7, 1823, Patience died at the age of fifty-three. His publicly expressed grief, nevertheless, did not prevent Moses making a trip back to Batavia less than eight months later to marry the widow Charlotte Moore, whom he had known for some time. The second Mrs. Rathbun, though looking far younger, was about forty-seven years old. A mere thirteen months after their marriage found Mrs. Charlotte Moore Rathbun in her grave, her death occurring in Batavia on July 25, 1825.

Moses waited less than three months before he took a new wife, an event that caught his children completely by surprise. His third wife was a thirty-two-year-old widow, Roxanna Bates, whom he married in Buffalo on October 14, 1825. Even in the rather crude world of the Niagara Frontier at that time, this sequence of events was decidedly unusual. No matter how his family tried to explain it away with such casual remarks as "He needs a woman to take care of him," his marrying ever-younger women and not spending much time grieving attracted comment.

Moses had yet one more surprise in store for his children. On January 28, 1829, Roxanna bore Moses a daughter, whom they named Elizabeth. The new child was almost twenty-seven years younger than her youngest half sister, and was thirty-eight years younger than her half brother Benjamin.

Benjamin felt he had to find a way to keep Moses busy. In late 1824 or early 1825, Benjamin set up "Lyman Rathbun and Company." Moses alone was the "and Company" part of the firm. No special formalities attended the start of this new retail establishment, which opened in an old building a block or so below the Eagle.

At the same time Lyman and Moses were a useful "front" for Benjamin's own desire to expand his activities in new directions. His credit was strained at that moment, and he did not wish to appear to be expanding his own affairs relentlessly. Perhaps, too, he lacked faith in Moses' ability to stick to anything, and wanted him at a distance from the Eagle's affairs as well as busy. At any rate, Benjamin felt that a separated establishment was advisable. It might protect him emotionally and financially.

Dry goods, groceries, shoes, glassware, curtains, liquors, and rum made up the stock publicly featured at the new shop. Many of these items were "imported," not from Europe, but from New York, as was the bulk of manufactured articles for sale in Buffalo at the time. Lyman Rathbun and Company used the fact that its goods were "imported" as a selling argument to lend a certain cachet that would attract purchasers. The fall of freight rates as the canal neared its completion at Buffalo made it practicable to bring in more and cheaper goods from the east than Buffalo stores had carried.

The establishment had barely opened when competition appeared in the person of Erastus Gilbert, who opened a similar general store immediately north of Rathbun's. Gilbert carried dry goods, hardware, groceries, crockery, and shoes.

Lyman Rathbun and Company, helped by strong recommendations from the supposedly disinterested Benjamin, was able to keep its shelves stocked with a representative line at almost no actual cost outlay. Moses' glib geniality in dealing with sales representatives of eastern concerns and Lyman's skillful arguments convinced sellers that they were good risks on their own notes.

Prompted by Benjamin, Lyman tried various gambits—they were innovations in selling then—to bring in trade. One was the purchase in New York of a lot of French-made wallpapers, which an importer had been unable to sell in the metropolis. For some time thereafter, Lyman Rathbun and Company featured notice of a fine stock of a thousand pieces of French wallpaper in its advertising. But this was either too fancy for the Buffalo trade, or the price was too high, for the paper had to be marked down drastically before it was sold.

Another purchase, more successful, was of large quantities of imported rum. Part of this purchase was distributed readily at the Eagle's own bar. Other taverns in the area were offered reduced prices for quantity purchases of the rum.

Benjamin instructed Lyman in the wisdom of buying in bulk. Sound as was the principle, the fact remained that the Buffalo market was not unlimited and the store did not have credit or capital enough to buy in extremely large quantities. Moreover, Moses bought too much of some very slow-selling stock. The difficulty in putting his ideas into practice convinced Benjamin that the only way real profits could be made would be by owning a number of stores—in effect, a chain store operation, in which he could shuttle inventory among the various units. But, as yet, that was out of the question.

As time wore on, Benjamin grew more and more dissatisfied with the way his father was running the store. Moses paid scant attention to details and Lyman had to spend too much time straightening out neglected records and stock. Moreover, Moses was wasting too much of his own time, to Benjamin's mind, in being pleasant to individual customers, especially if they were good-looking women.

When Benjamin built the Eagle buildings, he had contemplated using one of them for Lyman Rathbun and Company. Both Lyman and Moses pressed him to put the store farther up Main Street and nearer the courthouse. They claimed that it would be advantageous because it was easily accessible to the farmers who came in to pay taxes, attend court, and record deeds.

Late in 1826, Lyman Rathbun and Company moved into a new store in a location of the sort the two had urged. Its advertising announced that it was getting a new fall and winter supply of goods from New York to celebrate. The interior of the small, narrow building must have been jammed with its "fine assortment" of chintz, calicoes, silks, dry goods, groceries, teas, coffees, sugar, liquors, crockery, glassware, and carpeting. In view of the store's size, it could have carried only a minimal line of any one of them.

Despite the good location, the improved business climate in the town, and the obviously rosy future, a now-inexplicable trouble arose with Lyman Rathbun and Company less than a year after it had moved into its new quarters. Creditors were having more and more trouble getting their money from Lyman and Moses Rathbun.

There is no evidence that a failure was premeditated and that money which might have been used to meet the notes they owed was diverted elsewhere. Yet, in the light of the affair in Otsego County and of later events in Buffalo, it is certainly conceivable that their failure was a result of a deliberate plan. A number of judgments were filed against the two men.

The judgments themselves suggest what may have happened: prevailing interest rates were too high and the store got caught up in its escalating debts. Financing in western New York then permitted veritable usury—huge penalties and extra charges to be exacted commonly for the loan of money. Lyman and Moses, for example, gave a note for $269 to Aaron Arnold and George Hearn, payable at the Chemical Bank in New York City in four months. When Arnold and Hearn sued four months later, they asked for $500, although the

court cut the amount down to $296. Lyman and Moses gave a note of
$80 to the Oneida Manufacturing Facility for goods, payable in five
months. The Oneida firm assigned the note to a Thomas Metcalf,
who sued a year later for $200 and got a judgment, which was never
paid, for $105.

Stories that then circulated about the rotund Dr. Ebenezer Johnson, who gradually worked his trading in money into a private banking business, epitomized the prevalent practice of making loans.
Contemporaries spoke highly of Johnson and said that he was always
extremely law abiding and driven by a deep sense of duty "except
when it came to usury and shaving[1] notes." Money was so scarce and
much of the paper in circulation was of such questionable value that
lenders naturally anticipated handsome profits. Sharp practices with
credit were the basis of current business and, although widely condemned as unprincipled, were accepted as commonplace.

Benjamin knew what was happening to the store, and probably
knew what moves his brother and father were making to deal with
the situation. He had Lyman turn over to him the ownership of the
Eagle buildings' adjacent property, the record stating that he paid
Lyman $4,000, which undoubtedly wiped out the mortgages. Only a
few months later when Leonard P. Crary, an old friend of Benjamin's
who was now operating an auction store and serving as deputy sheriff
part-time, went to collect judgments against Lyman and Moses Rathbun "being copartners in trade and doing business under the name,
style and form of Lyman Rathbun and Co.," he "could find nothing to
levy on," according to his own notations upon the judgment papers.

Lyman Rathbun and Company had gone out of business and
Benjamin was in direct control of the store, which continued to operate at the same location, in the building he now owned, but under the
name of "B. Rathbun," as he always wrote his signature. He had
acquired the stock at a bargain rate, and was now, through this fina-
gling, a retail merchant.

Exactly how or when Rathbun got into yet another, far more
lucrative, business, that of a builder-contractor, which came to take up
so much of his time then and later, cannot be determined accurately.

---

1. "Shaving" was the popular term then in use to describe the practices of assuming the debts of others at higher than the initial rates of interest at the time the debt
was incurred. The term also was employed simply to describe charging higher interest
rates to someone badly in need of money or credit. Benjamin Rathbun had to deal with
both practices, but especially the latter.

Indirect evidence would suggest that it was about the time he first began enlarging the Eagle, two or three years after his arrival in Buffalo. He may well have been inspired by the experience of thinking through the improvements to the Eagle to go on to seek other opportunities to do the same work.

His first jobs must have been extremely small—for example, the tiny frame and brick dwellings for the growing population of the village that were going up everywhere. In a few years he was constructing slightly more elaborate houses, which Lyman advertised and sold for him. Benjamin found that it was useful at times to have people do their business with him through Lyman. It saved his own energy and time for the Eagle. Besides, what Benjamin liked most was consummating deals and projecting schemes into viable projects.

The scarcity of credit in the village made extensive operations impossible. With the only bank so feeble during most of that early period, credit was hardly obtainable at all. Men who had any money loaned it themselves on mortgages, built buildings, or started new businesses. Few loans of any consequence were obtained outside the community for years, despite the town's promise. Distant banks and investors were wary of chancing their money in a place they could not watch closely. This shortage of credit led Rathbun to become especially skillful in creating credit for himself. His flair for salesmanship, the genius of the born promoter, gave him convincing skill in negotiating with others and selling himself to them.

The experiment in erecting the profitable Eagle buildings assisted him in gaining a reputation as a builder and in getting contracts to put up other commercial properties. As time wore on, Rathbun controlled more and more of the construction work that the growing town required. Often he supplied everything the project required. He provided the idea, the plans, the supervision of the laborers, and the material. Also, he became adept at what would later be called "the deal": getting men together to finance jointly a new building or improve an existing one.

Scarce credit forced him to become skilled in trading: services for bricks, stabling for the use of oxen and wagons, goods for buildings, and so forth. These multitrade arrangements, which grew into a complicated barter system, helped increase construction jobs. Rathbun's retail store provided the perfect outlet for goods taken in trade.

His deftness at weaving one operation into another gained the admiration of his contemporaries. As his authority and power grew, so did his management skills. Though his jobs were small, he was learning how to gain trust and cooperation of those he needed to realize his goals, to find employees who were faithful and loyal, and to make the most of extremely complicated trades.

His complex bartering and his irregular employment of labor sometimes did produce arguments, and the breakdown of agreements took him occasionally into the courts. When that happened, Rathbun's friendship with lawyers and judges proved useful.

One of his first (of many, eventually) court appearances was in 1824 when he sued Samuel E. Barnes for $75. Barnes was defended by the hulking "Counselor" John Root, a lazy and convivial jokester whose fondness for drink was already speeding him toward hopeless alcoholism.

Rathbun's lawyer was Joseph Clary, partner since 1823 with the young Millard Fillmore. Clary, a native of Oneida County, had come to Buffalo to read law in 1820 at the age of twenty-eight, after working on a farm and in a store. He had been in the office of his brother-in-law, Asa Rice, but in 1823 went into partnership with Millard Fillmore, who had hung out his shingle in the village of East Aurora, eight miles from Buffalo. Clary was handling the Buffalo end of the firm and Fillmore took care of rural cases.

During his early years in the law, Clary, like so many other unattached men, boarded at the Eagle Tavern, and only left it when he married and set up his home on Franklin Street. Clary married in 1830, and his wife was Maria Theresa Rathbun, daughter of Samuel Rathbun, a New York City wholesale dry goods merchant who was a younger brother of Moses Rathbun. It is not certain, but it is likely that this romance blossomed when the twenty-nine-year-old Maria Theresa was visiting her first cousins, Benjamin and Lyman, at Buffalo.

The solidly built, up-and-coming Fillmore handled some of Rathbun's business himself in succeeding years, particularly after he joined Clary in Buffalo in 1830 after a term in the New York State Assembly.

While Rathbun's construction activities were getting a good start, he decided that it would do him no harm locally to become a candidate for public office. The villagers showed their confidence in him by electing him a village trustee in 1827 and then reelecting him the next year. (These, however, would be his only excursions into politics.) Village elections were then virtually nonpartisan so that Rathbun's refusal, as a hotel keeper desiring everyone's trade and a deal maker seeking credit and capital from anyone who could be persuaded to work with him, to associate himself with a faction did not count against him.

Perhaps it was the increasingly divisive and all-consuming nature of politics that caused Rathbun's retreat from public service. Politics at every level in western New York convulsed as new personalities and forces split the once dominant National Republicans into diverse warring groups.

On the national scene, forces loyal to Henry Clay contended with the Jacksonians. In 1822, Van Buren loyalists trounced DeWitt Clinton, whose personal magnetism could not attract enough votes to compensate for political ineptitude. Clinton recovered the governorship in 1824, and won reelection in 1826, but these contests were costly. Buffalo was left politically divided. Former followers of the defunct Federalists had always had a large voice in western New York, and now, increasingly, Buffalo voters translated these traditional tendencies into opposition to the Van Buren "Albany Regency" and the Jacksonians. The differences helped bring on a violent political explosion, called the Anti-Masonic movement, which originated in the nearby Genesee Valley. Fueled by real events and imagined conspiracies, Anti-Masonry assisted in breaking New York's established political solidarities. Alignments forged at this time affected state and national elections right up to the Civil War.

Underlying this emotional outburst was a widespread democratic and religious opposition to the growth of the Masonic fraternity. The belief spread that Masonic lodges exercised sinister power over politics and business affairs. It is true, too, that the bulk of the leading politicians and landed gentry were Masons. Masonic lodges were strong in western New York; Rathbun himself may have been a member, though no evidence remains today to prove this supposition. Many of his associates, such as Dr. Chapin, Granger, Landon, Caryl, Pomeroy, Townsend, Forward, Benjamin Hodge, Dr. John Clark, and Dr. Josiah Trowbridge, certainly were, as were such Rathbun relatives as his affluent kinsmen John and Ranson Rathbone of Oxford, New York, and others, as we shall see, in western New York.

The controversial abduction and probable murder of an unprepossessing Batavia resident, William Morgan, provided the spark for the rise of Anti-Masonry. Morgan was not one of the lucky men on the make. Despite his induction into a Masonic lodge at LeRoy, he had a penchant for contracting bills he could not pay.

Perhaps because he was envious of the success of powerful local people around him, Morgan had written a book purporting to expose the secrets of Masonry. Learning of this, Masons harassed both him and the Batavia printer who was setting his book in type. Finally Morgan was arrested on a trumped-up charge, taken to Canandaigua, and lodged in jail in default of bail. On the night of September 12, 1826, Morgan was abducted. Masons took him to Fort Niagara on Lake Ontario, which was then temporarily unoccupied by the military. A number of Masons saw him while he was imprisoned there. What happened thereafter is obscure—but he disappeared completely. The facts of his disappearance have never been established beyond dispute.

Rumor of these illegal activities spread. The scandal built slowly. David E. Evans, who had inherited a fortune from Ellicott after his aged uncle committed suicide in a New York City sanitorium, headed a committee of Batavia citizens in behalf of Mrs. Morgan and sent out circulars appealing for Morgan's discovery. Thurlow Weed, now part owner of the *Rochester Telegraph,* printed a story on the subject. Hounded by Masons, Weed sold out his interest and threw himself into the Anti-Masonic movement. Politicians sensed a good issue. Governor Clinton, the most distinguished Mason in the state, personally offered a reward for finding Morgan and the perpetrators of the crime. The lieutenant governor of Upper Canada (now Ontario) offered a reward. Mrs. Morgan became a recipient of bounty from numerous Anti-Masons. In an ironic twist, four years later Mrs. Morgan remarried: a Batavia Mason whose lodge then expelled him.

Nearly a year after the crime, the pressure was so great that legal prosecutions became unavoidable. In the interim, however, witnesses had disappeared. Now, too, evidence was distorted or falsified. A series of trials took place in Genesee, Niagara, and Ontario counties, the last of them in 1831. A number of Masons, including the sheriff of Niagara County, went to jail. Subsidiary trials, such as those on charges of libel, continued for years.

The storm whirled and eddied around Benjamin Rathbun, as it did around nearly every person of prominence. Two of his brothers-in-law were involved. One, Orange Allen, husband of Rhoda Rathbun, who had lived in Buffalo and was later postmaster of a small town near Batavia, had been one of two men who put up bail for Morgan on a suit for debt just before his abduction. Another, Bissell Humphrey, who had married Jeanette Content Rathbun, was the proprietor of Batavia's Eagle Tavern where the Batavia lodge, of which Bissell was a member, often met.

Many of those Rathbun knew well narrowly escaped going to jail.

Chauncey H. Coe of Canandaigua, with whom he was associated in the stage business, and James Ganson, tavern keeper at LeRoy and a former brother-in-law of Mrs. Israel Rathbun, were acquitted. Whitney, militia general and operator of the tavern at Niagara, escaped because a jury disagreed; Samuel Barton, son of the Porters' former partner and a stage operator at Lewiston, and his brother, James L. Barton, Wilkeson's partner in a forwarding business, were identified as having been closely involved.

Seth Chapin, a thirty-six-year-old Buffalo merchant who died late in 1826, was accused early the next year of Morgan's murder in a report prepared by the Lewiston (Anti-Masonic) Committee of Investigation. Dr. Cyrenus Chapin, a Mason himself, rallied to his son defense with a ringing charge that it was a "vile slander on the dead."

As the politicians channeled these emotions to their own ends, towns became warring camps. By 1828, the movement was strong enough to hold a state political convention. Although its force declined in the 1830s, "political Anti-Masonry" continued into the 1840s and many of its followers found haven among the Whigs, who were growing in opposition to the Jacksonian and Van Buren Republicans, or "Democrats" as they came to be called.

Although Buffalo escaped some of the most bitter of the upheavals, men like Rathbun, who usually benefited by being neutral in public affairs, had a difficult time staying uninvolved. Roswell W. Haskins, editor of the *Buffalo Journal* and proprietor of a bookstore that was a rendezvous for the village wits and intellectuals, was accused of being involved in one of the attacks on Morgan. Haskins conducted a vicious print war with the Anti-Masonic *Buffalo Patriot.* Rathbun's friend, Congressman Tracy, was among the Buffalo leaders of the new movement and it carried him to leadership of the New York State Senate. Thomas C. Love went to Congress on the Anti-Mason's ticket. Dr. Stagg and Noah P. Sprague, a broker and businessman, helped head the Buffalo movement. James Wadsworth of Geneseo, Batavia's James Brisbane, and Francis Granger of Canandaigua, son of Gideon, were among other outstanding leaders in the statewide Anti-Masonic movement.

❧❀◗

This case brought tempers to a white heat, estranged lifelong friends, and caused bitter tavern disputes. It was the most serious public cleavage yet in the young town. But it slowed Buffalo's dramatic growth not at all. Its harbor far outdistanced Black Rock, which had lost the Niagara portage business. In the winter of 1826, Black Rock's pier broke under ice pressure and its leaders became discouraged. Sheldon Thompson, who was later to serve as mayor, now moved his forwarding business to Buffalo, merging part of its operations with the Townsend and Coit firm. Others followed, vacating Black Rock for Buffalo. (Eventually that village would be annexed by Buffalo.) Because it was deemed crucial to the defense of the international border, the federal government put more than $71,000 into construction and repair of the Buffalo harbor in the five years after completion of the Canal. Stone replaced wood in the piers. Warehouses sprang up between the canal and harbor.

Use of Buffalo's harbor doubled in 1827, rose another thirty percent in the next year, and twenty percent in the following year. Canal clearances doubled between 1826 and 1830. The rise in business brought many new activities. Houses mushroomed where just a few years before there had been stump-filled fields, and they expanded into the surrounding forest. Supplying wood from these urban forests to fuel the steamboats being built at Black Rock and other lake ports became an important occupation, for each consumed one hundred to two hundred cords for a round-trip up the lakes.

The canal permitted mass shipments of goods. Bulk cargoes and weights of unprecedented size could travel at a fraction of their former cost. Commodities such as timber, once unshippable because of its bulk, now had commercial value to eastern contractors and shipbuilders. Once travelers were subjected to the ordeal of pitching stagecoach rides over bad roads. Canal packets now carried much greater numbers in greater comfort.

Spring, summer, and fall found the docks on Commercial Street near the foot of Main Street humming with activity. Sailing brigs, schooners, drays, and wagons loaded with goods for canal boats shuttled back and forth between the docks, warehouses, and canal. "Runners," who earned commissions by snaring travelers for particular hotels, lake boats, stage lines, or canal packets, ran shouting and cursing through the throngs. Life slowed down greatly in winter when lake and canal froze over, usually between mid-December and mid-April.

Ancillary businesses snowballed as commerce and population increased. Tanneries began near the port. Trade in cattle and breweries grew from trade in grain. In 1827, General Porter, Heacock, and others organized the Buffalo Hydraulic Association to extract mill power from a modest fall on a three-and-a-half-mile canal connecting Buffalo Creek with Little Buffalo Creek. This corporation, which had $25,000 capital, was a big enterprise at the time, and it gave rise to a new industrial neighborhood, popularly known as "The Hydraulics."

Rathbun was now making very good money as Buffalo prospered. His tavern filled with free spenders. His store, once he had it finally under his own thumb, did well. The growing town provided endless opportunities for the versatile, enterprising, and lucky contractor.

True, he had personal problems, particularly those caused by a broadening circle of relatives who clustered at his heels ready to benefit from his loyalty. Not only was he surrounded throughout much of this period by close relatives with their in-laws and children but also by distant cousins who were stonemasons, painters, and carpenters drifted into Buffalo. They, too, looked to him for work.

Because of his irregular work habits, Moses remained a continual worry. His most recent wife, possessive and endowed with a strong will, now at least helped keep him out of the sort of trouble to which he was prone. Indispensable as bookkeeper as his brother's interests expanded, Lyman was at times also a worry. Lyman was twice brought to court for assault: once, in 1829, along with Moses, and again, more seriously, in 1830. The second charge was lodged against Lyman and two others by a grocer who complained that he was beaten, threatened, held against his will for two days, and dragged for ten miles through public streets, thus "injuring his body, credit, and circumstances." The court records yield little about this bloody affair.

Benjamin's personal seriousness and desire for respectability made him take these incidents as grave affronts to his dignity and public image, but he need not have been concerned. It was a measure of frontier Buffalo's relative indifference to law and order that they did not injure even Lyman's standing. Indeed they seem to have enhanced his reputation in the rude male society of the frontier. He was promoted in the militia to the rank of major, then to lieutenant colonel, and when a senior officer was elevated from colonel to brigadier general, Lyman succeeded him. Lyman's skill in organizing parades and in managing the details of celebrations resulted in his selection, year after year, as marshal of the civic gatherings in which the militia took part.

Though his family and relations proved at times improvident, Rathbun showed that he was a systematic planner. He learned rapidly to pick the skilled architects and mechanics he needed for detail work.

The salesmanship involved in every contract and the many-sided barter-trades that entered into most of them Benjamin handled alone. His slight figure, a white cravat always topping his careful dress, was one of the most familiar in town, observed as he hurried to call on clients, to oversee jobs in progress, to discuss contracts and barters with the men who supplied the lumber, bricks, mortar, and metals that he required.

Although his business was still scattered and small when judged by his own later standards, he had already mentally formulated the principles of large-scale production and economies of scale that few of his contemporaries understood. He conceived of vast construction programs that could be directed by a small trained staff. Elimination of middlemen, more efficient use of equipment, and other steps to trim overhead were part of his entrepreneurial vision. He envisioned enormous profits, flowing steadily and richly into one till, as a result of coordinating a variety of operations. Such integration of operations later became the principal strategy of industrial monopolists like Andrew Carnegie, who had much more capital to play with than did Rathbun in the primitive but rapidly growing economy of his time.

He did what he could to put these ideas into practice by getting many contracts at once so that he could buy materials for many jobs at one time, thereby obtaining the benefits of buying in volume. People were willing to sell bricks at a lower price, he found, when he could order enough to keep their ovens busy for months. Cut stone was cheaper when he could assure a quarry operator that he would take his entire output for a year. Rathbun's tactics were many years ahead of his period.

As the 1820s drew to a close, he was still far from the goal he envisioned. Work was much more plentiful, but with money hard to come by it took days of arguing to round out the details of even the smallest project. Yet he was using his time to the fullest; every job gave him added skill and assurance both of which he would mobilize when soon his business would really begin to expand.

5

Stagecoach Entrepreneur

From the day that Rathbun secured control of the dilapidated Eagle, he was casting about for ways to link the tavern into the stagecoach business, the fast transportation medium of the time. An official connection with the principal lines, to his mind, was vital to make the tavern a success, for the great bulk of passenger travel to Buffalo came by coach over the eastern turnpikes.

Halting the coaches briefly at the Eagle's door to discharge or take on passengers was not enough. They also stopped at all the other major taverns along their routes as travelers requested. Moreover, operators of the official stage houses and, even more important, the well-instructed drivers, naturally only advised their passengers to use the taverns associated with the line. Travelers in a strange area usually allowed themselves to be herded impersonally into the official stage houses.

Taverns and stagecoaches had been closely related from the earliest days. In many places, taverns existed only to serve the stages by providing places where travelers could obtain food, drink, and overnight accommodations and where the horses could be refreshed or relays provided. Frequently, the tavern keeper was a principal or agent of one or more stage lines.

Rathbun had had one of those connections in his first hotel venture, the tavern at Monticello. Without the transient travel, that stage house would have been limited to relatively unimportant patronage of local origin. His instinct for tying related activities together drove him to take every possible measure to assure a stage connection for the Eagle.

New roads had been built and old ones improved as the state's population increased. The best highways, poor as they were, were the toll roads, which were built by private corporations under stage government franchise and financed largely by stock sales. These became the major routes of highway travel.

Coinciding with the improvement of roads was the rise of the stagecoach business, which began, as did the railroads later, merely as a series of short runs, operated by independent owners to serve the immediate needs of their area. By subsidizing speed and efficient operation, federal mail contracts promoted consolidations of the independents, thereby encouraging the development of monopolies along the major routes. Because political connections were important in obtaining the post office contracts, the combinations were soon closely tied into the political life.

The consolidations were just crystallizing fully when Rathbun went into the Eagle. On the great main lines of travel across the state, a consortium of tavern keepers and livery stable owners was gaining a near-monopoly of the stagecoach business on the Albany to Buffalo Turnpike. This "Old Line Mail," as the loose merger of interests along the Albany-Buffalo turnpikes was called, held most mail shipping contracts, and controlled many of the less important side runs as well. "Parker, Powell and Sherwood," the consortium's principal identity in mail contract bidding, had members who had been handling some of the passenger and mail routes since 1795.

Old Line Mail stages ran on schedule from Albany to Buffalo and Niagara Falls, at various times, by both the northern route (through Utica and Syracuse) and the southern route (through the Cherry Valley), both roads becoming one at Auburn and running westward through Geneva to Canandaigua and Buffalo.

Oliver Phelps and Company at Canandaigua in 1818 began a competing line from that village southeast across the Catskill Mountains to Newburgh on the Hudson River about sixty miles north of New York City. Its run, faster but much rougher than the turnpikes from Albany, cut fares to get business and shortly forced similar reductions by the Old Line, thereby speeding the consolidations already in progress.

Buffalo's Old Line mail franchise was owned by Sylvanus Marvin. Marvin was driven to the brink of bankruptcy in the depression, and the line was rundown when Rathbun arrived. Rathbun tried to persuade Marvin that their futures were linked and that Marvin should hold on until the Eagle began to pay. Rathbun lost his opportunity to merge with the line when Marvin sold out in 1827. The new owner, Chauncey H. Coe, hired his own agent at Buffalo, tough and taciturn Edward L. Stevenson. Coe then returned to Auburn where he owned an inn at the key stage junction point.

It looked as though a direct approach to Coe would fail, so Rathbun, always prepared with an alternative idea in reserve, opened an indirect attack. He began to sound out possible backers of a new stage line with the argument that the stage business, now that times were getting better, was an excellent investment. He claimed that with a new organization and up-to-date coaches and first class horses, he could effect an agreement with the Albany-Utica-Geneva members of the big combination to get control of the western end. Rathbun appears to have believed that Coe was not solidly entrenched in the stage business. Moreover, Rathbun knew that stage operators, as a whole, were tough men for whom sentiment played no part in business. If he could offer something better, Coe's new western franchise might be upset.

A relic of his successful assault is one of the many letters that Rathbun sent to prospective partners in the stage business. The following letter was addressed to Leonard P. Crary, later one of Rathbun's Buffalo associates, who was then living just north of Buffalo, in Williamsville, which was on the principal coach road. It was dated March 16, 1823.

> Sir:
> I am requested to enquire of you whether you would do anything toward incorporating a new line of stages. If so, please write me for return of mail—what and how much you would do towards starting a new line of Post Coaches to be run in an Elegant and Expeditious Measure.
>
> Yours etc.
B. Rathbun

Whether Rathbun would or could have carried this elaborate project to completion is conjectural. He was doing much better in the tavern, but he was using all his profits in improvements, and he was beginning to spread his efforts into house building. Under any circumstance, we have evidence here of Rathbun's propensity for overcommitting both his energies and his capital, habits that would soon get him in the most profound difficulties. In this case, however, Rathbun was allowed to get out of this situation without sustaining any harm.

Upon learning what was afoot, Coe hurried back from Auburn. It must have looked like quite a challenge to him. Perhaps he was on uncertain ground with the members of the combination. At any rate, he capitulated and negotiated an agreement with Rathbun to make the Eagle the headquarters of stage operations in Buffalo and to accept Rathbun as a partner in the control of the franchise.

Rathbun's cash contribution toward this valuable concession was apparently limited to the erection of the "stage office" on the south side of the Eagle and to the clearing and leveling of the big stage yard in the adjoining vacant lot. He built, at Coe's expense, the barns for the stages and stage horses in the rear of the next lot, which opened into the back of the Eagle's stage yard.

This tactical defeat, though taken with good grace, was a blow to Coe. He had underestimated the problems he would face in taking over the Marvin establishment and abandoning a paying tavern and stage business in Auburn. Travel was increasing so rapidly that the business inevitably prospered, but still Coe was dissatisfied. He doubtless discussed this thoroughly with his older brother, Bela D. Coe, former proprietor of Coe's Stage House in Canandaigua and agent for the Old Line there, and they came to an agreement satisfactory to both of them.

In 1825, the two brothers exchanged agencies, Chauncey Coe moving to Canandaigua and Bela Coe coming to Buffalo to take over the Old Line operation there. Bela Coe brought with him Isaac T. Hathaway, who had been his stage agent at Canandaigua, and, under this arrangement with his brother, also retained Edward L. Stevenson in his employment. Both employees were extremely capable persons in their own right and, though somewhat jealous of each other, contributed to the strength of the Buffalo stage business.

Bela Coe and his wife had bought from the pioneer merchant, Ebenezer Walden, and immediately moved into, a two-story buff brick house on Main Street near the northeast corner of Eagle Street, diagonally opposite Rathbun's tavern. Coe began a relationship with Rathbun that was to last many years.

A decided conservative, who spoke slowly and made up his mind with care, Coe respected Rathbun's acuteness and competence. Rathbun recognized Coe's shrewdness and the uncanny way in which his predictions seemed to prove accurate. Annoying as were Coe's protracted mental deliberations, their results were too often right to be ignored.

When Coe came to Buffalo he brought with him more capital, all of his own making, than most Buffalo merchants could command.

He added to it slowly and methodically. His investments were careful and closely watched. Bela Coe was not one to succumb to the unwise speculations that ruined many of his associates as these boom years went on.

Coe was a skillful stage operator, whose political friendships protected him from loss of the mail contracts and whose knowledge of stage operations made the Buffalo end of the combination one of its most productive parts. The success of the line helped the Eagle immeasurably.

Both Coe brothers had had the best available training in the stage business. Natives of Trenton in Oneida County, they had begun in a small way and then branched out for themselves. Bela, who was Rathbun's age, removed to Canandaigua in 1814 and invested $3,000 in a lot facing the town square. There Coe erected a tavern early the next year that immediately became the center of village life.

In 1816, he sold the tavern for $14,000. He took the money and joined by his brother, Canfield Coe, bought William Bostwick's tavern in Auburn, center of stagecoach operations in that village. There he was closely associated with J. M. Sherwood, a major partner in the Old Line combination. Three years afterward, he sold his interest in the tavern to his brother Chauncey and returned to Canandaigua, repossessing the tavern upon which the buyer had been unable to complete payments. Because this unsuccessful tavern keeper had lost the stage rights, Bela had to buy these back in 1821 from the Marvins and their heirs. He first leased the Canandaigua tavern and then sold it, spending all his time in the stage business before removing to Buffalo.

Despite his association in the stage business with Rathbun, in 1827 Coe made a sufficient down payment to become owner of Buffalo's Mansion House. He saw what Rathbun had accomplished at the Eagle, and he believed that Buffalo's hotel business had increased to the point at which another hotel, even if it were just the second best, was a good investment. Much as it might have benefited his investment, however, Coe could not successfully prevail on Rathbun to let him move the stage terminus to the other building.

Coe had no intention of treating the Mansion as anything other than a source of revenue. In the next few years, he renovated, improved, and enlarged the establishment, giving Rathbun the contract for at least part of the work, and keeping himself in the background. Coe installed a series of managers, but eventually leased the hotel to others to run.

While Rathbun and Coe were intimately related in business, they shared few private social relations. Coe and his wife attended St. Paul's and there they and the Rathbuns often met in fund-raising or charitable activities. But, unlike the Rathbuns, the Coes were active in forming the town's "high society." Elizabeth Coe became the genteel leader of what would later have been called a "set," and her parlor was constantly filled. Always on hand was the formidable William A. Moseley, whose sharp and sarcastic wit made him famed in the law as well as in parlor conversation. The Reverend Addison Searle, the convivial high churchman and rector of St. Paul's, also favored them with his attention. What promising young authors and poets Buffalo possessed usually graced the Coe salon. Members of Mrs. Coe's attractive family from Holland Patent, New York, often visited her, among them her sister, Millicent Ann, thirteen years her junior. When she appeared, so did Orasmus Holmes Marshall, Moseley's young partner. When Orasmus eventually married Millicent, few were surprised.

Despite Rathbun's very real and active partnership in the stage operations, his name never appeared publicly in connection with this enterprise. Advertisements for the Buffalo-Canandaigua and other runs of the Old Line from Buffalo were always signed by "B. D. Coe and Others." For the Canandaigua-Auburn run operated from Canandaigua, they were advertised by "C. H. Coe and Others." In Batavia, Rathbun's brother-in-law, Bissell Humphrey, the tavern proprietor, was the Old Line agent.

Before 1828, the stages on the main cross-state turnpikes expanded to two major runs daily, the Pilot and the Diligence. The Pilot mail coach, which took three days to cover the 298 miles to Albany, was the standard, four-horse post coach. Built egg-shaped of perfectly seasoned and matched wood, it had ample inside space for nine and outside for six passengers. Leather cargo "boots" fastened below the driver and at the rear held mail and baggage. The whole vehicle was slung on leather straps, which acted as springs to cushion the shocks of the road and to protect the horses from severe thrusts. The Diligence coach was a smaller vehicle that imitated the conveyance long familiar to travelers in mountainous regions of Europe. It was more comfortable than the standard coach, but took four days to make the Albany trip.

In 1828, the Buffalo and Albany Coach Lines, as the Old Line was now advertising its services, faced new, threatening competition from the Pioneer Line. This competitor was an entirely new combination, financed by a few wealthy individuals, who were assisted by humble contributions from Sabbatarian Protestant groups throughout New York. It was dedicated to operating only six days a week, halting completely on Sundays.

Its appearance was a result of a wave of religious piety in the backwoods,[1] which was manifested chiefly by a public demand for rigorous Sabbath observance. Ineffectual attempts had been made to get Congress to prohibit the stage lines with mail contracts from operating on Sundays. Setting up the new lines was the way these religious zealots thought they could effect that purpose.

Inauguration of the Pioneer Line brought intense competition in service, prices, and operation. Were it not for the growing volume of travel, both would have been ruined in short order. Battles for control of taverns, hotels, inns, and coaching stations along the highways brought the dispute into every village and town. The Old Line cut prices, so the Pioneer had to reduce them, too. The Pioneer offered more convenient hours of operation; the Old Line had to change its established times to compete. When the stages met on the road, as they often did, competing drivers lashed their teams into a frenzy to race each other, not only to the discomfort but also occasionally the danger of their passengers.

As part of this competition, in 1828 the Buffalo and Albany Coach Lines offered a real innovation in establishing the Telegraph Line, a completely new run on the routes covered by the Pilot and the Diligence. The Telegraph Line, according to the *New York Tribune*, was Rathbun's inspiration. It marked a definite departure from conventional stage operation, appealing to those in a hurry by laying emphasis on speed and efficiency. It met a hitherto unrecognized need that the public appreciated—or at least the part of the public that could pay the relatively high price.

1. Whitman reveals something of the old, but hardly moribund, liberal, secularist bias against evangelical religion, which he associates here with unenlightened, unprogressive—i.e., "backwoods"—populations. We now know that evangelical religion took firm root in antebellum cities, where periodic revivals were no less intense than those held in the countryside. It is to be expected, therefore, that historical research in recent decades has found substantial support in cities for such parts of the evangelical platform for social reform as Sabbath closing laws. And not only support—the leadership for that particular campaign came from prominent people in the urban North. See, for example, Bertram Wyatt-Brown, "Prelude to Abolitionism: Sabbatarian Politics and the Rise of the Second Party System," *Journal of American History* 58 (1971), 316–41; and Paul Johnson, *A Shopkeeper's Millennium: Society and Revivals in Rochester, New York, 1815–1837* (New York: Hill and Wang, 1978).

Using lighter vehicles, the new line carried only six passengers inside and traveled day and night, cutting the trip to Albany in good weather to forty-eight hours. Its strict rules provided that passengers could not stop over en route, unless they were willing to make the remainder of the trip on one of the slower Pilot or Diligence coaches. The Telegraph's stages started on time, would pick up passengers only at fixed points, and stopped only at specified places. The charge was $15, fully twice the rate for the slower vehicles.

The ruinous competition between the two combinations could not be continued for long, especially because the more comfortable, although slower, canal itself reduced the potential business. Coach travel was frequently uncomfortable. Often the coaches became stuck on muddy roads, and passengers had to move themselves and stand, sometimes knee deep, in mud, while the driver swore and beat the horses in an endeavor to free the wheels. Accidents were not uncommon, the coaches sometimes overturning because of the driver's carelessness or the roughness of the road. A broken axle, a smashed wheel, a snapped strap might mean a fatality. All the stage roads were usually poorly maintained, and the more traffic they had on them, the worse their condition. The busy stretch between Batavia and Buffalo was paved in rough "corduroy," a road design in which logs were laid crosswise to the direction of travel. Experienced travelers called it the worst road in the world.

Operations of the four-horse post coaches that carried the main line mail were always under great pressure, regardless of the weather. Under the terms of the program of government subsidies, missing a connection or bringing damage to the mail led to immediate financial penalties. Keeping the equipment in good condition and the hardbitten (and in some cases, hard-drinking) drivers on the job was a highly specialized task.

In Buffalo, the Pioneer Line first set up an office with David E. Merrill, proprietor of the Steamboat Hotel, as its agent. The Steamboat was not a temperance house. But then most of the Pioneer's drivers were drinkers, although the religious folk backing the line would have preferred to pick out sober Christians as its representatives. Merrill was the last of his Buffalo associates with whom Rathbun kept contact in his old age. The Steamboat was a roughcast stone building, with a cupola belfry on its roof. Near the docks, it possessed few of the pretensions to elegance displayed in the uptown hotels. Later, the Pioneer turned the agency over to Ira Merrill, who had some previous staging experience. His headquarters were at the Buffalo House. Under Merrill's supervision, competing stages operated to Niagara, on the Canadian side of the river, and between Rochester, Lockport, Niagara Falls, and Buffalo. The Old Line had to add parallel runs to each place to prevent its business being wiped out.

After about two years of this wasteful competition, the Pioneer Line collapsed suddenly. A combination of fervor and inexperience ultimately had cost its backers tremendous sums. Three men in Rochester alone were reported to have lost $60,000.

The competition started as a result of a meeting and of agitation at Auburn. Opposition, which also developed in that village, helped break it. Those who objected to banning Sunday operations on either financial or theological grounds called public protest meetings. William H. Seward, the Auburn lawyer who was a rising star in the state's political firmament, and one day to be its dominant figure, was the chief spokesman for the opposition. The enrollment of good citizens and "practicing Christians" in the ranks of those in favor of seven-day operations confounded the Pioneer's backers and disheartened them.

After the demise of the Pioneer, some of its stages, employees, and runs were taken over by the Old Line. But even with this competitor out of the way, the remaining lines had to maintain their services and operations at a high point. Travelers had grown to expect it, and with the threat of business going to the canals and even to the slowly proliferating local railroad carriers, there could be no letup. They had passed the pioneering stage in their development and could now stay in business only by giving good service.

As Rathbun's entrepreneurial ideas widened, he concluded that full ownership of the stages, with their mail contracts and the political connections of the Old Line organization, would be useful in furthering his plans. Many of the stage lines, he could easily foresee, would be doomed sooner or later by the newfangled railroads. Full ownership, publicly recognized, however, would serve his purpose by so closely identifying him with transportation interests that he would have something to trade upon as they sought entrance into the railroad business. At the same time, the stages would temporarily supplement his other interests.

Surely Rathbun approached Bela Coe with this idea many times before Coe made up his own mind. That astute businessman, still making good money from his stage operations, also saw the shape of the future. Profits had declined from their earlier high points. The stage business would never regain its former earning power. Moreover, Coe himself was interested in railroads, and he was satisfied that the main stage lines, the best paying runs, would soon be outmoded as railroads were completed.

Coe's decision was hastened by the sudden death of his brother at Canandaigua in late April 1835. Hannah Coe, widow of Chauncey, could not continue in the stage business. It was probably clear that the tough drivers would not work for a woman. Under any circumstance, she needed money to care for her two fatherless children. The business would have to be sold.

This event convinced Coe that the time had come to accept Rathbun's offer. After months of dickering on details, on October 31, 1835, the negotiations were completed and he sold Rathbun his entire Buffalo stage property for $20,000. The sale included some real estate as well as the barns and stables, the horses and stages, and the part of the franchise that Coe owned himself. Two weeks later, Coe also sold his half interest in the stage franchise at Canandaigua.

The shrewd Coe, who had always protected himself in his dealings with Rathbun after Chauncey's difficulty, did not make any errors this time. He accepted a $13,300 mortgage from Benjamin and Alice, for that part of the sale price, and made sure that the mortgage was doubly guarded by a $20,000 bond. Moreover, he directed that Rathbun insure the property for $12,000 and turn the policy over to him, a most unusual requirement at that period.

Part of the Rathbun-Coe contract required Coe, with his political connections, to remain as the official mail contractor. After the sale, therefore, the Post Office Department continued to deal directly with him, even though he no longer operated the stages.

Rathbun put the livery stable part of the business under the direction of Benjamin F. Hadduck and Granville Kimball, stable proprietors who had been working for him for some time. He not only retained Stevenson to direct the stages from the headquarters at the Eagle, but kept Hathaway, Coe's second foreman, to handle the business that had developed around the Mansion House.

Rathbun ordered that the coaches be repainted as they were overhauled. In the coach manufacturing shop, which he had recently taken over, the vehicles were colored a bright red. On the door panels, inside a decorated floral leaf border, was painted in dignified script, "B. Rathbun."

In 1835, Rathbun's stage service covered these main route runs: Eastern Telegraph, Eclipse and Pilot; Western Mail; Eagle (to Rochester); Mail (to Niagara Falls), and Mail (to Canada). Each left at a different hour, from the Eagle at 5:00 A.M. to the Western Mail at 8:00 P.M.

For the first time now, as sole owner instead of silent partner, the name "B. Rathbun" appeared as the signature to the stage line advertising. Already familiar to the public of western New York in many other ways, the Rathbun name now came to represent an almost complete monopoly of public transportation by highway.

6

Banking and Building in Buffalo

As its prominent businessmen were aware, Buffalo lacked money for current enterprises and capital for expansion. Barter, which had sufficed for ordinary business in early days, was awkward and time-consuming. Wealth amassed in land and buildings was not capital until it could be translated into currency. Investors complained that "speculation," a term that then really meant "investment" and hence bore little of the derogatory connotation it acquired later, was severely curtailed. Without a reliable currency, few expected that their land would rise systematically in its value, even as population grew and trade increased.

It was difficult to raise money for new undertakings. Small private mortgages were practicable, and so were advances on notes, but interest rates remained high. Exchange and discount brokers, such as Noah P. Sprague, Henry Seymour, Ebenezer Johnson and Company, and others demanded so substantial a share of the principal for discounting notes that few could hope to raise sizable capital on the basis of their services.

These exchange and discount offices, however, were the only "banks" in Buffalo after the final suspension of the feeble Bank of Niagara in 1828. The farmers who had been inveigled into accepting the bank's depreciated bills, which were hawked for months at 62½ percent discount, lost heavily. Few in Buffalo suffered, for those with money had already been hurt once before by that bank and they were determined not to be victimized again. Philander Bennett and William Williams, appointed receivers of the defunct bank, closed the doors of the one-story building on Washington Street and began the decade-long job of settling its tangled affairs.

The money stringency handicapped Rathbun along with everyone else. It prevented him from carrying out many of the bigger schemes he was considering. However, men with money were putting it into construction of homes and stores, as investments, and they were paying off their friendship with Rathbun by giving him more and more building work. He could discount his own notes, based on these contracts, and raise some money. Also, he made at least one connection outside Buffalo that he retained and increasingly used. This connection was with Robert L. Steele, a New York City broker. He arranged with Steele to accept his notes, a service that enabled him to pay quickly for goods bought in the markets of the metropolis.

The tight situation began to change in 1829, a very important year, as residents looked back on it later. Building and improvement projects seemed to be taking off everywhere. The first evidence of change was the largest federal expenditure, up to that time, on improvement of the harbor. Some of the more important buildings, such as the Eagle, were now being supplied with running water. Pumps and wells had failed to meet the growing needs and the Jubilee Water Works Company, capitalized at $20,000 and the first such enterprise in village history, piped water through wooden tubes to the center of town. The source was in the eastern Black Rock area at the Jubilee Springs, which was owned by General Porter. The system produced a thirteen-foot head of water at the Eagle, about two and a half miles away. Within three years, sixteen miles of wooden mains, a number of them put in by Rathbun, were in use.[1] The Buffalo High School Association, organized at a meeting at the Eagle two years earlier, had been campaigning for a goal of $25,000 to finance the opening of such a school. With $10,000 pledged, members now decided to realize their project.

There also was a singular, lucky coincidence having to do with an Englishman's tooth, specifically a molar belonging to Wilfred Parkins, former sheriff of London. Parkins had come to Buffalo and stayed longer than he intended. Breaking a tooth, he found himself in agony, unable to eat, and without the services of a dentist. Sheriff Parkins heard of Dr. George E. Hayes, who had done some dental surgery and was experimenting with artificial teeth. Although he

---

1. Most residents, however, continued to be without running water. Those who needed water, for whatever purpose, continued to buy it from "Water John," the Alsatian immigrant whose spavined horse pulled a wagon on which there was a large barrel of fresh water.

went to Dr. Hayes with trepidation, Hayes not only extracted the root easily but also devised replacements for that and other of the sheriff's missing teeth. Parkins swore that his new teeth looked and worked better than nature's originals. Dr. Hayes prospered from the testimonial, and Buffalo benefited because the broken tooth delayed Parkins long enough to allow investors to persuade him to finance a block of stores. The sheriff loaned Ira Blossom and Lewis Allen the fabulous sum of $20,000 at an even more incredible, mere seven percent interest. Rathbun was the builder of the fourteen stores known locally as Ellicott Square.

The event in 1829 that seemed most pregnant with meaning for economic development, however, was the establishment at Buffalo of a branch of the Bank of the United States. Nicholas Biddle, president of the bank, was then engaged in an expansion program, partly to meet the obvious needs of newly settled sections of the country for banking facilities but mostly to counteract ideological opposition to the very idea of a central bank. He had, from his inauguration in 1822 as bank president, until 1827, kept its activities within the chief commercial cities. The bank's stability, the prestige it had developed, had greatly improved the general banking situation and had made the currency firmer than it had ever been. State banks reflected this improvement by functioning better than they had in the past.

Buffalo's leaders, like their counterparts in other recently settled New York State towns, clamored for a branch bank. Proponents pointed out the village's advantages, its assured future, the fact that the Bank of Niagara could never be revived, and the certainty that the great amount of accumulated wealth gathering in the area and hidden in private safes and locked drawers would flow rapidly into a stable bank.

In the summer, Biddle and several of his associates visited western New York, not only to examine the ground themselves but also, incidentally, to see Niagara Falls. At the Falls, Biddle was so impressed by the scenery that he offered to pay Augustus Porter from his own pocket to build a circular wood stairway down to the gorge for public use. Porter accepted, and the stairway perpetuated Biddle's name among visitors for nearly a century. At Buffalo, he gave General Porter and David Evans assurances that establishment of a branch in western New York would be approved by the bank's directors.

Biddle's visit inspired ambitions to compete for leadership of the new branch, a post that it was rightly assumed would give numerous opportunities for profitable inside manipulations. If the branch were to be in Rochester, the obvious choice was the reformed Van Burenite and eminently respectable figure, the conservative Judge William B. Rochester. As his name suggested, no finer genealogy existed in that Lake Ontario city. If it were to be at Buffalo, the obvious choice seemed General Porter, who had recently served as secretary of war under John Quincy Adams. State Senator Tracy also dreamed that he might have a chance in view of his political connections, which had led President Adams to offer him a cabinet post.

But when the bank's directors decided on September 15, 1829, that the new branch would be in Buffalo, Biddle's astute hand nonetheless fell on former Judge Rochester, the least politically embroiled of the candidates. The judge still believed that he could keep the bank out of politics. He also cleverly convinced both Porter and Tracy that, though an outsider, he was the only possible choice under the political circumstances, a selection in which the influential Evans also strongly concurred.

Judge Rochester moved to Buffalo and, with the aid of a Philadelphia-trained cashier, opened the new branch in the fall. Well before the start of the new year, Biddle was assured that the branch was in complete operation and was fully accepted in the community. Opening of the branch brought more credit into the village than the Bank of Niagara had offered even in its best days.

The branch bank's board was composed of some of the strongest figures in the area: Tracy, Townsend, Thompson, Evans, Augustus Porter, William Peacock, and James Wadsworth. The others were Joseph Stocking, Buffalo's leading hatter and furrier, and Lyman A. Spaulding, a mill and land owner at Lockport in Niagara County, men of great wealth, if less eminent and powerful.

Few were surprised when the *Buffalo Journal and General Advertiser* announced on March 24, 1830, that "B. Rathbun, Esq., of Buffalo" had obtained the contract to build a handsome new home for the bank. The paper's editor said of Rathbun his "proverbial good taste, in matters of this sort, we are glad to see called into action upon the present occasion." By mid-July, Judge Rochester could advise Biddle that the building was on schedule and that the design "presents a fair earnest that we shall have quite a handsome house."

The boxy stone building, relieved only by massive white pillars in front, was at the northeast corner of Main and South Division streets, in the heart of the business section. Rathbun had done all his building jobs thoroughly and well. He put his heart into this one, determined that it would give satisfaction—and it did. The directors were pleased and the public impressed with what Rathbun conceived: a tasteful adaptation of the Grecian style, which was then coming into fashion for American public buildings.

This contract for the most important institution in town gave a tremendous boost to Rathbun's reputation as a contractor and architect. He was established. He was a man of ability and taste. He was employed by the men whose opinions counted. Buffalo's affluent residents no longer had to worry about their own lack of architectural knowledge and cultivation. They had, at the call of their pocketbooks, a contractor to whom they could turn in designing their homes and businesses with full assurance that his job would be done right.

Rathbun's home was just a block away from the new bank. On the second floor facing front, his office was the site of many candlelight meetings where devious and complicated schemes were now increasingly determining the financial future of Buffalo and much of the New West. If his planning and scheming were done at his home, his detailed business was done in the countinghouse in back of the store in the Eagle block, where Lyman could watch it. Lyman was his brother's adjutant and head supervisor now, as well as chief bookkeeper. Lyman checked and counterchecked, hired the lesser employees, and paid off the workmen.

Emboldened by his success, Rathbun engaged in his first important promotion. He acquired by some process (for the transaction was never recorded) a large and centrally located piece of land extending from Main Street west as far as Delaware that was right in the path of the northerly movement of the city's development. He broke this into a number of small lots, and for the next several years, he was engaged in erecting and selling houses. As land values rose, so did Rathbun's fortunes. Indeed, this venture proved to be financially successful and it established his reputation as a developer of real estate. He also gained experience in promotion techniques that he would put to use on a larger scale as soon as the opportunity arose. Rathbun directly profited from the growth of the cities' social problems as well. More people meant more crime. More transactions meant more bad debt. His recent successes in hand, it was natural that Rathbun be selected to build the new jail needed to house criminals and debtors. The old jail, appallingly unsanitary, was sold to private developers.

For some time, as these new and bigger matters filled his head, Benjamin had given almost no attention to the Eagle. Only occasionally did he drop in to make sure that it was operating properly. Late in 1830 or early in 1831, Rathbun sold the Eagle and the Eagle buildings. The tavern had given him his start, yet he probably felt little sentiment about abandoning it. It had served its purpose, and the money from the sale could more usefully and profitably be employed elsewhere.

The purchaser who gave Rathbun $10,000 in cash and a $3,000 mortgage on the land covered by the Eagle buildings was Isaac R. Harrington, who was active in the Anti-Masonic movement and later in the Whig party, a devout Presbyterian, and a moderately successful businessman. Harrington, who would be Buffalo's mayor and later its postmaster, probably peered through the spectacles that were always halfway down his nose as he signed the deed, glancing up and over them to make sure that this sharp Rathbun, for all his pleasant manners, played no trick on him.

Harrington made few changes in the Eagle, continuing the practices Rathbun had instituted that had made the place famous. Many visitors who had known the Eagle under Rathbun did not even realize that its ownership had changed. Everything, with one exception, was the same. Hawkins, who had been spending less and less time at the Eagle anyway, left its service and became Rathbun's full-time valet, private agent, and messenger. Hawkins was particularly useful whenever Rathbun wanted something done quickly by one whose loyalty could not be doubted.

Simultaneously with his disposal of the Eagle, Rathbun bought land and erected a four-story sturdy commercial building, with a bluish cut-stone front, on the west side of Main Street midway in the block below "The Churches." At 230 Main Street he installed a fancy dry goods store, under his name, and next door at 230½ Main Street, he moved the whole stock of the store from the Eagle block, together with Lyman and the rest of the countinghouse staff. His presence in the central business district was expanding, even as he gave up the Eagle.

While "B. Rathbun" the business concern and Benjamin Rathbun the person were busy carving a real niche in Buffalo's business life, other self-made men were also moving ahead by shrewd exercise of ingenuity, ability, and bluster. Inevitably these up-and-coming men had close contact with Rathbun.

One whose activities and personality brought him in frequent contact with Rathbun was Hiram Pratt, youngest son of Capt. Samuel Pratt, Buffalo's first merchant. Ten years younger than Rathbun,

Pratt could recall how his father brought him into Buffalo at the age of four, with the rest of his large family. They came in the first carriage to bounce over the rocks and stumps on the old Indian trail, much to the amazement of the handful of settlers, most of whom had walked across New York State to get to frontier Buffalo.

When Pratt was a boy, the elder Pratt's business failed. The father died while still relatively young, and the children were forced to support their mother and each other. Hiram's first ambition was to be a physician. As a youth, he became an apprentice, studying medicine with Dr. Cyrenus Chapin, whose medical work was largely in his apothecary shop. Young Pratt's medical apprenticeship comprised little more than learning how to mix herbal brews and clerking.

Ready to turn an extra penny when the chance occurred, Chapin gradually expanded his stock along general lines. Pratt and a fellow medical apprentice, Orlando Allen, found that they liked selling goods better than puttering with medicines and advising the sick. When Dr. Chapin opened a second store and gave Pratt the opportunity to take over the original establishment, Pratt seized it. He took Horace Meech as partner, and Allen remained in association with them.

A couple of years later, Pratt dissolved this partnership and formed a new one with Allen, who in 1826 had become his brother-in-law by marrying Marilla Pratt, Hiram's younger sister. Operating as Hiram Pratt and Company, their business was chiefly in groceries. About the same time, with Asa B. Meech, Pratt organized Pratt and Meech, a general forwarding, storage, and commission business in which he showed his skill by competing successfully with the earlier established firms.[2]

The same year that Allen and his sister were married, Pratt married Maria Fowler at Northampton, Massachusetts. Ambitious and aggressive, Maria complemented her husband's restless drive for success by furthering his interests among the arbitrators of taste and the conveners of fashionable soirees. Her strong character and commanding presence made her, for years after Pratt's death, the stern and uncompromising dictator of the local elite's social life.

Like all the Buffalo men who were accumulating wealth, Pratt combined shrewd opportunism and entrepreneurial zeal that took

2. As common an enterprise as forwarding, to which it was closely related, the commission business comprised the forwarders who were hired not only to ship but also simultaneously to sell goods or commodities on behalf of their suppliers.

him into a variety of fields. Recognizing Rathbun's skill from the start, Pratt hooked himself to Rathbun's projects whenever he could and benefited from several joint projects in which they engaged with others. Rathbun was impressed with Pratt's astuteness and ability to make money. He saw in him a likely collaborator in some of the schemes he was hatching.

Their first major joint venture was the creation of the Bank of Buffalo. Established under the recently enacted State Safety Fund law, this institution had been in contemplation when Biddle opened the branch of the Bank of the United States. Rathbun had been a principal in the organization of the new Bank of Buffalo and was appointed one of the commissioners to establish it. With him were Evans, Pierre A. Barker, Israel T. Hatch, Guy E. Goodrich, and Stephen G. Austin. Hatch was a young lawyer then serving as New York's assistant secretary of state. He had been appointed by his half-brother, Enos T. Throop, who in 1829 had succeeded Van Buren as governor when Jackson made Van Buren his secretary of state. Goodrich had a dry goods store, and Austin was a lawyer.

Subscription books for the purchase of stock in the bank were opened on May 16, 1830, in the Eagle Tavern. Capitalization was set at $200,000, but the public was so convinced that banks were a sure investment that subscriptions of $1,654,250 in stock were taken in less than two weeks, forcing the commissioners to apportion the mandated amount of stock among all these eager investors.

Pratt had not been one of the prime movers in planning the bank, but through Rathbun's influence he was elected to the first board of directors, on which Rathbun also sat. Goodrich was elected president and, again with the help of his friend Rathbun, Pratt secured the important job of cashier. The bank began business on September 6, 1831, and Rathbun built its headquarters, a "gem of architecture," on the west side of Main Street immediately below St. Paul's Church. In contrast to most of Rathbun's buildings, this two-story stone structure was utterly plain except for a stone railing around the top. Its business floor was approached from the outside by a flight of stairs, under which could be found the candy store that rented the basement.

Although there were a few other "great men," the officers and directors of the United States Branch Bank and the Bank of Buffalo were the chief figures of their time in Buffalo. They were the men who had the trust of those who owned the stock, and they were also those who benefited most from the operation of the banks. Possession of a seat on the bank's board made it easy to arrange the negotiations and the loans by which they themselves could benefit in one way or another.

The opening of these banks gave Buffalo the credit that could help relieve pent-up pressures for expansion. Conditions were propitious for the start of an era of investment and dealing. Local businessmen had not yet become fully aware of the inevitability of the cyclical cataclysms of the capitalist economy that would afflict finance, and they were quite sure that Buffalo's future held unending opportunities.

7

Booming Business

A "bull market" in western lands, as it would have been described later, was already under way as the 1820s closed. Throughout the United States, a speculative fever—more akin to gambling than anything else—was beginning to take on momentum. Promoters were now hawking village lots and farm property all around the lower Great Lakes.

Banks were busy loaning their paper money, which borrowers could use at face value as a down payment on government-owned western land. Borrowers used as collateral the land they had just bought and got new loans to buy more land, a process that seemed as if it could go on endlessly. The paper money that paid for the land remained in the financial stream. Very little of it found its way back to plague the issuing banks with calls for redemption, because increased trade gave rise to an intense demand for currency.

Land values were rising fast enough to give those who bought and sold a substantial quick profit, and the continued rapid westward flow of population convinced investors that land values would go on rising indefinitely. Making money on land appeared not only sound but also eminently patriotic. It demonstrated a conviction in the promise of the ever-unfolding future that lay before the United States. In addition, the growth of towns such as Buffalo, which would soon provide numerous examples of mammoth increases in the value of particular pieces of land, proved the point that promoters were emphasizing in their advertising.

In Buffalo the rise in land values did not at first advance spectacularly. But the steady growth of its population (from about 2,500 in 1825 to 8,653 by 1830), the substantial increase in forwardings on the canal and the lakes, and the mercantile business transacted in local stores all gave a firm basis for optimism. Rathbun and other business-men were thriving.

Above all else, it was the changing of the interregional trade that boded spectacularly well for the future. More and better household goods and farm supplies were being moved for settlers. Fabricated articles from eastern factories and more of the best American and European products were being shipped westward over the great ar-teries of transport, replacing the bare necessities and the coarse, utili-tarian trade goods, which had formerly been freighted with such labor. More wheat flowed out of Ohio, precursor of the flood of grain that was soon to present Buffalo for a time with the distinction of being the world's busiest grain port. Sailing vessels were hauling the grain, grown on newly settled farms along the shore of Lake Erie, to Buffalo for transshipment by canal. Although these vessels were small by later standards, there were many of them. Capt. Levi Allen, for instance, commanding the 113-ton brig *United States,* brought in six thousand bushels of sound western wheat in one trip. Because the technology had not yet been perfected, there were no elevators to simplify grain handling. It took five days of backbreaking hand labor to empty the ship. When a method could be found to speed this essential work and thereby increase the volume of traffic, Buffalo's prospects would be even brighter.

Also moving east in greater quantity were cargoes of timber, chiefly for ship construction. Some timber came from western New York and some from farther west. There was plenty of it. Farmers considered most of these stately trees of the region's vast virgin forests little more than obstructions a cruel fate had placed there to worsen their lot. Farmers wanted only to chop them down, blow them up, and, in whole sections, to girdle them, so that they withered, died, and crashed to the ground to be dragged off and burned as time permitted.

Quantities of potash, leached from the ash of the burned forests and from the wood fuel consumed in homes and factories, were also going eastward constantly, and turned out to be one of the best cash products of the farms. The stores accepted potash in barter for goods and then forwarded it to the East. Shiploads of potash came into Buffalo, and boat after boat, loaded with the barreled alkali, floated east on the canal to the soap and other manufacturers who needed it. Mixed in with the lumberyards along lower Delaware Avenue were the small soap factories that belched smoke.

As Rathbun hurried on his errands, he doubtless noticed that Buffalo was getting a different look. Travelers mingled with country people and villagers in the streets, giving the town a cosmopolitan and slightly exotic air. The transient visitors and the locally affluent stood out in the crowd, the women in bright Italian silks, colorful shawls, and bonnets or leghorns in summer; the men in black frock coats, with figured silk waistcoats, pleated shirt fronts, and flowing cravats, their blue cashmere trousers tucked into their boots. Contrasting with these elaborate costumes were the assorted garb of sailors and the miscellaneous rough clothing of wagon drivers, farmers, and laborers and leather-dressed hunters. Many workers wore the comfortable moccasins that they bought from the Indians or made themselves. Throngs of Indians from the nearby Seneca Reservation at Buffalo Creek crowded the streets, too—the women in bright calicoes and often bearing papooses on their backs, the men wrapped in traditional blankets or the rough workingman's clothes of the time.

Yet for all this gathering prosperity and even sophistication, Buffalo was a rough-hewn place. Streets remained muddy and unpaved. Only a few oil lamps broke the darkness at night. Places such as the Eagle, the Mansion House, and taverns and restaurants were unique havens of brilliant light to the occasional wayfarer out after sundown. Cattle and hogs were at large on the streets. Bears could still be shot in nearby woods. Only a few board sidewalks on Main Street gave sound footing in the frequently wet weather when streets became seas of mud.

Fire was ever a danger to life and property. Watchmen making their rounds in the jerry-built town were on the lookout for fires, for the combination of defective chimneys, flying sparks, and wooden buildings created a constant hazard. With an inadequate water supply, the volunteer bucket brigades could do little to stem flames in windy weather. The best way to halt their spread was to pull down all buildings in the immediate vicinity. One windy day in November 1829, a number of stores on the west side of Main Street burned, with a loss of $25,000. Two years later, the "Kremlin Corner," wooden structures owned by William Peacock at Main, Niagara, Pearl, and Eagle streets, burned. The most damaging fire came in 1832 when flames gutted several whole blocks in the heart of town, from Main Street back to Washington on one side and Pearl on the other, between East and West Seneca streets, with a $250,000 loss. "Cheapside," a popular-priced buying area of clothing wholesalers near Main and Seneca streets, was cleaned out together with its many little shops. The fires finally frightened the municipality into paying the Jubilee Water Works to build and keep filled four underground cisterns in the built-up part of town. But this offered false security, for it was discovered, when it was most needed, that the water was either too low to be rapidly pumped out or that there was too little of it. Part of the year, too, it was simply frozen rock-hard.

Serious as these fires were, at least for builders they had a positive side. They brought business to Rathbun and other contractors who got the job of replacement. The "Kremlin Corner" fire was an especial benefit. On January 1, 1833, Rathbun leased the whole fire-ravaged area from the Peacock Estate and built a series of new stone stores for tenants. This property then became one of the chief business blocks of the town. Various stores occupied the first floor, Main Street front of the Kremlin. Upstairs the offices tended to be occupied by lawyers and brokers.

The flood of newcomers, particularly working-class ones, in 1830 astounded older residents. These laborers and other migrants crowded into existing buildings, into shacks and hastily erected huts, creating for the first time large slumlike sections. By the end of the year, the village population had risen to 15,661, thus nearly doubling in one year. The influx was a bonanza for Rathbun. From then on, as long as he was in business in Buffalo, there was a shortage of dwellings, a lack of commercial facilities, and a heavy backlog of demand for almost every sort of construction. Despite new and even more skillful competition, Rathbun's commanding lead as the town's chief builder brought him business and the magnitude of his construction work rose astronomically.

Moreover, the large population and the tremendous multiplication of its requirements benefited his stores to such an extent that he felt justified in opening another retail operation on Main Street. The new one specialized in dry goods. With larger stocks in its line than any other store could boast, it offered a wider selection for the differing tastes of more shoppers, giving Rathbun a chance to buy in greater volume and increase his profits. Retail specialization was novel for Buffalo where most stores carried a little of almost everything, but not much of anything except groceries.

Because of the shortage of small-denomination currency, largely because of state laws restricting its issuance, Rathbun served the convenience of his employees and customers alike by issuing scrip signed with his name and redeemable at the "House of B. Rathbun." In denominations of $1, $2, $3, and $5, the scrip was widely accepted as valid currency, testimony to the general confidence in his prospects and in his word.

The tremendous population growth necessitated a more active municipal government, and gave rise to a new civic pride among those who wanted Buffalo to look and to act more like a mighty metropolis. Soon agitation arose to replace the village structure with a more powerful city form of government, free of township, and freer of county, interference. Because Buffalo controlled the county in votes, opposition was negligible, and the state legislature was induced to pass an authorizing act on April 8, 1832, creating the City of Buffalo.

Dr. Ebenezer Johnson, now the solemn and irascible senior partner of the banking and exchange firm of Johnson, Hodge and Company, was elected the first mayor of the new city. He took his job with the same sense of duty that he always displayed, a seriousness greater than that of many of his constituents.

Rathbun profited here, too. The second floor of one of his dry goods stores became the Council Chamber. Mayor Johnson and the city clerk, Dyre Tillinghast, doubtless had to twist their rotund frames awkwardly to squeeze between the two stone piers at the bottom of the narrow stairs when they went to council meetings.

One of the mayor's first tasks was to quell a street brawl among dock laborers. Waving his cane and ordering them to desist, the authoritative Johnson was worth a battery of police. He was less successful, however, at enforcing an order against fireworks and firearms on the Fourth of July that had been enacted because of the danger of fire. Attempting to stem such time-honored American customs was impossible. Gangs of youths defied him, exhausted the mayor, forcing him to dash from one section of the town to another following the noise of their guns and firecrackers.

The city's real test of its new responsibilities in its first year came with the appearance of cholera, the most dreaded scourge of the age. That first outbreak was to be the worst of three nineteenth-century cholera epidemics. Death swept away rich and poor alike, until its sight became a casual matter.

Without a reliable cure for cholera, or even a clear notion of its cause, officials could only hope to manage the epidemic. Assisted by a quickly appointed board of health, Mayor Johnson quieted the fearful, arranged for the handling of the sick, and bought five acres to start a new cemetery. The mayor's stout figure, it was said, thinned noticeably during the ordeal. Dr. John E. Marshall, the municipal health officer, worked tirelessly throughout the epidemic. Roswell Haskins distinguished himself as a member of the board of health by entering the houses of the sick when others were fearful, and carrying victims in his arms to the hospital. Some rose to new heights of humanity. Some shamelessly showed their cowardice or superstition. The best known in her profession, the madame of a house of prostitution near the waterfront volunteered her services in the hospital. She was one of the few women to do so, and she worked heroically until she fell victim to the disease. Before it was over, at least 120 had died, and many, many more had been sick.

The epidemic with its horrible deaths apparently sharpened moral sensibilities, at least among local editors. The newspaper claimed that most of the eight thousand who braved the rain to see the city's last public hanging in 1832 came from the country. Buffalonians, it was maintained, were shocked to see mothers nursing their babies in the shadow of the gallows, and sickened by the rude jests, coarse revelry, and commercialism of the scene. But Buffalo had come only so far, it seems, despite the desire in some quarters to boast of civilization. Enterprising businessmen sold seats on stands they had erected. Others did a brisk trade in liquor at temporary booths.

There were now a few healthier entertainments, for no doubt a market was taking root for art for the first time. The firm of Gilbert and Trowbridge had taken over the Buffalo Theater opposite the Eagle and was regularly presenting some of the plays then in vogue. Trowbridge, a general utility actor, took many roles and his vivacious wife had female leads. In 1832, a second theater, which soon supplanted the old Buffalo, was opened by the firm of Dean and McKinney on the second floor of a Seneca Street building.

Other cultural stirrings were also evident. Charles Anderson Dana, afterward the famed publisher of the *New York Sun*, recalled that he gained an important education in Buffalo at the meetings of a literary group, the Coffee Club, in one of the taverns. Dana was then clerking at Staats and Dana, a dry goods store where his uncle, William K. Dana, was a partner. Another effort, like the Coffee Club, eventuated in the organization of the Young Men's Literary Society, where these young clerks and bookkeepers could find an outlet for their literary productions in congenial and supportive company. This organization, which lasted many years, provided part of the initiative that eventuated in the founding of the Buffalo Public Library and the Buffalo Historical Society.

Financial conditions were so bright that the few who recalled the long-past depression felt that a new era had dawned. Prosperity was merely in the air from 1829 to 1833. After that, at first only imperceptibly, the pace quickened. Then almost moment by moment, business became better and the values of local property escalated beyond the wildest imaginings of the past.

This dramatic change in tempo was largely traceable to the controversy between President Andrew Jackson and the Bank of the United States. In his 1829 inaugural address, Jackson had roundly attacked the bank. Bank director Nicholas Biddle awaited his chance to respond, and in 1832, an election year, foolishly decided on an immediate test of the bank's strength in Congress. An act extending the bank's twenty-year charter, which still had all of four years to run, was passed, but was vetoed by Jackson.

The campaign of 1832 closely reflected this issue. The Buffalo conservatives, numbering the Rathbuns among them, united with others throughout the country to denounce the Jackson administration and support the bank. Lyman Rathbun was enrolled as one of the leading "Democratic Republicans who have been friends of Jackson but oppose the reelection of any man." Rathbun Allen, Rhoda Rathbun Allen's eldest son and now an employee of his uncle, joined in calling the youths of Buffalo together to oppose Jackson's reelection. The Rathbuns were now no longer middle-of-the-road tavern keepers, but were ready to commit themselves publicly as supporters of the system that was bringing them wealth.

Jackson's victory that year, in a campaign that saw Biddle reverse the bank's neutral policy by actively throwing its strength against the administration, spelled doom for the bank. Even while a special congressional committee was reporting the bank sound, Jackson was planning to dismantle it. This took the form of an order effective October 1, 1833, directing the removal of federal deposits from the Bank of the United States and putting them in state banks. Foreseeing this action, Biddle determined to create a business panic and in August began a sharp contraction of credit, which dislocated the general economy, causing widespread failures. But the state depositories, with huge new funds at their control and no established tradition of responsibility, soon countered the effects of the central bank's contraction by offering loan capital at an unprecedented rate, thereby giving an inflationary boost to an entirely new group of borrowers.

The economic storm agitated the entire country. In Congress, Samuel Beardsley, the younger of the two brothers who had been neighbors of the Rathbuns in Otsego County, stood as one of the major Jackson defenders. In an antibank speech, he coined the burning phrase "perish credit, perish commerce" in preference to the "tyranny of an irresponsible corporation."

The conservatives were losing political ground. The reaction against Biddle became so strong that he almost as suddenly reversed the bank's policy and began pumping credits and paper money into the already inflated economic stream until finances began to spiral upward at an incredible speed. The new waves of credit from the state banks, plus the revived tidal wave from the central bank, brought an unprecedented boom. Throughout the country, speculations in land, buildings, railroads, steamship lines, and similar enterprises assumed huge proportions. Federal land sales, which totaled $5,000,000 in 1834, were nearly five times greater in 1836.

The good tide of speculation struck in Buffalo with Rathbun in an outstanding position to benefit. In six months, it had carried him to the apex of his career; lots were changing hands with incredible frequency. Men who had always been conservative in their investments were found to be putting money into new buildings and other construction with what seemed complete abandon.

In synchrony with the central bank, the Buffalo branch of the Bank of the United States contracted its credit in 1833 and then the next spring opened the floodgates, assisting in precipitating the dizzy spiral until Biddle ordered the branch closed on August 1, 1835, in anticipation of a windup of national operations. Momentarily, as its capital then began to flow out of the city, financiers grew fearful. But Judge Rochester and some of his fellow directors, who knew the value of the branch's assets, bought them and began to function as a private banking firm called William B. Rochester and Company. Alanson Palmer, the amusing Eagle taproom denizen whose speculations were growing extraordinarily successful, bought the handsome branch bank building with the idea of leasing or selling it. Palmer was already boasting that he was worth a million dollars. His method was to buy and sell real estate, using one property as security for the purchase of the next.

The Bank of Buffalo's business was also expanding fast in those halcyon days. Rathbun was no longer on its board. There were other changes too. Even though it was a "Safety Fund Bank," meaning that it had been organized under a law sponsored by Governor Van Buren that was supposed to assure conservative operation, and had the relatively small sum of $164,100 in bank notes in circulation in 1834, it got into difficulties in early 1835 and temporarily suspended specie payments. Because of this trouble, Goodrich stepped down as president. The calculating Hiram Pratt succeeded him and continued to run the bank just as he had, for all practical purposes, when he was its cashier. The machinations which had led to Pratt's elevation were rumored throughout the city but none dared to voice them publicly. Pratt treated the bank as though it were his own property, approving speculative loans to those who were most closely tied to him in his business projects, especially forwarding, steamboating, and land speculating.

Because the city's rapid expansion warranted it, the legislature in 1834 incorporated a second local bank, the Commercial Bank of Buffalo, with $600,000 capital. Rathbun made a gesture of subscribing for some of its stock, but the control of the new institution went to Israel T. Hatch, Pierre A. Barker, and others Rathbun felt certain would support his projects, whether or not he had tied up his own money in the bank. In the next few years, this bank became the chief source of speculative funds in Buffalo.

Barker, one of Rathbun's best friends and his colleague on the old Bank of Buffalo board, became president of the new Commercial Bank and served two years until an internal dispute led to his removal and Hatch's appointment as his successor. While Barker was in office, Rathbun was closely associated with him in several speculations, and, for a time, had upward of $40,000 in loans on the bank's books.

The new bank joined with Johnson, Hodge and Company, the private firm that held a good chunk of the Commercial Bank's stock, in hiring Rathbun to erect a joint building for them, an elaborate, solid stone structure on the west side of Main Street, midway between Seneca and Exchange streets and set back from adjoining buildings. The Commercial had its offices in the south half of the building, and Johnson, Hodge and Company in the north half.

Buffalo financiers as well as borrowers such as Rathbun were also dealing with other nearby banks that were springing up. The Lockport Bank, at that village, became notorious for the carelessness of its investments, a notoriety that a little later was destined to put Lewis

Eaton, one of the three New York State banking commissioners, in a most difficult ethical and political position. Eaton, a founder of the bank, served as its first president before receiving the appointment.

Early in 1836, the legislature incorporated the City Bank of Buffalo with a $400,000 capitalization. People were by then so sure that bank stocks offered the road to riches that they subscribed $1,771,500 before the books were closed. However, the bank did not get under way until the boom had passed and the economy was already showing signs of sharp contraction. Philander Bennett, the storekeeper who had now served for many years as the "first judge" of the Court of Common Pleas, was the inaugural president. The bank was always accused of being politically dominated by the "Albany Regency," and its officers were looked upon as Van Buren henchmen.

Rathbun, Palmer, and some others got the idea of starting a savings bank and whipped up sentiment for an institution that they thought would open a new source of loan capital for land. It is possible that the inspiration was entirely Rathbun's. A letter published by the *Buffalo Daily Commercial Advertiser,* signed with a cryptic "R," began the campaign on the ground that workmen should have a place to put their money. Though he was one of its incorporators in April 1836, Rathbun himself was by then already in the business difficulty that would ultimately destroy him.

There were other banks in organization, among them some in nearby Canada. Rathbun himself had discovered that Canadian laws on private banking were most conveniently lax. The Niagara Suspension Bridge Bank was opened at Queenston, a village twenty miles north, directly across the international border from Lewiston, New York. (There was talk of connecting the two nations by a bridge at this location, a project that would not really begin in earnest, however, for many years.) Bates Cooke, a lawyer who had distinguished himself in the Anti-Masonic cause, became its head.

Construction and real estate deals brought Rathbun into contact with nearly every member of these regional bank boards. No bank could afford to ignore the man who appeared to possess such a Midas touch. Rathbun was involved in so many different projects during the boom that his days were never long enough to do all that had to be done. He rushed from one construction site to another and seemed ever between important meetings. Local bankers and competitors alike must have been amazed that one mind could encompass the variety and complexity of the projects in which he was engaged.

There was a shift, however, in Rathbun's activities. Unlike many of his fellow speculators, Rathbun's primary interest had always been in the development of productive enterprises. Now there was so much quick money to be made that he, too, drifted with the tide into speculation for its own sake. The desire to make money rapidly was overwhelming the belief in the obligation to create soundly operating as well as profitable businesses. He still built substantial structures that did him credit, but his enterprises were becoming so large and complex that mere craftsmanship and skill were less consequential to him than management and acquiring capital he could use to extend his enterprises. If something he undertook did not show immediate signs of profit, he was ready to unload it.

As his enterprises grew bigger, efficiencies of scale became increasingly possible. Part of his mind was now engaged constantly in devising ways to reduce the costs of his huge operations.

His preoccupation with transportation, which was looming as a vital factor in his farflung jobs and stores, suggested one form of savings. In transportation, Rathbun found ways to eliminate middlemen by making agreements with owners of horses and wagons, such as Noyes Darrow, to give him nearly all their services. Because of the volume of his trade, he practically controlled Jacob S. Miller's big Buffalo livery. Now he began to buy horses and wagons himself and to house them in barns and stables he built behind the old Bank of Niagara building. Rathbun worked the same idea to cut costs on long-distance hauling. He bought into the Buffalo and Rochester Packet Boat Company, and when this was no longer useful in meeting his needs, he also bought several canal boats of his own and leased others. He used these to bring material and goods from the seaboard and also to haul eastward products that he had accepted in barter arrangements.

Rathbun's operations had become so complex that he was now forced to departmentalize his growing empire. Agents had charge of purchasing; others of architecture; some of stagecoach businesses, and still others, diverse activities. Subject to his orders and policies, these deputies directed and supervised large segments of his work. Just handling the payroll for so many men in such widely scattered jobs was complicated. But that and other detailed financial problems primarily came under Lyman's sharp-eyed scrutiny at the countinghouse.

Rathbun, with his brother's assistance, held the financial strings tightly. He would loosen his grasp only when it came to especially trusted family members. Hawkins, the link between his private office and the countinghouse, was one of the few outsiders privy to his secrets. He had added Rathbun Allen, then eighteen years old, to his staff in 1832. He had always felt affection toward the good-looking, even-tempered, and mild-mannered youth, and was glad to put him on the staff of the dry goods store. Gentlemanly in appearance, with a florid complexion, young Allen had shown enough ability that Benjamin felt safe in adding him to Lyman's countinghouse staff in the innermost recesses of his empire.

Another nephew admitted into the charmed circle was Lyman Rathbun Howlett, son of Polly Rathbun and her husband, Benjamin Howlett. Employed when he was about fifteen, young Howlett was a favorite of his Uncle Lyman. A clever and handsome boy, at fifteen he was made chief messenger of the countinghouse. Young Howlett speeded his work by riding a little pony, which made him the envy of the other boys throughout the city.

Messengers were being kept busy by the House of Rathbun. Contemporary accounts indicate that Rathbun was engaged extensively in land transactions. These were handled largely as options or direct transfers, without the formality of filing deeds. They were often involved, too, with improvements that Rathbun made and for which he took or gave mortgages. When it was necessary to consummate a contract, he still was willing to work on the barter system, accepting part payment in cash, notes, and concessions and the rest in goods, which he traded again or sold through his stores.

By 1835, Rathbun had so far outstripped every other merchant and contractor in Buffalo that he was widely looked upon by outsiders as the most important and best-known entrepreneurial figure in the Niagara region. His life and habits had become of public interest. He had begun to exhibit the traits that others would most recall, many years later, when thinking about him as he was at the height of his power. The most often commented on was his insistence on the utter loyalty of every employee. Any questioning of his orders, any departure from his ideas, and an employee was discharged and, in effect, "blacklisted." He could never get another job from Rathbun no matter how he, his friends, or his family pleaded. Rathbun had the power now to cause ruin or prosperity to those around him. But he paid a price for the isolation in which he lived, for few questioned him to his face in fear for their livelihoods.

Rathbun was now at the zenith of his success. This was clear in his changed conception of himself—somewhat pompous, certainly proud. One of the most prominent of the structures he built, which remained in use more than a century later, was a relatively smaller job. It was a building he erected for the First Unitarian Church at Franklin and Eagle streets, afterward remodeled and enlarged into an office building. He participated proudly in the laying of the cornerstone on July 11, 1833, and made sure that the silver plate telling of the event bore the self-important notation: "Benjamin Rathbun, Master Builder and Architect." Later in the century Henrik Ibsen would use a part of this professional title to symbolize the hubris of the bourgeois man of professional authority. Rathbun was just the type the Norwegian dramatist had in mind.

8

The Great Speculation

The invention of the steam locomotive in England fired imaginations throughout the world. In America, trains promised speedier transportation and a relatively cheap way to span vast distances and open fertile lands for settlement and development. Railroad promotions spread like wildfire. Extravagant claims of profits combined with appeals to local pride to bring greater numbers of investors together in larger enterprises than ever before. Railroad development soon became a basic force in the swelling business boom.

In western New York, which owed its prosperity to a fortuitous location on natural highway and water routes, the revolutionary significance of railroads was instantly recognized. Steam-drawn trains, hauling freight and passengers to new places, could positively affect the area's development if brought into an ancillary, supportive relationship to water routes—for, as yet, no one doubted that railroads would be the servants of the great canals. But if the steam-drawn trains bypassed the city, Buffalo's dominance of the lakes would be threatened. Besides, railroads certainly looked like a way to make money.

Wilkeson, Townsend, Coe, Rathbun, and many others whose businesses depended directly and indirectly upon transportation canvased every aspect of the subject in anxious discussions. Though none had more than vague ideas of what railroad building entailed, they agreed that Buffalo must be in the vanguard of the new movement. They calculated and drew up tentative plans, but even their most extreme guesses, they were to discover later, grossly underestimated the costs and complexities of railroad projects.

Only a year after the first train ran in England, and before the first American steam train operated on the hastily built Albany and Schenectady line, Buffalo entrepreneurs were attempting to organize their counterparts in other upstate towns to develop a line that would connect Buffalo to the Hudson River. Coe served as chairman of a meeting at the Eagle on September 6, 1831, to consider this possibility. Delegates, including Judge Rochester, Wilkeson, and a few others from Buffalo, attended a meeting of similarly minded promoters at Syracuse a month later. There they set up an association that announced its intention of applying for the incorporation of a "Schenectady and Buffalo Railroad."

The plan was ambitious, and made such good sense that the idea sold itself. Every crossroads hamlet wanted a railroad. Promoters discovered that they could raise immense sums, at least in pledges, for anything advertised as a railroad. Enthusiasm could be found everywhere except in the legislature, which, fearful of competition with the Erie Canal, would approve only short-line charters.

Rathbun needed little convincing. Railroad building and the development it would inevitably stimulate would make his contracting business soar. He remembered the effect of Fulton's *Claremont* on water transportation, and he sensed the arrival of another feverish era of economic expansion spurred by transportation technology. But the rate at which he was developing his own building operations and promotions took every cent he could raise. All he could do was hope that a personal connection or a low bid might get him railroad contracts.

Many of his contemporaries were in far stronger financial positions. Goodrich, Barker, Pratt, Judge Rochester, and Dr. Johnson had access to ample bank credits. David Evans, Brisbane, the Granger family, and the Porter brothers could raise credit on their lands. The forwarders and even some of the shopkeepers were in a much more liquid condition than he.

The merchants, bankers, landowners, and others in Buffalo and vicinity were already promoting many other, shorter lines by the time the "Schenectady and Buffalo Railroad" was abandoned as hopeless. Even the names of the bulk of those embryonic dreams have been forgotten. Still, before the end of 1832, the legislature's consent had been given to four western New York projects: the Albion and Tonawanda (to connect Albion and Batavia villages), the Aurora and Buffalo (to link East Aurora and Buffalo), the Buffalo and Erie (to connect Buffalo to Erie, Pennsylvania), and the Tonawanda Railroad (to link Rochester and Buffalo by way of Batavia). Financing problems wrecked the first three; much of the money was wasted in promotion and planning. The fourth, the Tonawanda Railroad, conceived by James Brisbane and some associates, became the first western New York project to get under way.

The Tonawanda Railroad's authorized capital of $500,000 was raised by stock sales along the route. Evans was selected as president and Elisha Johnson, the first mayor of Rochester and a brother of Buffalo's Dr. Ebenezer Johnson, became its engineer. Johnson began construction at the Rochester end. Plagued by financial problems and engineering difficulties, the work proceeded slowly. It was 1837 before the tracks reached Batavia and another four years before they were laid to Attica, a village southwest of Batavia. Buffalo was finally linked to Attica by another, entirely separate, railroad corporation in January 1843.

Two groups almost simultaneously came up with the idea of connecting Buffalo to Niagara Falls. One, headed by Dr. Johnson, applied for several charters under different guises in the hope that at least one would be successful. The other was sponsored by Augustus Porter and his brother, the general, who now threw himself into business again to forget the untimely death of his wife in 1831. The Porters made their application for a charter indirectly, requesting approval of a manufacturing corporation whose authority would be so loosely written that it could legitimately be construed as giving permission to finance a railroad.

For Peter and Augustus Porter, the prospect of a successful railroad was attractive enough, but they had other reasons to gamble. When the canal came to Buffalo, it had left the Porters with some unfinished business: unproductive land along the Niagara, too removed from the canal route to profit from the growth of trade. The Porters were amazed that mills could line the shores of Rochester's Genesee River Falls with their relatively trifling hydraulic flow, when the greatest waterpower potential in North America went undeveloped. Even at Lockport the trickle of surplus water from canal feeders powered new factories. A railroad line might open the way toward settlement, land sales, and waterpower. Long-delayed profits would finally reward their foresight in investing in land at the rapids of Niagara Falls and in the vicinity.

Rathbun knew both the Porter brothers well by this time. He had done much considerable work for Peter, including developing the Jubilee Water Works, which Porter headed. He had been associated with Augustus on the Bank of Buffalo board. Earlier the brothers had looked on him as a financially inconsequential newcomer who knew how to run a tavern. They saw him now as a clever businessman and an effective promoter. The general, especially, liked Rathbun. He probably admired the way the younger man forced his will on others, smoothly, delicately to be sure, but nonetheless powerfully.

There was little gossip in the Niagara region that Rathbun missed. His friendships, his business agents, and Lyman's associates in the militia kept him informed of what was going on. He had heard when the Porters made their first move to get a railroad charter. He knew of the conflict with Johnson and how both sides were using every means to influence members of the legislature in their favor.

He put himself forward, in close contact with each of these budding railroad projects in the hope of winning a profitable construction contract. With that in mind, too, he judiciously began to cultivate the Porters' friendship. It was then that he discovered their desire to sell most of their Niagara shore lands.

This discovery soon led him into his greatest speculation. The idea no doubt appealed to Rathbun's growing sense of his ability to engineer grand schemes. Why should *he* not be the one to promote the sale of these valuable river properties and reap the benefits of the construction work that would certainly follow their settlement?

Up to that time Rathbun had confined his operations to Buffalo and its immediate vicinity. He refrained from speculating in Ohio lands, as many of his associates were doing. His speculations, in fact, were more oriented to property improvement than to mere gambling on the value of unimproved land. It was less the land itself than what could be built upon it that interested him.

At the time he got the great idea, he could do nothing to further it. Because he had always expanded his operations just as far as his credit would comfortably permit, borrowing against a current job to start another and borrowing against that to start a third, he had practically no cash at all to contribute to what he already envisioned as a gigantic promotion. It would have to wait for later, when he would be in a better position to make a concrete offer. Meanwhile, however, he could keep in the good graces of the powerful Porter brothers.

In the manipulations at Albany, Dr. Johnson and his associates in 1833 won the first round. They got authority for the Buffalo and Black Rock Railroad, connecting the towns whose rivalry continued, though with Buffalo now so clearly in the lead. Though this line was capitalized at $100,000, the cautious Johnson wisely only expended

$15,000. The principal investment was a three-mile track of strap-iron spiked to the top of wooden sills laid along the highway near the canal. Finished in 1834, it was the equivalent of a horse-drawn street-car line. It had two horse-drawn cars—one for stormy and the other for fair weather. It operated on regular schedules and met a real need, even if the area it served was quite small.

Johnson, who did allow others to subscribe for a minority of the stock, kept control himself, and he gave his brother Elisha the job of installing the line. Rathbun got a few minor contracts, but he came to feel that the whole job was inconsequential.

Rathbun more or less officially had become aligned now in the Porters' camp. He had pursued his associations with the brothers, on one pretext or another, until they gave him a fair measure of their confidence. Moreover, he shrewdly won a valuable ally in Peter B. Porter, Jr., the young attorney who was a son of Augustus. Peter, Jr., a lighthearted youth who amused his uncle, but whose lack of steadiness worried his father, had studied law in the general's office and had then struck out for himself in Buffalo. Rathbun calculatingly turned much business his way. Young Porter served as intermediary between the elder Porters and Rathbun on many matters.

This time-consuming groundwork bored Rathbun, who preferred operating independently as the chance offered. But private reports made him sure that the Porters were likely to get a railroad contract and he hoped that he would then be repaid for his friendship. Moreover, he would be in a much stronger position to broach his big idea if the opportunity arose.

The Porter brothers had worked well together through the years. The more spontaneous and polished of the two, Peter supplied the ideas and the legal skill that had helped carry them from modest beginnings to the position of great landholders. Ponderous and conservative, Augustus had been the balance wheel, the man of business detail, who kept track of their joint operations and supervised some of the segments. Mechanically minded because of his surveying training, he built the power canal at Niagara Falls that operated the few mills at the hamlet. Augustus also built bridges over the rapids, to Bath Island and Goat Island. He and his brother owned these islands, which were at the very edge of the cataracts. The fees charged visitors for crossing these bridges provided the steadiest income the Porters had from their land at the Falls after the canal ruined the forwarding and portaging business of Porter, Barton and Company. At Black Rock their interests were more varied, touching the steamboats, the waterworks, and some mills.

Although nothing spectacular had happened on the Porter properties, several projects were being promoted on the Niagara River
near the Falls. On the Canadian side, two promotions were undertaken in 1832 and immediately afterward. At the top of a high bank
that overlooked both cataracts, Samuel Street, an American, and Col.
Thomas Clark, a Scotsman, joined forces. The partners bought five
hundred prime acres, and also purchased the Pavilion Hotel, and
they began to lay out lots under the colorful name of "City of the
Falls." Just north of this development and extending to the brink of
the gorge, a Canadian, Captain Creighton, and some associates,
staked out the village of "Clifton." Within this development on the
gorge bank overlooking the road to the rowboat ferry that ran to the
American shore, Harmanus Crysler started erecting "Clifton House,"
which was destined to become one of the continent's great resort
hotels in later years. In Lewiston, New York, a group was applying
for a charter to build the long-discussed suspension bridge to the
Canadian shore. Related to all these works was another project, sponsored by a group of financiers in Lockport, who planned a railroad
association to seek authority to run a line to Niagara. Lockport was a
major location on the Erie Canal, and the effect would have been to
divert some of the tourist traffic away from Buffalo. Another group
at Lewiston was working to organize a railroad to connect with the
Lockport-Niagara line, if that should be built.

While all these plans were in progress, the argument between the
Porters and Johnson over the Niagara Falls Railroad continued. The
Porters advised their friends in the legislature of the defects in John-
son's plans. His scheme would interfere with the canal and docks at
Black Rock; as it passed through outlying farm districts, its engines
would frighten horses and cattle; its financing was absurd.

The Porters and Rathbun and their associates made numerous
trips to Albany during these maneuverings. When it finally appeared
as if neither party would get a charter, the realistic general compro-
mised with Johnson and let him and his associates have enough stock
in the Porter-sponsored company to meet the expenses they had already incurred. This sensible solution paved the way for approval of
a charter for the Buffalo and Niagara Falls Railroad on May 3, 1834,
with Johnson as one of the commissioners authorized to set it up.
Augustus Porter was elected president of the new company. Rathbun
sat on the board.

The railroad's authorized capitalization was set at $115,000, for
General Porter had calculated that it would cost $4,000 to $5,000 a
mile to construct. This would have been insufficient if the company

had to acquire a right-of-way, but the general had made sure that the charter authorized the company to use about twenty-five feet of the ninety-nine-foot highway right-of-way between Buffalo and Niagara Falls. Once he had the charter, the general conveniently forgot his fears that locomotives would frighten cattle.

Rathbun was now assured of having all the major construction work. He was responsible for the surveying, grading, and construction of the line. He was awarded the contracts to build the cars and supply motive power. Most of the money expended passed through his hands. The line was financed, supplied, and surveyed in 1834. Crews graded the roadbed in 1835 and began building the two principal bridges on the line. One bridge was to take the railroad over Tonawanda Creek near where it emptied into the Niagara, and the other, farther north, was to cross Cayuga Creek near its junction with the Niagara and close to the spot where the French explorer LaSalle built the first European vessel ever to operate on the Great Lakes. The road generally followed the main highway, passing through Black Rock to Niagara Street in Buffalo and then to the Terrace, where it paralleled the Black Rock Railroad before reaching its terminus at Pearl Street.

Early in the spring of 1836, Rathbun's work gangs began fastening the strap iron track on top of a wooden framework, most of which was laid directly on the surface of the rough right-of-way. The workmen laid heavy wooden crossties on the roadbed, then spiked upon them the six-by-six wooden stringers that became the base for the track. On top of all was spiked the strap iron track, two inches wide and half an inch thick. It seemed so firm and solid then, none foresaw that the strap could break loose, derailing trains. Nor did anyone foresee that loose track would buckle under a train, and also cause a derailment. There were other perils. Tracks laid flat on the poorly smoothed roadway or across holes hastily tamped full of earth would be tossed and heaved by the snow and ice in winter.

Rathbun divided the track-laying operations into three major sections, each to be carried on simultaneously from points accessible by riverboat to his supply warehouses in Buffalo. The first point was at Black Rock, from which work went northward toward Tonawanda Creek and southward toward Buffalo; the second at Tonawanda where the construction of the principal bridge and the track laying was the biggest job of the project; and the third at Schlosser Landing, two miles south of the Falls, where the old Porter-Barton warehouses and docks were located. This had been the portage road where bullock carts crossed the country with goods from Lewiston on the lower river.

Rathbun could take pride in the way he had worked out the details of his construction program. From top to bottom, this project was a model of the mass production methods that he had been developing. He acquired gravel pits to furnish fill for the roadbed; he obtained control of quarries to furnish stone for bridge abutments, retaining walls and buildings; and he leased or bought timberlands and sawmills to supply large quantities of lumber. He contracted with Abraham Witmer, a farmer near the falls, to turn out three hundred thousand bricks in his oven for the railroad and the new buildings he was planning. He contracted with William Young, another Niagara farmer, to provide all the lime his small kiln could burn. In Buffalo, he greatly enlarged his warehouses and dockage facilities. He brought trained mechanics from the East to fabricate the railroad cars in the Bush and Spicer coach works, which he himself now owned. On Buffalo's Main Street opposite the Eagle, these shops were augmented by blacksmith shops nearby, which forged the wrought iron parts for the cars.

His now enormous construction operations in Buffalo were coupled with the railroad work. He made skillful use of his equipment, utilizing the same wagons and men, as far as he could, on construction of buildings and railroad. His payroll of two thousand to twenty-five hundred men was the largest in the history of the Niagara region, and the efficiency of his operations amazed his competitors. His independent purchasing of supplies without dependence on subcontractors and his absorption of massive numbers of artisans, carpenters, joiners, blacksmiths, painters, and mechanics into his working force made many mumble "monopolist" under their breaths. Small men outside of his employment were growing envious and afraid of him, while those who had steady work on his payrolls began to be vociferous in his praise.

Everything had changed radically for Rathbun in the last few years. His speculations had grown. He was risking more on each new enterprise, but with the confidence that the profits would more than compensate for the added risks. Successful new ventures enlarged his prestige. People clamored to sell him their schemes and even their enterprises. Yet public perception did not square at all with private reality. Every added project deepened his financial problems. He never seemed to have enough money to sustain his projects. Always the next speculation promised to be so profitable that it would wipe out the gathering debts from the preceding one; and yet almost invariably his situation grew worse.

It was not surprising then that he labored intensely on his schemes for promoting the development and sale of the Porter lands, for they offered the prospect of the windfall that would solve his problems. There were two possibilities for development: the still busy port at Black Rock and the land around Niagara Falls, which was nearly as untenanted as it had been a decade before. Because there were so many speculative opportunities arising and his money was always short, he deferred broaching the subject to the Porters. Then, suddenly, it was too late for the Black Rock development. Early in 1835, General Porter assembled a group of associates from past projects, and proposed a joint promotion under a twenty-year agreement. His scheme was to organize a Black Rock Land and Railroad Company. This group would both hold the Porter share of the Niagara Falls Railroad and pool certain of the Porter properties at Black Rock with those of other landowners for development and sale. If the new company succeeded, the Porters would offer it additional lands later. This was not Rathbun's style. He was accustomed to personal control and close personal supervision of important detail. He depended on others for money, and offered in return his skill at deal making and promotion. Rathbun regarded the general's men as incompetents.

But to show his interest, if only in a limited way, Rathbun entered the agreement, subscribing to eleven shares, a minor interest. Isaac S. Smith and his corpulent partner, John B. Macy, divided eighty shares. Hiram Pratt, Rathbun's friend who was increasingly competing with him for control of desirable promotions, split another eighty shares with William F. P. Taylor, his partner in a steamboat firm. Lewis F. Allen, the insurance agent for an eastern company that controlled a major share of local fire and marine business, was now blossoming into a financier, and was also part of this agreement. The Porters and their relatives, together with Benjamin Barton and one of his sons-in-law, held a major interest. Rathbun also bought some seven acres of land at Black Rock, figuring that the promotion would boost the price enough to give him a quick profit.

Renewed interest in Black Rock stirred ancient rivalries. Samuel Wilkeson, father of the Buffalo harbor, was shocked. To him, any improvements there would ultimately be at Buffalo's expense. Haskins, Barker, Heacock, and other investors who had been left out of the transaction agreed, and carried their protests to the halls of the U.S. Congress. But the plan went ahead.

Rathbun felt he could no longer delay. He had to make his first direct approach to the Porters on the subject of a Niagara Falls promotion. He proposed that they lay out a village and that he undertake the promotion of the village lots, in return for which he would obtain an assurance of a share in the profits.

Rathbun was very discreet. He revealed as little as possible. He neither wanted to frighten the brothers with some of the grandiose features of his scheme nor inspire in them too exalted an idea of the value of their property. He offered enough to convince them that he had a sound idea and that he alone could carry it out successfully.

Eventually his many discussions with the Porters crystallized in an agreement. Rathbun was not entirely satisfied, but it was a start. He hoped that he might be able to induce them to go further as time passed. For what they considered a nominal sum, the brothers let Rathbun purchase some land outright and go into equal partnership with them on the projected industrial development of Niagara Falls.

While he was negotiating with the Porters he began to expand some of the subsidiary plans that he did not reveal to them. Samuel DeVeaux, who had the largest general store at Niagara, owned the lot where Parkhurst Whitney had long operated his tavern. Rathbun negotiated with DeVeaux and contracted to buy Whitney's tavern and the two adjoining lots.

Whitney had enlarged his log cabin and boardinghouse, and had christened his establishment with the by now popular name Eagle Tavern. It was the best the hamlet offered, facing east on Main Street at the north corner of Bridge Street, which ran to the bridges to Bath and Goat islands. The American cataract was only a quarter of a mile or so to its rear, in full view from the porches that surrounded the two-story, gable-roofed structure.

In 1829, Whitney had bought "The Columbian," a larger building a few rods south of his Eagle, as an annex. The whole establishment, to Rathbun's critical eyes, was little better than a backwoods stage house. Travelers to the American side of the great Falls who wanted better accommodations had to stay at the "Pavilion," "The Ontario," or the "Clifton House" on the Canadian side of the river.

The moment Rathbun reached agreement with DeVeaux, he ordered Whitney to vacate the Eagle. Then Rathbun sent in one of his own managers to take it over and install the same type of service he had offered at the Buffalo Eagle. Whitney, discomfited, transferred his hotel operations to "The Columbian," renaming the structure "The Cataract House." In later years, he and his successors made the "Cataract" a famous resort hotel, the American counterpart of the Canadian "Clifton." It would operate profitably for more than a century.

Once in possession of this promising property, Rathbun started his architects working on an extension to the hotel. He wanted a building that would also house stores. On the unoccupied lots north of the Eagle, extending to Falls Street, he initiated plans for the erection of a mammoth new hotel. This would be, he projected, the most splendid building he had ever erected, a luxury hotel that would attract trade from all over the world.

Rathbun signed his agreement with the Porters in November of 1835. Together they hired Jesse P. Haines, a Niagara County surveyor, to plot a map for a village, which would provide the manufacturing sites he had envisioned, the residence lots, and the plan of the major streets. Years before, Augustus Pòrter named the village "Manchester" in the hope that waterpower would transform the outpost into a rival of the seat of the English Industrial Revolution. By now, however, that name had become a symbol for the miseries associated with England's industrialization. The village would be called simply "Niagara Falls," which masked the massive industrial establishment projected for it, just as it would later when industry came to the place. Haines plotted a new village map to give the maximum number of industrial sites along the extended hydraulic canal that Rathbun proposed building. The approximately rectangular pattern of village streets filed the right angle bend at the cataracts, where the river changed its course from almost due west to a northerly flow. Except for the area right at the cataracts, which was reserved as a scenic park, mill sites were mapped along the riverbank, above and below the Falls. Each was designed to be linked to the main canal by a short feeder canal, with the mill's spent water flowing over the bank into the river.

For $23,500 (only $2,000 of it down) Rathbun acquired one-third interest in twenty-two and a half acres jointly owned by the Porter brothers, comprising the major rivershore manufacturing sites in the new village and the Prospect Park scenic area at the brink of the cataracts. In addition, he acquired full title to more than twenty-eight acres in the heart of Niagara Falls that Augustus had owned.

These were indeed modest prices, at least as land values were going at the time. Rathbun himself valued his one-third interest at $75,000 and the property he had acquired from Augustus Porter at $60,000. The profits he expected, when the property was sold, were to be his compensation for the promotion. Yet the brothers were hardly losing by the deal. They had, after all, paid less than $5 an acre for most of these lands. The highest price had been for the land and water rights at the Falls themselves. For an area slightly larger than Niagara Falls' scenic Prospect Park, they had paid only $342!

Even before these deeds were filed, Rathbun had agents at work acquiring additional land in the area from other owners. He hoped to be able to acquire still more of the Porter property before the promotion was begun.

The filing of these deeds created a sensation among western New York financiers. Although no announcement of their plans had been made, it was quite obvious what kind of promotion Rathbun and the Porters were projecting. Pratt, Allen, Smith, Macy, and some of their associates were nettled at being left out of a most promising speculation. Excluding Rathbun this time, they now developed a new and larger plan for Black Rock, which they hoped was in a form that would tempt the Porters to accept it.

The first Niagara land acquisition, beyond the transaction with the Porters, was announced by Rathbun in January 1836. It embraced some sixty-six acres of farmland, located five miles north of the new village. He got it for $500 down and a $4,000 mortgage. This lot, which other financiers had considered nothing more than farm property, was from the standpoint of tourism and commerce one of the choicest spots on the whole Niagara, for it offered the only scenic view from the American side of the river of the great whirlpool below the Falls.

In the next few months he bought 875 additional acres of riverbank farmlands north and east of the new village. This land cost him nearly $43,000, but he had to expend only $13,000 in down payments, which was the measuring stick he used in all his land dealings.

His new mile-deep acquisitions extended from the whirlpool for a mile southward, past the site where the famous Suspension Bridge to Queenston in Canada would later be erected. They included a sulfur spring, just north of the eventual location of the bridge, which Rathbun envisioned as the potential site of a health resort; the vantage point where travelers from the north could get their first glimpse of the spectacular cataracts in the distance; and the land around the whirlpool, where he planned a scenic resort. The right-of-way of the Lockport-Niagara Falls railroad extended across all his property, assuring its accessibility. It is conceivable that he even envisioned taking on the building of a bridge to Canada.

In addition, Rathbun acquired between a quarter and a half mile of upper river shore property, just above Schlosser Landing. This purchase anticipated his most grandiose project. This was to be a broad canal, shorter but like the Welland, which had been completed in 1833 on the Canadian Niagara peninsula, to carry boats around the cataracts, making a passage from Lake Ontario to Lake Erie possible on the American side. A feasible proposal had already been outlined by a federal engineer in 1835. His report called for the canal to begin at the Niagara near Rathbun's upper river property and would have extended to Lewiston, crossing all the lots he owned below Niagara Falls, where it would join the Niagara again. The main navigation canal would have been tapped easily for shorter canals to run toward the gorge bank, and supply a large number of mills. Rathbun had now acquired as many potential water-driven mill sites served by a railroad as then existed in the entire United States.

While he was securing these properties, which he intended to develop and offer for sale after the completion of the promotion at Niagara Falls village, Rathbun continued his negotiations with the Porters. That situation was changing, too. The unexpected interest in their lands led the brothers to decide that the time was ripe to sell and let the promoters take over. As long as they received top prices themselves, they did not care much what these land speculators did with their holdings.

On May 1, 1836, the Porters and their relatives and associates sold all their properties and manufacturing interests at Black Rock and Buffalo and their control of the Black Rock Land and Railroad Company to a group newly organized by Hiram Pratt. For their interest, they received $383,250 in bonds, of which $300,000 went to General Porter. The general even turned over his mansion, abandoning forever the home to which he had taken his bride. Associated with Pratt in the new promotion, as equal partners, were Allen, Taylor, Smith, and Macy.

Rathbun could not make as good a contract as this, but competition was forcing his hand. He did not feel he could let anyone else get the Porter interests at Niagara. When he signed a supplementary agreement with the Porters on May 6, 1836, he obtained the bulk of their property at Niagara Falls. But he had contracted to pay them the enormous sum of $470,000!

He realized that he had paid a stiff price, but the contract was still to his liking. It became binding when he made a down payment of only one-tenth of the principal on July 1. After that, succeeding annual payments of one-tenth each year would be required. Under any circumstance, he was confident that he could raise enough from the sale of these and other lands he owned at Niagara to give him a handsome profit. He counted on this profit to stave off the potential disaster that might be caused by his growing indebtedness. He figured that he would gain at least $300,000 from the lots he would sell in the first offering.

The supplementary agreement gave Rathbun title to nearly all the lands the Porters still owned in Niagara Falls, including the two-thirds interest in both the manufacturing sites and the scenic area that they had retained in the original agreement. This cost him another $30,000, and required a payment of another $3,000 annually. The agreement excepted only Goat and Bath islands, with their bridges and the lane leading to the bridge, Augustus's home and outbuildings, the site where Peter planned to build a new house, the village cemetery, and a few other lots.

For all practical purposes, Rathbun was now the owner of Niagara Falls.

Rathbun made sure that he would have the right to provide for navigation into the heart of his new industrial settlement. He insisted that the agreement contain a clause giving him the right to "take out" a canal on lands that the Porters owned on the upper river shore west of Schlosser Landing, to be extended through any of their lands to the new village.

The first public announcement that something important was afoot at the Falls appeared in newspaper advertisements late in May and in a widely circulated two-page printed leaflet. This announcement, in grandiose language supplemented by a simplified version of the Haines's map, invited would-be buyers to a sale to be held at Niagara's Eagle Tavern beginning on August 2.

These notices, which have the characteristic effusive style of one of Rathbun's press agents, the local Presbyterian minister and guidebook author Horatio A. Parsons, were signed by both the Porter brothers and Rathbun, who were listed as the "Proprietors." This was a delicate fiction, and correspondents for distant newspapers properly described Rathbun as sole proprietor.

The announcements emphasized the solidity of the Niagara project as compared with other contemporary developments along the lakes that were said to vastly overrate the endowments and potential of their lands. Niagara Falls and vicinity "combined more of the natural advantages which tend to invite, cultivate, sustain and adorn a great population than fall to the lot of any city in the civilized world."

The leaflet stressed the transportation advantages enjoyed at Niagara. It was the center of the New West. It was connected to both the Atlantic and the Great Lakes by water. It would be linked to other places by three railroads. Moreover, the leaflet declared, a ship canal around the Falls was in contemplation. Stretching the truth to outright falsehood, it said that the new proprietor had already built "a new and capacious canal, capable of any required extension," and was daily opening new brickyards and quarries, a new sawmill, and other facilities. The leaflet breathlessly concluded, "We trust that many of the substantial manufacturers of the Eastern States will avail themselves of this favorable opportunity to establish themselves at this place, where labor and provisions, as well as most of the raw materials for manufacture are abundant, and cheaper than where they now reside, and where they will find a ready sale at advanced prices for all their fabrics." Hopes, promises, projections, some plausible and others a leap through a void, it was more or less what many local entrepreneurs wished to be true.

To avert the usual hue and cry from his Buffalo colleagues, Rathbun had cautioned the Buffalo editors before inserting his advertisement to make sure they fully understood that the new development would not injure Buffalo. Indeed, he claimed, it would add to its prosperity, for it would increase Erie Canal traffic and regional demand for Buffalo's goods. The *Commercial Advertiser* dutifully editorialized along these lines.

Even before his sale announcement, Rathbun's workmen had completed building a four-story brick annex against the north wall of the Niagara Eagle. This almost overshadowed its tiny parent. The upper floors of the annex were sleeping chambers, permitting most of the original building to be devoted to public rooms. In one of the two stores on the ground floor, Rathbun opened a new "B. Rathbun" general store, with $15,000 in stock, which made it by far the largest store in the village. DeVeaux, who had sold him the site, was undoubtedly in despair at the appearance of this competition across the street from his own store.

Yet DeVeaux, a shrewd trader of French Huguenot descent, acknowledged genuine ability when he saw it. Although living at Niagara over many years, he had never recognized the opportunities for profit that Rathbun discovered on every hand. DeVeaux was amazed, he confessed later, by the acute vision Rathbun displayed in every purchase.

Though the Eagle would serve for the present, Rathbun now

approved the plans his architects had prepared for the superluxury hotel he intended to erect along Main Street between the end of the Eagle property and the corner of Falls Street. This hotel would be in an ideal location, right at the junction of the Buffalo and Lockport railroads. One side would overlook the cataracts, the other side would face the end of the lot where General Porter was making plans to build his new mansion.

Rathbun's architects designed a building to house six hundred guests on the grand lines he desired. The new structure would be of brick, 174 by 190 feet, the main building four stories or sixty feet high. A dome, the final touch of elegance in Rathbun's judgment, would tower over the central section 120 feet form the ground and provide a vantage point for visitors to view the cataracts. Two tiers of heavy Doric colonnades, each two stories high surrounding the building, would provide Rathbun's interpretation of the classic style.

When the design was announced, the *New York Times* exclaimed in envy that the proposed structure would be larger than the Astor, then the greatest and most modern in the metropolis.

Rathbun started a whole series of other improvements. He considerably extended the earlier Porter canal. He built a rustic summer house near the Whirlpool to lure more visitors to that spot and to shelter them in case of rain. Over the sulfur spring he erected a wooden Grecian-style shelter and inaugurated plans for development of a health resort, complete with hotels, at the spot.

Years before, Augustus Porter had attempted to build a road large enough for carriages to lead from the top of the gorge bank to the riverfront landing place nearly two hundred feet below of the rowboat ferry to Canada. Even though Canadians had built a similar road on their side of the gorge, Porter had to abandon his project because of the difficulties in gouging out the solid rock of the cliff face. Rathbun set a gang at work, with orders to build a road inclining toward the ferry landing from the foot of what he named Ferry Street. Though the workmen made progress, it was a difficult, expensive job. Rathbun discovered, to his annoyance, that a powerful stream of water diverted from the lower end of the canal had no material effect in removing the rock. Every inch had to be blasted.

With these activities superimposed upon his Buffalo construction, and the exhaustively detailed problems of his financing, Rathbun himself worked frantically throughout this period. Pressed financially as he was, the Niagara Falls sale had to be a success. He needed the money.

Moreover, Rathbun had always welcomed correspondents for the New York, Boston, and Philadelphia newspapers when they came to western New York to get material for the then popular travel articles on Niagara. Stories in Buffalo newspapers were often copied verbatim in the eastern and southern press. His candid explanations of his plans, the generosity of his welcome, and the trouble to which he went to see that they were well accommodated paid bountifully in additional newspaper space. These accounts all helped whip up the enthusiasm of the investing public.

Reading of these developments and hearing by word of mouth of Rathbun's plans, financiers also came personally to Buffalo to meet the great promoter. As far as his time permitted, he saw them himself and conducted them on personal tours of the developments he was charting.

Every news story emphasized not only the magnificent schemes ahead but also the work already in progress. They cited the railroad construction, the new hotel, the woolen plant, flouring mill, sawmills, cabinet factories, machine shop, and other industries already set up. They pointed to the establishment of a weekly newspaper, the *Niagara Falls Journal,* as final proof of the enterprise of the new village. They did not reveal, if they knew, the fact that the editor of this publication was on Rathbun's payroll and that Rathbun was also subsidizing the publicist, Rev. Parsons. The great speculation had its own self-verifying momentum.

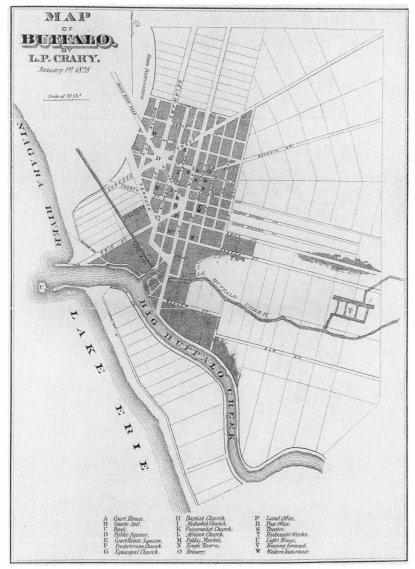

1. Map of Buffalo, New York, in 1828. The Eagle Tavern (N) was at the corner of Court and Main Streets.

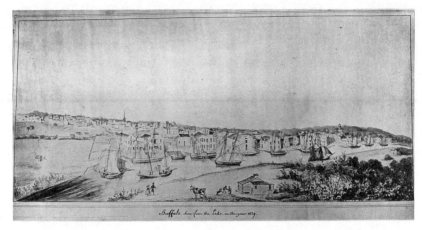

2. A view of Buffalo's central business district from the docks along the Buffalo River, 1829.

3. Buffalo, from Lake Erie, 1833, illustrating the rapid growth of commerce and infrastructure that resulted from the settling of the West and the expansion of trade via the Erie Canal.

4. Rathbun's Eagle Tavern, his first successful enterprise.

5. An early nineteenth-century surveyor's instrument of the type Rathbun would have used in his land development projects.

From a Drawing by W.R. Callington, Engineer, Boston, from an Actual Survey made in 1837.

A Birds eye View of the river Niagara from Lake Erie to Lake Ontario shewing the situation and extent of NAVY ISLAND, and the Towns and Villages on the banks of the river in Canada and the United States.

UNITED STATES.		CANADA.	
1 Town of Buffalo	6 Hotel at the falls	A Lake Erie	F Rapids
2 Black Rock	7 Lewiston	B Fort Erie	G Islands of Niagara
3 Grand Island	8 Fort Niagara	C Waterloo	H Queens Town
4 Tonawanda Creek	9 Lake Ontario	D Navy Island	I Fort George
5 Grand Canal		E Chippewa	J Welland Canal

Published by J. Robins, Bride Court, Fleet Street.

6. A bird's-eye view of the Niagara River and Falls, 1837.

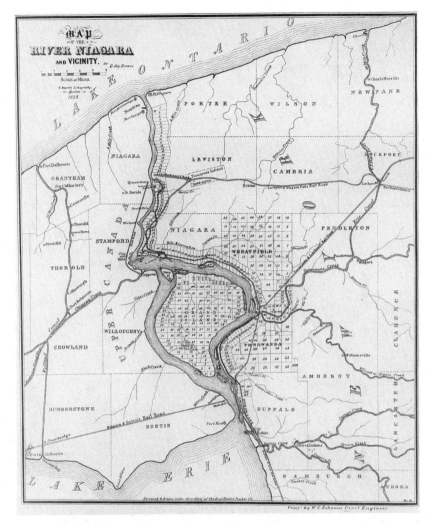

7. Map of the Niagara Frontier of the United States and Canada, 1838. In 1836, Rathbun obtained possession of a number of township sections at and north of Niagara Falls. The falls are several miles north of Grand Island.

8. Printing plates for paper money circulated by the Bank of Niagara and representing currency used in the region during the 1820s and 1830s.

9

"Experiment," "Enterprise," and "Encouragement"

In the 1830s, speculative fever spread like a contagion. Money could be made so quickly that even the most conservative began to abandon the old ways of thrift and caution. Inflation was the inevitable consequence of such fevered prosperity. Before 1833, prices rose steadily, afterward they rose sharply—doubling in just three years. Money bought only half what it had shortly before.

Railroad corporations, with relatively great capital, urged investors to think in larger terms. Merchants, artisans, and landowners who were suddenly transformed into bankers and financiers as a consequence of their speculations could not realize what was happening. Huge issues of paper currency poured into the financial stream, often propelled there by banks that were themselves capitalized on a handful of promissory notes. Their wages and incomes rising, debtors found it much easier to pay old obligations. The rising tide of prices, wages, and property values lifted all boats, small and large. Interest rates soared. At the small brokers' offices, "shaves" were illegally high. Even on commercial loans a borrower judged a good risk could expect to pay three percent a month. The less credit-worthy would pay five percent, a whopping sixty percent per year. Brokers charged one and a half to two and a half percent a month just to endorse notes. Onerous as these rates were, borrowers paid them because they could make such huge profits by the appreciation of their principal.

Though the greatest speculation centered on land, buildings in Buffalo also changed hands at a startling rate. As soon as construction began, the owner could sell an unfinished structure at a handsome profit. It might be sold several times over before it was completed. Structures already in existence experienced a similar popularity, and their prices rose as they were frequently sold for quick profits, in the way that stocks and bonds were traded at a later period.

The speculative habit, by which bold persons were making fortunes overnight, was not confined to the rich. It infected artisans, laborers, widows with a little property, and others who, under normal conditions, would never have considered hazarding their small means. Even some laborers and semiskilled mechanics refused proffered jobs because they were making much more money speculating than they could possibly earn with their hands. Prices and profits were the talk of the day in taverns, stages, canal boats, homes, and other gathering places. Brokers' offices, where some of the transactions were consummated and where notes were taken for discount, were filled with throngs of speculators. The new rich wanted fine homes, clothes, and carriages, and their demand for luxuries further increased prices.

Rathbun's remarkable rise in Buffalo was not only an inspiring lesson to the ambitious, but had brought profit to many. The interest on his notes, income from mortgages he had given, and paper profits gained by selling him businesses compelled a measure of respect for one who was responsible for such bounty. The increasing roll of his relatively well-paid clerks, supervisors, and laborers helped build up a huge class of working men and their families. All of them had a vested interest in his continued success and looked on him as their benefactor. By early 1836, about one-third of all the inhabitants of Buffalo were directly dependent on Rathbun for their livelihood.

While Rathbun was the outstanding example, many others in western New York had built astounding fortunes in this period. Alanson Palmer, whose hearty laugh and heavily handsome figure were familiar adjuncts to the Eagle's bar each afternoon; Evans, James Brisbane and his son Albert, in Batavia; Hiram Pratt, Dr. Johnson, and many more had doubled, trebled, even quadrupled their fortunes. Everyone wanted to emulate them. Youngsters sought to follow in the footsteps of these financial geniuses, who seemed to be able to turn every venture to their profit. But Rathbun and Palmer were the most spectacular, for people considered each of them very probably a millionaire.

As the fever spread, speculators began to buy in larger and larger quantities: instead of a store, they bought blocks of buildings; instead of a city lot for their new home, they bought acres. Men with almost no capital and without even the ghost of an office ranged the streets in the role of broker, negotiating "deals," buying and selling property for which they levied fat commissions.

Newspapers were filled with offers of land sales and auctions of lands in the West along the shores of the lakes. There, promoters were staking out new cities in the wilderness for the great populations they confidently predicted were certain to settle, on the promise of industries and transportation facilities still unborn. Profits made on land sales in Buffalo financed purchases of these lands, and, in many instances, when land resold at a substantial appreciation, the seller reinvested in more western land.

Buffalo deeds in the quarter century preceding 1835 totaled nine thousand, according to Guy H. Salisbury, a contemporary Buffalo newspaper editor, but in the next two years they totaled twelve thousand. On the conservative assumption that *recorded* deeds probably represented less than one-half of the land contracts made in 1835 and 1836, Salisbury computed that at least twenty-five thousand sales, representing a turnover value of perhaps as much as $25,000,000, took place in Buffalo in those years.

Almost all the land was encumbered with one to three mortgages. Frequently no money changed hands in a sale. Promises replaced it, and the only expense in a huge transaction might be in the small fee paid to a commissioner of deeds for witnessing the contract.

Staggering profits made overnight were lost just as quickly in these two years. There were many $100,000 transactions and a few of $200,000. One tract, worth $2 a front foot, or $500 an acre in early 1835, sold in 1836 at $10,000 an acre or $40 a front foot. A quarter of a century later, the land was worth only $18 a foot.

James L. Barton, who had abandoned his forwarding business for speculation, later entertained his friends with an illustration of this speculative mania. Barton bought two lots at Black Rock in 1815, before he had even reached his majority. A decade later, he assumed that they were worth about $4,000 on the basis of then current prices. But in April 1836, just back from a trip to New York City, he met a man on the street in Buffalo who asked him to sell the lots. Because Barton had not given it much thought, he said that he would be willing to sell for $6,000. The prospective buyer then said that he wanted time to think the price over. A few minutes later, another man accosted Barton with a similar inquiry. This time, Barton, alert, asked $7,500. A third man, further down the street, asked the same question, and now Barton offered the lots for $20,000, ten per cent down and the remainder in four annual payments. The man was keenly interested and they dickered a few minutes, agreeing finally on a price of $2,000 down and $18,000 to be paid in six annual payments, a completed transaction. In traversing a city block, Barton had made as much as $16,000!

The boom spread to every field. Steamboats were being built as fast as financiers could raise the money; there were thirty-five in operation on the region's Great Lakes by 1836. Though they were still being turned out at Black Rock, other places were building them, too. Charles M. Reed, who did much business with Rathbun, was entering the field from Erie, Pennsylvania, paying to have hulls laid down in various places. His bold operations were destined to make him one of the richest men west of the seaboard.

The old forwarding firms consolidated and expanded their operations on to the lakes and into steamboats as well as on the canal. Steamboats stimulated the fuelwood supply business as their boilers consumed upwards of 150,000 cords annually. Railroads demanded wood too. Farmers were getting more from the sale of their trees for fuel or ashes than they could earn by raising a planted crop.

The relative scarcity of labor attracted immigrants, including many Irish who were beginning to flood into the port of New York and to move westward over the canal. Their wages rose slowly, despite rising prices, because frequently there were labor surpluses in many urban centers, and because the newcomers often were desperate enough to work for whatever they were offered.

Against the background of these prices, the first tentative breath of organized labor was finally heard in 1836. The "Journeyman Operative Building Society of the City of Buffalo," a small union of carpenters, passed a resolution asking $1.75 for a ten-hour day for "good carpenters and joiners" and promising to support other building mechanics in similar demands. To bolster their claim that building mechanics' wages were too low, they said: "Land speculators are making one hundred to 2,000 per cent and landlords are raising rents one hundred to two hundred per cent; farmers and wood merchants have raised prices twenty-five to one hundred per cent and grocers twenty-five to one hundred per cent; butchers the same; the money shaver takes three to six per cent [per month] . . . and yet labor has no increases." Labor made no headway through organization, however, and the shadow of poverty crossed the door of many a working-class cottage.

If any of these or other miseries swirling around him bothered

Rathbun, he gave little sign of his concern. He participated in civic mobilizations, such as raising money for the American rebels fighting for independence in Texas against the Mexican dictator Santa Anna, only when he believed he was expected to for appearance's sake, or when the issue at stake directly involved the preservation of the local status quo. He was too busy, too enmeshed in financial detail, to give any time to matters that did not bear directly on him.

Indeed, Rathbun had his own troubles. He was as chronically short of cash as he was pressed for time. In buying stock for his stores he had to pay the whole account in a limited period. He had to have cash to meet the overhead on his mortgages and to meet current wages for the clerks and laborers he employed. When he sold property, he rarely got more than a small percentage in cash. On the other hand, he had to make only a relatively small down payment when he bought land. But any payment at all required cash and Rathbun had too little of it. Most financing at the time was in renewable notes. Rathbun would take a contract to build a structure, take notes in part payment as the job progressed, and discount these notes to raise cash for current needs. Sometimes he would take a contract and issue his own notes. These were endorsed by others—especially by those for whom he was doing the work. Rathbun would then discount them for cash. But it was the fearful rate that brokers and others collected in "shaves" on these notes that caused the greatest difficulty. The few local commercial banks could absorb only a fraction of his notes. Too often even these banks, which charged the maximum legal rates of interest, would demand endorsement by selected private brokers. Some bank directors were in informal collaboration with these same brokers to squeeze money out of debtors before they would discount a note. Simply getting that endorsement might then add from twelve to thirty percent per year to the cost.

Because all these notes were short term, usually three months or less, every day or so some of the many outstanding notes came due and money had to be on deposit at specified places for payment. When payment could not be made, arrangements to replace the expiring notes by new ones were negotiated. Buffalo's streets were crowded with Rathbun's messengers and those of other businessmen who were doing extensive financing as they rushed notes to endorsers, brokers, moneylenders and banks. The more the volume of these transactions rose, the more casual they became and the more confident these otherwise wary businessmen attempted to appear in each other's good faith.

These common transactions, so ambitious and so casual, became the lifeblood of local commerce. They grew from a prevailing habit of confidence that had developed among merchants in Buffalo. Because the banks discounted notes only at the formally scheduled times when their discount committees met, between times merchants were frequently strapped for cash. It became the custom, when a merchant needed money immediately, to assemble surplus cash from fellow shopkeepers merely by sending a messenger around. These informal loans were generally repaid without argument.

By 1835, Rathbun's mercantile volume was by far the greatest in the city and very probably in western New York. Rathbun was responsible for Buffalo's facelift, and the scale and scope of his construction projects amazed even jaded Buffalonians. Outsiders were thunderstruck. No one had ever seen so much building going on at one time anywhere in the United States. Rathbun was erecting buildings, and then tore them down just as quickly to build others as owners demanded more space.

Exactly how much construction took place in Buffalo in 1835 and 1836 cannot be computed accurately. The only statistics were compiled carelessly by public-relations-conscious newspapers wishing to prove to the world how prosperous Buffalo had become, and in some newspapers 1836 figures overlap those of 1835 (and probably 1835 overlapped 1834). It is difficult to believe that such inflation of the annual totals was completely innocent in the light of the editors' boomtown mentality.

The 1836 *Gazetteer of New York* gives the figure of $1,130,300 for the value of Buffalo construction in 1835 and the *Buffalo Whig and Journal* in 1835 stated that Rathbun alone erected $500,000 worth of that year's new building. In October 1836, the *Buffalo Commercial Advertiser* valued city construction completed in that year at $1,720,000 of which Rathbun had built over $600,000 worth before August 1. Even a century later, those figures would have been impressive for a city of sixteen thousand to seventeen thousand persons.

Several writers indicate that in the years of Rathbun's construction operations, the "Master Builder and Architect" built more structures than all other Buffalo contractors combined. This may be true, especially if more of the other buildings were erected by their owners instead of by contractors, but it is no matter. What is certain and significant is that he did erect most of the major and highly visible structures that transformed the raw frontier outpost into a city of "elegant" brick and stone buildings.

Rathbun began two of his major Buffalo projects in 1835. One of them was the Eagle Street Theater that contemporaries lauded as "unsurpassed by any [theater] in the United States." The stone building, 70 by 100 feet, and 47 feet high, attracted financing from James Brisbane of Batavia, and Albert, his son. Albert's travels in Europe acquainted him with modern Europe, where ideas of social reform (which were to make him the best-known American disciple of Fourier) and also taught him about European architecture. The two Brisbanes built the theater to lease to Dean and McKinney, the theatrical firm that had been presenting stock shows in the small theater on Seneca Street.

The centrally located new theater had a gallery and four tiers of boxes. It boasted all the latest improvement, such as a drop curtain and Buffalo's first gaslights. The "olefiant" gas was produced in an "elaboratory" on the Washington Street side of the building. The presentations of two plays, *The Hunchback* and a selection from *The Taming of the Shrew*, marked its opening to enthusiastic local audiences on July 20, 1835.

Because he felt it necessary to control the adjacent land in connection with the second big project, a huge hotel-office-store complex begun in 1835, Rathbun found himself in the odd position of buying back his old starting place, the Eagle Tavern. He had no sentiment about the transaction, though it probably annoyed him to pay far more than he had received for it four years earlier.

Once again in possession of the Eagle and adjacent properties, Rathbun razed the barns and set his men to excavating the basement for a new hotel designed to be the most sumptuous establishment of its kind west of New York City. (This was, of course, before he planned erection of the huge hotel at Niagara.) South of this site and right alongside it, he demolished the small structures that had long stood, and began construction of two four-story commercial buildings to be attached to the hotel.

The new hotel was the greatest piece of construction work yet undertaken in Buffalo. Including the two adjoining commercial buildings, the top two floors and attic of which connected to the hotel to enlarge its capacity, the structure was 150 feet wide, and 130 feet deep. It was five stories high, of cut gray stone, surmounted by a circular cupola, which formed an "elegant observatory" jutting 120 feet into the sky. A spacious dining room was built on the ground floor rear, and a grand ballroom with a domed ceiling laid out on the floor above.

Rathbun intended to sell this hotel as soon as he could. Looking about for a buyer, he fixed on his rich fellow speculator, Colonel Palmer. Rathbun did not like Palmer but the strutting Palmer could be useful.

"Lance," as Palmer was known to a wide circle, was then almost thirty-two years old. A poor boy, he had begun business as a grocer in the Kremlin building in 1817, setting up shop with $13 capital at a time when many merchants were failing. Palmer, however, had run the capital up and up. In the late 1820s, he branched into timber and sawmill operations. He now called himself a land broker. An inveterate braggart and joker, when he boasted that he had $2,000,000, some of his intimates laughed. Still, most were awed by his rise.

Lance was a natural gambler, ready to take a chance on anything. Of course, it helped that his wife had some money, but there was no doubt that the man had a genius for making money. His speculative instincts were so well known that once, when he proposed with utter seriousness to buy up the city of Troy, New York, lock, stock, and barrel, its public officials deliberated the offer at public meetings. When word leaked out that Palmer was merely joking, the officials were somewhat chagrined.

Rathbun and Palmer were both self-made men, and both were gamblers. But the similarity ended there. Rathbun was noted for his sobriety and restraint, the oversized Palmer for his enthusiastic drinking and buffoonery. Though opposites, the personalities of the two men served them well in the boom years. Palmer cultivated the image of the lucky simpleton by wearing a portrait of his hero, Andrew Jackson, done in diamonds, on his ruffled shirt front. A ready laugh and inventive practical joking kept him popular with a wide circle. Palmer's personal generosity in endowing a school for boys and his drive to establish a comprehensive "University of Western New York" added to his popularity. Always the poker face, Rathbun privately described Palmer as "pompous and ridiculous." This underestimate would later prove fateful for Rathbun. For the present, however, Rathbun's impatience with the younger extrovert did not keep the two from doing business.

Rathbun knew that Palmer was now ready to buy almost anything. Palmer had bought the brick building that Rathbun had erected for the Bank of the United States, even though he knew that it was doomed to be demolished shortly. Palmer had also bought the Baptist Church, built in 1829 at the corner of Washington and Seneca streets, and was reconstructing that for commercial purposes. One of its first uses was as a popular museum, a sort of touring cabinet of curiosities. Through his political connections, Palmer was now lobbying to get the federal government to lease the church's main auditorium. He succeeded and soon "United States Postoffice, Orange Dibble, Postmaster" appeared on the old church doors.

Palmer was no match for Rathbun. It was a simple task to convince him that the new hotel, to be known as "The American," was just the thing he needed to add to his prestige and to make more money. Rathbun gave him a bargain, too: the lease of the whole building for 999 years, and of the upper floors, intended for shops, for ten years, all for the paltry sum of $100,000. Palmer paid him $40,000 cash and gave him notes for $10,000 and a $50,000 mortgage.

Though the newspapers were by that time accustomed to large figures, this transaction amazed editors. The editor of the *Buffalo Commercial Advertiser* gushed:

> Buffalo may well be proud of such citizens as Messrs. Rathbun and Palmer. They have participated largely in the prosperity of our young city and have always shown themselves ready with a liberal hand in advancing her causes. To Mr. Rathbun's energy and skill, we are indebted for a style of building unsurpassed in any city of the United States.

At the same time, Rathbun was building Palmer a fine new home for Julia Palmer to spread herself socially. The contract called for a $42,000 structure. This was then an almost unprecedented expenditure for a local residence, but hardly too large for a man to whom wealth largely meant an opportunity to display his already ample person even more prominently.

In the two stores adjoining The American, Rathbun opened a second dry goods store, which he enlarged to carry groceries and hardware, and a carpet store, which was one of the first in Buffalo. The general store was particularly designed to meet the needs of his mechanics and their families, although it was open to the general public as well. The Rathbun wives—Benjamin's, Lyman's, and Moses' third spouse—did not hesitate to push their way ahead of more poorly dressed workers' wives to do all their own family purchasing there.

Counting the new carpet shop, Rathbun had four stores under his direct control in Buffalo, and he was about to open another in

Niagara Falls. Rathbun could buy at lower prices because he bought in large quantities, putting most of his retail competitors at a disadvantage. The second floors of the new Buffalo stores rented as offices. The increasingly eminent Millard Fillmore had his law offices there. The store at 304 Main Street, two doors south of The American, also housed part of Rathbun's "countinghouse" staff as well as offices where his workmen reported weekly to get their pay.

Besides these elaborate commercial structures, in 1835 Rathbun built forty-eight other first-class brick stores, each three to five stories high. He built a four-story brick warehouse. He erected thirty-one fine dwelling houses valued at from $4,000 to $15,000. He also built four commercial buildings, a four-story stone warehouse, a very large barn, and five other frame dwellings of good size.

In the barn and the warehouse, he housed the horses and vehicles for a new service he inaugurated in the middle of the year: the city's first omnibus line. Sixteen passenger buses, with drivers and conductors in uniform, made regular trips along the length of Main Street. For a small fare, a passenger could ride from the docks at the foot of Main to a couple of blocks above the Eagle Tavern. For several cents more, one could travel the entire route to Cold Springs on upper Main Street, just beyond the town's northern boundary. Each bus bore a name that offered inspiration. These included, for example, "Experiment," "Enterprise," and "Encouragement." Rathbun wanted to be identified with progress. He constructed a similar vehicle to pick up patrons at the canal terminal and haul them directly to the Eagle's door.

He also experimented in street paving, an entirely new construction field. A few alleys had been paved, with the assistance of the city, solely because they were otherwise impassable. But the streets, much of the time, remained in terrible condition. The Scotsman, McAdam, had devised a way of surfacing a road. News of the new technique inspired a group to organize the Buffalo and Williamsville McAdam Road Company, to build an improved toll road on the Scotsman's principle. Rathbun decided to show Buffalo what he could do. He laid a wooden block pavement at Main and Eagle streets, the section going halfway across each street. This solitary solid section in the sea of mud that formed Buffalo's streets remained for some time an object lesson in what could be accomplished for a price.

During this period, Rathbun was erecting many of the fine residences for the great figures of his time. Some of these survived into the next century, though they were often converted into stores and offices as the city's areas of residence moved farther uptown.[1]

The range of Rathbun's work was impressive, as were the identities of his clients. He built an elaborate home for his friend Pierre A. Barker, when Barker was president of the Commercial Bank. Rathbun built a $20,000 home for Martin Daley, brokerage partner of Charles Taintor in C. Taintor and Company, whose services Rathbun was utilizing constantly. Taintor, a former clerk in the United States Branch Bank, was considered an excellent financial manipulator. He built a two-story brick house for Congressman Love, who had done extremely well in the law and speculation. Love was one of Rathbun's friends, too, not as close as Tracy, but he was willing to endorse notes occasionally on Rathbun's behalf. For Henry H. Sizer, the broker, Rathbun built a two-story brick home on the northwest corner of Delaware Street, just across Niagara Square from the handsome colonial homestead Judge Wilkeson had occupied for some time. For Thomas Blossom, of Blossom and Luden, a commission firm that dealt in produce and whiskey, he built a two-story brick residence. Thomas was the brother of Colonel Blossom, the handsome man who had profited extremely well on his business connections with the Holland Company. Many other lawyers, bankers, and brokers came to Rathbun for the construction of their homes.

His commercial property constructions were also impressive. For the firm of Walter Joy and George B. Webster, forwarders, he built in 1835–36 for $100,000 the massively constructed and long-lived Webster block of seventeen four-story stores on the east side of Main Street near the canal. The block measured 337 by 50 feet. Its walls were sixteen inches thick all the way to the top. This job, which he agreed to do in three months, was finished on time, and on the very last day itself, he turned the keys over to the new owners with the laconic, "The stores are completed, here are the keys," according to one chronicler.

---

1. However, of the approximately eighty-four blocks of stores, private dwellings, public institutions, and office buildings Rathbun designed and constructed at Buffalo, only one remains standing in the 1990s. The structure that Rathbun raised for the First Unitarian Church in 1833, in an elite residential neighborhood, is now the headquarters of the Title Guarantee Company. It is in the heart of the city's central business district, and is the oldest standing structure in Buffalo. See Reyner Banham et al., *Buffalo Architecture: A Guide* (Cambridge, Mass., and London: The MIT Press, 1981), 44, 63.

In the banner year of 1836 when he sold the American Hotel, he built the United States Hotel, four stories of brick with eight stores adjoining, on Pearl Street at the Terrace, then considered a fine site because two railroads ended right at the door. The job was for Dr. Josiah Trowbridge, a socially prominent medical practitioner, who would soon be elected mayor. The doctor had $60,000 to invest and decided to use it that way.

Rathbun had one great project under way in 1836, a job intended to be the high water mark of his Buffalo construction career. It was to be a huge combined office, hotel, and auditorium for all the city's major commercial interests and would be called the Buffalo Exchange. It was intended to be the prestige address for Buffalo business. To be erected at a cost of $500,000, it would occupy the entire block on the west side of Main Street, between North and South Division streets, right opposite "The Churches," as prominent a location as then existed in Buffalo.

The block this was to occupy had originally been part of a large tract exempted from sale by Joseph Ellicott, who intended to build his own mansion there. The land fell into the hands of David Evans, a major owner of commercial real estate in Buffalo, who erected various buildings or leased it to others for building purposes. One of the structures on the site was the building of the former United States Branch Bank.

Rathbun had built most of the buildings already occupying the site, but now, in partnership with an enthusiastic Evans, these structures were to be demolished and excavations were begun for the foundations of the great building. It would extend 245 feet on Main and Washington streets and 200 feet on North and South Division streets. The plans provided for a cut-stone entrance with a dome sixty feet in diameter and thirty-four feet high, its top towering 222 feet above the sidewalk. The dome would surmount a huge rotunda. Four great "Grecian Doric columns ten feet two inches in diameter," as the newspapers reported, would completely surround the exterior, a design somewhat like plans for his hotel at Niagara. The main building was to rise four stories, then there would be a smaller floor on a setback, and finally, topping all, would come the dome surrounded by sixteen columns each more than four feet in diameter. The work on the building would require at least two years.

Rathbun was also commissioned by a committee, comprising such civic leaders as Heacock, Wilkeson, Palmer, Caryl, Barker, and Dr. Stagg, to erect another grand monument in the city's center, this one to Commodore Perry, victor of the Battle of Lake Erie. Rathbun's plans called for a white marble, Grecian column, one hundred feet high, on a square base thirty-four feet to a side, topped by a fifteen-foot statue of Perry. The memorial, which would cost about $75,000, was to be erected in the square opposite the new Exchange. The committee had worked four years raising subscriptions, and now approved of Rathbun's plan.

His was now the brightest entrepreneurial star in the Buffalo and western New York firmament. Travelers and businessmen carried tales to all parts of the country of his accomplishments and plans. They speculated on his wealth. He must be, it was often said, many times a millionaire. They viewed his buildings and projects as examples to the rest of the world of what could be accomplished by foresight and determination in the growing Republic.

It was now, in New York's financial circles, that he was dubbed the "Girard of the West." William L. Stone, the editor of the New York City *Commercial Advertiser,* who commanded a large following because of his own enterprise and journalistic integrity, was moved to unusual eloquence in writing of this latter-day Girard, entrepreneur, and community benefactor: "Mr. Rathbun is doing for Buffalo in his lifetime what Stephen Girard authorized to be done after his death. The citizens of Buffalo are greatly indebted to Mr. Rathbun for the extensive improvements [he has] made and [is] making in that extraordinary city."

It was high praise for Rathbun, who seemed the greatest entrepreneur of the postfrontier West, a "Master Builder," a grand schemer, a master of detail, of money, and of men.

10

"A Splendid Pyramid Based on a Peg"

Rathbun's ambitious building projects gave Buffalo the look of permanence and continuity of a great city, but the financial foundations of his own business empire were built upon the shifting sands of Jacksonian-era credit practices. Wildcat money issues from irresponsible banks sustained the trading in land and real estate. Interest rates rose to usurious levels more as a measure of the profits expected than as a projection of the risks. In the Niagara region even the most conservative began to cooperate with Rathbun's exotic money-raising schemes. From this distance it is easy to see how badly the jerry-built system was sagging under its own weight. But thousands were lured inside by the evidence that money was being made quickly and easily around them. For a long time they shored up the structure with their enthusiasm. They seemed delirious with the desire to gamble on the future.

The get-rich-quick virus changed Rathbun more than he recognized. His ambitions had been whetted into an overwhelming desire for money and fame. The gravity and reserve of his earlier years may have been part show and part personal aspiration. Now they were just a useful facade, convenient to cloak his confidential transactions and to impress others with the importance of his mysterious and extensive operations. While he maintained a pretense of his old public modestly, he constantly furnished news of himself to the newspapers; he "leaked" rumors and reports of what he was planning. He used techniques that a few generations later would have been recognized as stock-in-trade among press agents and public-relations specialists. His mastery of the press was uncannily modern.

He was clearly getting pleasure from the repetition of his name on stores and buildings, on stagecoaches and omnibuses. He appreciated the envy of his contemporaries. Public acclaim for his well-advertised largesse made his heart quicken. The more people talked about him, the wider he could expand his operations, for the more investors and creditors he could attract.

Rathbun no doubt continued to believe that he saw objectively and weighed and balanced every suggestion and its chances for profit. Suggestions were pouring in now from his associate, from other financiers, and from the general public. Here was a good speculation; there was a building whose owner had no idea of its real worth; this thing was a sure bet; that one could not be passed up. Almost no idea with even the slightest degree of merit could be proposed to him before he found himself grasping and fighting to get control and put it under his wing.

Rathbun's control over Buffalo's lands, its buildings, and businesses approached monopoly by the mid-1830s. Yet the gain to him was dubious, to say the least. As his operations grew, so did his obligations. Grand construction projects meant swollen payrolls, difficult supply problems, and enormous debt. Though at the peak of his power, Rathbun had never been in worse shape. Meeting the "shaves" on his retail operations and real estate investments demanded ever more creative financing. Rathbun paid his workers $10,000 a week. To supply his stores he paid $300,000 per year to his wholesalers in New York City. Rathbun had to grow to stay even, and he was forced to take on more deadweight in notes and mortgages. The pace left him no time to consolidate or to digest the new operations. As Rathbun himself later put it, the burden forced him to "twist and screw" every moment of his life.

He induced Buffalo banks to give him as much as, and then a little more, than the minority of prudent conservatives among the local bankers considered safe. He borrowed from officials of the banks individually, when he could, or from anyone else who would lend him cash. He backed his loans with notes, bonds, pledges of land, and interest in his properties. He gave first, second, and third mortgages, shuffling them back and forth, recording some and not recording others. Under such circumstances, those who loaned him money could not have had any real idea of the worth of the security he put up.

But his demands for capital were insatiable—far beyond the limited loaning capacity of Buffalo banks and individual leaders. He and his agents needed to reach out constantly to other banks in western

New York, central New York, New York City, Ohio, Pennsylvania, New England—anywhere that the capital could be raised. When finally he drained the Wall Street money market of all that he could get, his notes were hawked in England.

Rathbun had always worked hard; now he was on the job day and night. Daytimes, when he was in Buffalo, he raced about checking on the many activities for which he was responsible. When he was out of town, it was usually to see bank officials or wealthy men who might furnish him the money he needed to keep his huge machine in motion.

Each evening the foremen of his far-flung operations assembled at his house to get their directions for the next day. Always he was exhorting them, "in strong language," as they themselves testified, to new exertions. Jobs had to be finished on time; contracts had to be procured to supply timber, bricks, hay for the horses. His active mind seemed to encompass every detail.

Yet no matter how late these nightly meetings lasted, the next morning found him on the job before his men arrived for work. One day he would be waiting at a store for the clerks to show up; another he would be at the barns, long before the first teamster was on hand to start hitching the horses to the 150 or so wagons engaged on his jobs.

But overhanging all his work and all his ambitions was that constantly overpowering, stifling fear of being unable to meet his notes as they became due. Once he failed to meet a crucial note, there might be a general panic about his solvency. The whole credit structure might crack, and the great machine itself could drag him down to disaster. Occasionally a note would be missed, forgotten, and a protest would come through the mail. The note had to be made good immediately and all those immediately involved had to be assured that it had merely been overlooked, that his business was perfectly solvent, and that he could meet every obligation when it was due.

Part of this difficultly stemmed from a situation that Rathbun recognized, but apparently dared not change. Out of a need for secrecy as his affairs grew more complex and dubious, only his inner financial staff was given the information necessary to grasp the enormous detail of his operations and act upon the most sensitive business problems. At the center of Rathbun's operations were only his brother and his nephew—barely enough staff for a small-town bank, let alone for Rathbun's extensive operations. As a result, Benjamin was forced to drive the two to superhuman efforts, just as he drove his foremen and supervisors and indeed himself. He and Lyman especially were forced to strain every minute merely to keep abreast of daily work. Whether by design or inadvertence, all too frequently now they were failing to keep adequate records of outstanding notes. There were simply too many of them.

They faced potential disaster almost daily because of a forgotten note or notes. New emergencies piled on old ones. Either notes were protested or, as often happened, just on the eve of a note's due date they made the belated discovery that they had failed to provide for it. Then there followed a mad scramble to make money available to creditors.

This outstanding deficiency in his otherwise exceptional organiza-tion kept Rathbun in an almost continuous state of tension, though outsiders naturally knew nothing of it from their interactions with him. His letters reveal how close he often was to mental and physical collapse. He was fearful that his or his brother's health might give way under the pressure of their work and bring the House of Rath-bun tumbling to the ground. He told himself and his closest associates that the crisis ahead would mark a turning point in their affairs, and that things would be easier afterward. But the next day often brought problems that made yesterday's seem insignificant.

Only this tight hold of the reigns of his empire made many of his financial operations continue to be possible. Associates had only a vague idea of what he was doing. As he reached farther and farther away from Buffalo for money, his operations became more mysteri-ous to outsiders. Other financiers undoubtedly thought that they knew how he was doing business, but their knowledge proved to be quite incomplete. Rathbun was secretive about his borrowings. He was aided in his manipulations by the banks, which exchanged little information at the time, and by the fact that communications were primitive enough that both gossip and news traveled very slowly. This protected him. Rathbun knew how to take advantage of the financial game as it was then being played.

To the business community, he was a keenly alert, close-mouthed man of affairs, who knew his way through the deep maze of business practice. To his inner staff, he was the voluble spur who never let them forget that they had both to work and to scheme in secrecy.

His fear that details of his business operations might leak to his detriment were voiced in the earliest of his business letters still extant. This somewhat cryptic letter, written to his nephew, Rathbun Allen, whom he had sent late in 1835 to raise money in Ohio at Warren and

Cleveland, illustrates the complexity of the financing in which he was engaged. He was training the young innocent to handle some of these delicate tasks.

> Your several letters have been received with some of the needful [notes] by Capt. Stone. The object of this you'll see by the enclosed which I have just received. If you have not been to Warren you had better go there and get the proceeds of the note mentioned in the enclosed letter. But one word of caution: William Williams [then a Buffalo broker] is going out there to spend the winter. You must therefore be cautious of your paper [notes].
>
> I suppose you have my several letters sent to Cleveland. Redeem all you can of such paper as has been sent back to the banks. Navigation [on the lakes] is now closed, and what will make more difference in the circulation is that the money market will be easier in this State after the 1st January. All the Safety Fund Banks have sent home all the paper [notes from banks in other states] that they could possibly get hold of. It will not be so after the 1st January. You can inform the bank folks at the West that their paper will receive a much greater circulation after the 1st January.
>
> I sent Newell [S. Newell Brown, a confidential clerk used constantly as an agent in Rathbun's negotiations] to Cleveland, as you have learnt, I suppose, ere this. I have answered the enclosed letter of Mr. Fitch and have also wrote you at Warren, directed to his care, requesting him to send proceeds of that note by first safe conveyance, either directed to me or care of Edward Clarke, of Cleveland. Therefore if you do not go to Warren let Mr. Clarke know that a package may come to his care for me. If so forward it without delay.
>
> Hope you'll be home as soon as may be; but do up all your business right and straight before you leave it. You must know that this is a very important business you are on and much, very much, depends upon its being properly arranged.

The enclosure was a letter from Zalmon Fitch at the Western Reserve Bank at Warren who said that Robert Bush, a stranger to him, had forwarded one of Rathbun's $2,000 notes for discount. However, he would not furnish the money unless Rathbun himself identified Bush. Bush, from whom Rathbun had acquired the coach works, must have been doing some business for him.

Rathbun was experiencing more and more trouble raising money on his own notes. Occasionally he could market a small one, particularly on western banks or in his dealings with persons who were furnishing him goods and solely on the strength of his signature. But increasingly, most endorsements now needed the signatures of well-respected, substantial citizens, endorsements that guaranteed that the fortunes and reputations of the endorsers were thrown into the maintenance of the obligation.

In the light of its later bearing on Rathbun's affairs, the most important of these transactions was a loan of $15,000, which he obtained in the spring of 1835 to help finance the "Evans Hotel Block" (presumably the new Exchange Building). The existence of the notes backing the loan was bruited about Buffalo as time went on, although the details were not known until much later.

He required the money to meet pressing expenses, probably in connection with the acquisition and demolition of the various buildings then on the site. He sought assistance form Lewis F. Allen, the Buffalo loaning representative of the New York Life Insurance and Trust Company, who had been helpful to him in numerous other negotiations. Allen, then thirty-five years old, had ingratiated himself with leading financiers, and, after only eight years in the city, amassed a fortune. His helpfulness polished by intensive training in promoting insurance among people who knew little about it, Allen was ready to serve in finding a solution for the important Mr. Rathbun's problem.

When Allen delicately raised the matter of security, Rathbun told him that he could assign the front section of the Kremlin building to guarantee the payment of the notes. Thereupon Allen drew up the notes, and, on his own initiative, got twelve of the most solid local men as endorsers on an informal agreement, which stated that the four-month notes would be renewed periodically for two years. He returned the endorsed notes to Rathbun who tried, or said that he tried, to raise money on them. Allen then volunteered to get the $15,000 loan from the New York company he represented, using the notes as security.

When they were first issued on April 8, 1835, these notes bore on their backs a dozen names that were representative of a cross-section of Buffalo's power and wealth. Besides Allen himself, they included Colonel Blossom, Dr. Johnson, Congressman Love, Hiram Pratt, then the mayor as well as president of the Bank of Buffalo, Clary, former state assemblyman and Rathbun's cousin by marriage, Sheldon Thompson, dean of forwarders and chief partner in the newly organized Coit, Kimberly and Company, and Charles Townsend, Thompson's partner in the new forwarding concern.

There were also Joseph Dart, Jr., who had begun as a hat dealer and manufacturer and who was now financing grain shipments,

Henry Morris, an affable and successful entrepreneur, business firmament, Dr. John W. Clark, one of the five city aldermen and a speculator who, like several of the city's doctors, was making so much money outside his medical practice that he was among Buffalo's richest men, and Joseph Stocking, Dart's partner in the hat business. Stocking's death, that same summer, reduced the endorsers to eleven.

But even such massively supported notes did not provide the money Rathbun needed. Doubtless he had begun to wonder if there were not ways to raise capital faster and without so much preliminary work. In this search, a solution occurred to him, just as it would to others at the time who faced a similar dilemma. He would gain control of some small banks in states with lax regulatory standards. These needed to be institutions far enough separated by distance to assure that their note issues would have no apparent relation to each other. It was essential that his connection be concealed.

State-chartered banks were springing up everywhere at this time, primarily because their paper issues were being accepted at face value by the government in the purchase of federal lands. They loaned cash on promissory notes for the express purpose of facilitating the buying of western land. The borrower would get the land and then, on the strength of his title, might get new loans to buy more land. Money issued in this manner came back to the issuing bank for redemption very slowly with the result that the bank could maintain the appearance of solvency on its account books, even while possessing almost no specie in its treasury.

In 1835, Rathbun's search uncovered a bank that could be revived to serve his purpose. This was the Granville Bank, in a small village of the same name, in Licking County in the central Ohio countryside.

The Granville Bank, like many others at the time, was an institution with a checkered history. It had begun in 1815 as the first bank in the area, under authority of a charter granted to the Granville Alexandrian Society, which sounded more like a reading club than a bank. Because early legislatures had been distrustful of financiers and reluctant to charter banks, it was common to utilize loosely worded charters, granted for entirely unrelated purposes, as a sanction to engage in banking. The Granville Bank had built a stone building on Broad Street in Granville, just east of the village square, and then experienced a failure in August 1817. It had languished since that failure, and now awaited revival.

Granville had several advantages from Rathbun's viewpoint, notably its interior western location and its isolation in winter. It might benefit by making loans for western lands. More important for Rathbun, notes and loans issued by the bank could be handled farther east during the cold season with the assurance that banks and brokers would know little about the bank's condition until lake navigation opened in the spring.

In Rathbun's behalf, James Miller, who worked in the Buffalo brokerage office of Sherwood and Kinney, negotiated the Ohio transaction, stimulating interest in a revival of the bank in Granville and handling the acquisition of its old stock and its transfer to Rathbun. Miller managed the negotiation carefully, getting the stock cheaply before sellers became aware of the plan for the bank's immediate revival.

Working with Miller on the transaction was Henry Roop, who had been a partner of Merrill B. Sherwood in the grocery business that Sherwood continued as a sideline to his brokerage office. Roop spent all his time on the Granville project. Rathbun appointed him president of the Granville Bank when it was reopened for business in early 1836.

How much of its stock Rathbun controlled is not on record. He owned at least thirty-two hundred shares outright, which he valued at $77,000 in August 1836. Against this the bank had advanced him about $50,000 of its paper notes, which he planned to distribute widely, so that no great quantity would be returned for redemption at any time.

Even before this neat transaction was complete, Rathbun, now looking eastward, uncovered another possible banking connection in the Paterson Bank of Paterson, New Jersey. Now he used the confidential services of Lemuel White, who was a broker as well as a leather goods merchant in Buffalo, but was presently giving much of his time to Rathbun's business. White was a skillful negotiator, one of those Rathbun liked to describe as a "giant with money." Sent to Paterson, White succeeded in December 1835 in procuring a $20,000 loan to Rathbun from the bank. By using the loan to buy outstanding shares of stock at depreciated prices and by giving other notes to pay for stock in its treasury, Rathbun shortly held $130,000 of its capital stock and was in full control of the institution. He later used $30,000 of this stock to secure a loan elsewhere.

White handled most of this transaction directly with J. M. Redmond, cashier of the bank. He had convinced Redmond that his patron, Rathbun, was one of the greatest contemporary financial figures and that he would soon raise the bank to the first rank. Not until the negotiations were practically complete did Rathbun even meet the cashier.

The Paterson Bank to some extent resembled the one at Granville. It had also been founded in 1815, had put up a pretentious building, and had operated for a while with modest results, before getting into difficulties and having to close in 1829. Local capital revived it in 1834 with a Paterson man, John Travers, as president, but with Redmond really running it.

Early in 1836, while these banking deals were in progress, Rathbun concluded that yet another financial connection, this time an international one, was needed. He settled on Fort Erie in Canada, directly across the Niagara River from Buffalo. Here he intended to create the "Commercial Bank of Fort Erie." Canadian laws relating to private banks, under which this one was to be organized, were even more lax than their American counterparts. Through connections developed in Montreal, Rathbun obtained authority for its financing and got the bank going by midsummer. The local details of the transaction were handled by Merrill B. Sherwood, one of Rathbun's broker-agents, who publicly fronted as the bank's organizer and president.

Rathbun's role in these transactions was carefully hidden. But local bankers suspected that some influential entrepreneur—and surely an astute few might have privately suspected Rathbun—in the area was flooding Granville Bank notes into circulation in western New York. The *Niagara Democrat* in Lockport printed a vaguely worded article warning the public to be careful of accepting Granville notes until they knew more about the institution. This provoked immediate retaliation from Guy Salisbury's *Commercial Advertiser*, Rathbun's strong supporter. In an editorial, Salisbury stated that the Ohio bank had had a handsome start and gained legitimacy by being listed in various financial trade summaries. Moreover, the paper said, its notes were being accepted by banks throughout the region.

Though rumors of the sort circulating around Buffalo rarely were printed, Rathbun's desperate search for capital to keep his huge operations going, to pay off his mechanics and laborers, and to stave off the creditors who were harassing him could not long be kept secret from the brokers, bankers, moneylenders, and other financial experts who peopled New York's Wall Street. Suspicions soon reached the metropolis, where they were widely and openly discussed in the financial industry. Beginning early in 1836 they cut down his credit, except on the best endorsed paper—and only then at increasingly exorbitant rates. As their terms to him rose, so did their terms to all borrowers. Ample credit was available—but at a growing price.

The connection of these rising rates to Rathbun himself came out only later. At the time there was only the inexorable rise of interest to two, three, four, and even five percent a month, which nearly demoralized the money market. The charges to Rathbun, a major player, for the money he received were ruining other borrowers, stifling legitimate commercial loans, and impairing business operations elsewhere.

It was clear that some New York moneylenders had grown distrustful of the activities of Buffalo entrepreneurs, especially Rathbun. Most of them claimed later that they knew sometime the bubble would burst. But none admitted to the least suspicion of when or where the collapse would begin.

Word of the New York financial community's eroding confidence was carried back to Buffalo by Alanson Palmer, the one man Rathbun had probably never guessed could injure him. Benjamin and Lyman quickly convinced Palmer that he was in the wrong, but the rumor continued that the New York market, as Palmer had reported, was crowded with Rathbun notes. Local newspapers took no public notice of the gathering trouble and continued to praise Rathbun. For many Buffalonians there was, perhaps, too much at stake to acknowledge publicly the gathering crisis. In May 1836, Thomas Woodcock, an English visitor, described this mood of collective denial and fearfulness. Woodcock was astounded by the atmosphere of reckless speculation and by the superficiality of the boom.

This Buffalo is a most corrupt place as regards money matters. The whole of these fine buildings being built upon credit, should an alteration in the value of money take place, and it most assuredly will, then these men cannot pay their mortgages; the banks will claim them, and as I firmly believe the banks cannot redeem their paper now, how will it be then?

There is a person here by the name of Rathbun who they say has built up the place. He is the greatest builder, the greatest stage contractor; in fact he is at the head of everything, and I see by the papers he has lately offered Niagara Falls for sale for manufacturing purposes.

Now this man is admitted on all hands to be unable to pay his debts and yet his notes pass current for money, the people declaring that they dare not let him break as it would ruin the whole place. . . . To sum up the matter, it [Buffalo] is a fine place, a splendid pyramid, but it is based on a peg.

Astute an analyst as he was, Woodcock did not realize that the potential harm he associated with Rathbun's difficulties now extended far beyond the confines of Buffalo, and continued to reach further and further out to more institutions and locations. Even Nicholas Biddle was to become involved in Rathbun's frantic machinations, through the intervention of the prestigious Judge Rochester.

William B. Rochester and Company, the group that had purchased the assets of the closed branch, was doing much business with Rathbun in those days. Burt, Thompson, General Porter, Evans and Coe, who were associated with Judge Rochester in buying the old assets, viewed themselves now as a promising banking firm. Later they were considered the temporary saviors of many businesses that might have suffered by a too sudden liquidation of their obligations to the Bank of the United States.

That this was only a part of their purpose in buying the assets, however, was later admitted by General Porter in pleading for an extension of their obligations to the central bank. Pointing out that they had bought the assets of the branch when the country was very prosperous, Porter said that their primary motive had been to relieve their "friends and neighbors from an immediate and forced collection." He added that Judge Rochester all the while continued to tell them that, if the government's policy were changed, the branch might be revived.

Rathbun looked on Judge Rochester and his private bank as a link to Biddle in Philadelphia. He had sent Lemuel White to Philadelphia several times in the spring of 1836 to attempt to procure a substantial loan, as the start of a "permanent connection," as he expressed it. His own salesmanship was exercised assiduously on Judge Rochester. Rochester wrote an endorsement to Biddle, which helped enable Rathbun's New York agent to negotiate an $80,000 loan in the early summer.

Rathbun was further extending his business operations, even as he grew ever more desperate for the money to sustain them. He bought a place on Cattaraugus Creek, at what he called "Cattaraugus Falls," in the forest south of Buffalo, and there constructed sawmills, a gristmill, a storehouse, and other buildings essential to settlement. The sawmill, which he valued at $50,000 when he opened it, was kept busy shaping quantities of timber for his construction jobs. Lewis F. Eaton, the former president of the Lockport Bank and now a state banking commissioner, was associated with him in this investment.

He also acquired new stone quarries near Lockport to supplement the ones close to Buffalo that he had owned for several years. Getting these enterprises started took valuable time. He set a killing pace, rushing back and forth by carriage or stage to these operations, to Niagara Falls, to New York, to Montreal, his head whirling with the necessity of supervising construction, raising money, and seeing businessmen who might become partners in one scheme or another.

Rathbun's ability to keep his self-possession, to give the appearance of an unworried, confident businessman assured of success in his many undertakings, was certainly sorely tried by this point. Things were "squally," he admitted frequently to his brother, using a word that was as near an oath as he permitted himself. He acknowledged in private letters that he was "under whip and spur," that he was frightfully nervous, and that he was so tired he could remember only half the things he had to do. The exhaustion of one day carried over to the next. He could not slow his pace, for the success of each of his projects was so tied to the others that none could be curtailed or abandoned. On his seemingly endless journeys he tried to catch up on the many problems of his diverse interests, but the rolling, jolting motion of the stages gave little opportunity for real thought and none for rest. Regardless of his exhaustion, he seems always to have been able to pull himself together in time to be keenly alert, assuring the financiers and others with whom he had to deal.

He was especially anxious to begin selling lots at Niagara Falls. This new source of cash, he convinced himself, would enable him to meet his pressing obligations and provide momentum for the future.

Yet, in the mean time, he had difficult decisions to make. Because he could not really retrench without endangering all his operations, he finally settled on the only alternative. He ordered James DeLong, the former clerk he had put in charge of his construction operations, to refuse to take any new contracts and to cut down on labor and the costs of material on the projects in progress.

DeLong was one of the many time-tested men with carefully defined responsibilities who comprised the staff of the House of Rathbun. Benjamin had so departmentalized his operations that supervisors were delegated responsibility for large segments of the work and reported directly to him. Albert S. Merrill, for instance, directed the Bush coach factory where railroad cars, post coaches, wagons, and similar equipment were fabricated; Stevenson had charge of stagecoach operations and Hathaway was general travel superintendent. Thomas G. Perkins, a retail clerk who had been promoted to manager, was put in charge of most of the stores. Each construction job was headed by a foreman who reported to his next supervisor.

If his later description of his function can be accepted at face value, Benjamin served as, in modern parlance, "outside man" in this empire, making the contacts and handling the then equivalent of promotion and sales. Lyman, who was closely assisted by the nephew, Rathbun Allen, was the "inside man," with the responsibility, or so Benjamin would claim, of seeing that notes were paid or renewed on time to avoid protests, obtaining some loans, paying the workmen, paying debts, and handling the many similar "paper" details of such a complicated organization.

As the "outside man," Rathbun talked to financiers and kept himself available to callers from out of town who wanted information about Buffalo and his business. As he stated later, "Much of my time was necessarily taken up in attention to strangers from New York and elsewhere who were daily referred to me for information on subjects of importance—worth of lots, costs of blocks of buildings, etc."

Always in these contacts, he maintained the open, casual, and assured appearance that people expected and that helped build and retain confidence in him and his schemes.

❧❀◗

The money markets in New York and Buffalo went through a number of disturbing and frightening periods during the late winter of 1835 and the spring that followed. Each was reflected in Rathbun's financial situation. Crises occurred in his affairs in New York in January, March, and April, and then in May, when he was able to keep afloat only by the expenditure of tremendous effort and by calling on the support of almost everyone he knew.

He had a number of intimate broker-contacts in New York, among them Robert Steele, with whom he had been dealing since about 1829. Steele and Joseph Gauvier had discounted many of his notes. On the suggestion of New York acquaintances, perhaps one of these two men, in February 1836 he employed Horace Janes as his general agent in New York City. Janes opened an office at 8 Liberty Street, which Rathbun began to use as his headquarters when he went to the metropolis.

Originally Janes was hired to be mainly a buying agent, negotiating contracts with New York wholesalers and keeping track of bargains for the Rathbun stores in Buffalo and Niagara Falls and for the manufactured goods he needed in construction work. But with money problems so pressing, Janes's function was transformed almost immediately into that of a financial representative. Several times in the early spring and summer Janes saved Rathbun's financial life. Rathbun fully realized how essential Janes's activities were to his survival, for in writing to his brother he described Janes with that ultimate accolade, "a giant with money."

In April, Rathbun did something that he considered at the time an extremely clever, farsighted move to help relieve his difficulties. He was destined, however, eventually to regret it. He employed Richard M. Blatchford as his legal representative in New York City.

This choice was clearly a step in making a closer approach to Biddle. Blatchford was a social intimate of Biddle and was near the purse strings of that financial leader. Biddle was then in Philadelphia at the helm of the Bank of the United States of Pennsylvania, the successor to the former national institution. Blatchford was one of the best-known lawyers in New York City. He was so adept in manipulating the law for the interest of his clients that his talent was recognized a short six years after he began practicing when he was selected by the Bank of England as its American financial agent and legal counsel. Only a few years later, the Bank of the United States employed him for the same purpose. In the spring of 1836, he was busy settling outstanding accounts between the two banks in connection with winding up the affairs of the former Bank of the United States.

In late June, Rathbun was again in New York attending to another crisis, and conferred with Janes and Blatchford. He "found from the great amount of my paper afloat (the increase having been caused by enormous shaves) that increased exertion was absolutely necessary and a resort to a heavy loan then seemed most desirable."

Blatchford told him that he thought $500,000 could be obtained on adequate security, which would be "a bond signed by myself [Rathbun] and a sufficient number of wealthy persons of Buffalo." With the promise of a liberal commission, Rathbun turned over to Blatchford the responsibility for obtaining the loan, while he himself made arrangements for a bond to secure it. The House of Rathbun was delicately poised between success and utter ruin.

The next few weeks were hectic. From New York City, Rathbun had been pressing Lyman to pay some money to the Porters before July 1 to bind the Niagara Falls bargain in accordance with the agreement. But in Buffalo, Lyman was equally strapped for money. Nothing that he could do was adequate to relieve the stringency.

Agents were sent by fast horse to pump more cash out of Granville, to get what could be borrowed at any other western banks, and to pick up any loans that upstate New York banks there would grant.

Benjamin had to make an arrangement with the Porters. He could not abandon his great sale, which in combination with the $500,000 from New York would certainly extricate him from his difficulties. He had to explain something of his affairs. He emphasized the purely temporary pressure that made it impossible for him to pay. He persuaded the Porter brothers and they agreed to accept the $47,000 down payment, with interest from July 1, if he paid it by August 10. This allowed him enough time after the start of the sale to be sure that he would have the money available. But the brothers made him guarantee the payment by a mortgage on the lots that contained the Eagle Tavern and adjoining buildings.

Still, no hint of Rathbun's new difficulties was slowing the momentum of the local boom. Steamboats, sailing ships, and other craft crossed the harbor. Canal arrivals set a record. Increasing amounts of the raw materials being brought into the city now were remaining there, for the first time, to become manufactured or processed goods. Buffalo was experiencing the first evidence that it was industrializing.

Eastbound canal traffic had dramatically increased its volume. Shipments of fifty-four hundred tons of white oak shop planking from Grand Island in the Niagara River occupied 120 canal boats on their way to tidewater. In addition, $3\frac{1}{2}$ million feet went east by raft on the canal, lumber alone paying tolls of $15,000. Tidewater financiers, in cooperation with Lewis F. Allen, organized the East Boston Company, and in 1833 bought huge Grand Island, downstream from Buffalo in the middle of the Niagara, from New York State. They were now engaged in putting in sawmills and clearing the forest at a rate that would soon make fortunes for the owners.

The Buffalo and Erie Railroad, capitalized long before, called for new subscriptions to its $650,000 capital stock and raised pledges of over $1,000,000 from confident investors. Rathbun was reelected to the board of directors of the Niagara Falls Railroad at its annual meeting, where optimistic reports of the great profits that would flow as soon as the road was finished cheered every heart. A firm of land agents, acting in behalf of the Niagara City Association, announced that six hundred lots would go on sale at Black Rock on September 6. Few doubted that a great development for the Niagara region was in the making.

Then, on July 11, 1836, President Jackson issued his famous "specie circular," designed to halt the wild inflation by directing the Federal Land Office to accept payments for western lands in specie only. The inflationary boom in the West halted almost instantly. Speculators who had been buying and selling government lands in wildcat paper money had to cease their activities. A spasm of fear shook many western banks, and some failed. On federal lands, however, which had been already sold, the boom continued a little longer. But deflation had begun.

To all appearances Benjamin Rathbun was at the very peak of his career. He had surmounted financial crises of a magnitude that would have driven lesser men to insolvency or distraction long before. By August 1, workers finished demolishing structures on the site of the new Exchange and construction of the massive building began. Buffalo's momentum seemed irresistible.

Likewise, at Niagara Falls, evidence of solid prosperity was everywhere to be found. The basement for the huge new hotel had been excavated, and workmen were raising the foundations for the first floor. Work on the Niagara Falls Railroad ran ahead of schedule. Rathbun had participated in dedication ceremonies held at Schlosser Landing on July 29 and 30 to herald the arrival by barge of two of the fine new cars that had been fabricated in Rathbun's Buffalo factory. Horses hauled these cars from the Landing to Niagara Falls village, where they were placed on exhibit.

The eager speculators who assembled to buy lots at Niagara Falls on August 2 were unaware that these were the final moments of the spectacular boom of the 1830s. In the first few hours of the sale, $30,000 in lots sold. Those present believed that the sale would continue at that furious rate all week. So many were there, cash in hand and determined to buy, that one man compared the scene to a "camp meeting." The sale reached full stride the next day. Bidders, sure of a bright future, competed intensely for the choicest lots.

But by nightfall on the second day of the sale, August 3, Benjamin Rathbun was in custody in the jail he had built. Now in disgrace, a failure, apparently a felon, he was charged with forging the names of prominent local men as guarantors on a series of his promissory notes.

11

"Under Whip and Spur"

At the time, few were prepared to understand how the House of
Rathbun could have fallen, and the story can still be only partly recon-
structed. The real issue was and remains the extent of Rathbun's
legal and moral culpability. Was he personally responsible or were his
subordinates to blame? What responsibility did the "Master Builder"
bear for the activities of trusted employees, two of whom were his
close relations? The interpretation of these questions created tremendous controversy, for the significance of Rathbun's enterprises for
local prosperity guaranteed that many lives would be touched by
Rathbun's collapse and that emotions would run very high. Between
Rathbun's violent opponents and his unthinking partisans, there
would be little neutral ground.

Rathbun's only direct public defense was a long statement, issued
half a year after his arrest. He did not deny that crimes had been
committed. Instead he blamed the crimes charged to him on his
brother Lyman and his two nephews, Rathbun Allen and Lyman
Rathbun Howlett. Later, and until the end of his life, he would also
maintain that he was the victim of a conspiracy to seize his property,
engineered by Hiram Pratt and others. But his self-defense was rid-
dled with inconsistencies and false statements.

Rathbun's basic contention was that he had turned over the entire
financial management of his affairs to his brother and that he never
interfered with Lyman's management. He never even wrote to his
agents, he said, except at Lyman's dictation. So closely, he contended,
did he follow his brother's instructions, that "I seldom knew when,
where or how funds were raised and never when payments were due
but from him."

Rathbun's own letters, however, provide eloquent testimony that this was far from a precise statement of his financial operations.

His violent struggles to keep afloat in the shifting morass of finance are graphically pictured in the letters that intermittently cover his business from January 1836 to the day of his collapse. They mirror his fears, his hopes, and the multitude of increasingly dubious devices that he employed to stave off disaster. Their ambiguities were interpreted later by state prosecutors as evidence that he knew what was going on. In many instances the letters more reliably reflect the confused mind of the harried and increasingly desperate writer. It is difficult to deny, however, that the letters provide ample evidence that Rathbun was ultimately the architect of his own catastrophe. They certainly suggest the possibility of criminal behavior.

The first letter of importance was to his nephew, Rathbun Allen, when Allen was in New York in January 1836 attempting to provide for the many notes then falling due. Rathbun admitted that he had forgotten about $6,000 in notes discounted at a Connecticut bank that were already due for payment at the North River Bank in New York.

To meet this situation, he urged Allen to get a loan on what uncurrent money he had on hand. The loan would have to come from a "safe place," which would not send it back too soon to the originating bank for redemption. But he worried about the tightness of money, fearing that he would not be able to cover his obligations. He wrote that he had "never seen nor known money so scarce as now. It's impossible to get it on any paper or in any possible way."

Allen must have met the immediate situation and then returned to Buffalo. In March, with the purchase of stock in the Granville and Paterson banks necessitating heavy cash outlays beyond the already large obligations, Rathbun had foreseen difficulty in meeting notes due on the seventeenth and nineteenth of that month in New York. He dispatched Allen to New York yet again, to try to raise money along the way and to assist Janes in making sure that money was available at the various banks when notes were presented for payment.

While Allen was in New York, Benjamin wrote him some especially revealing letters. Rathbun later insisted they were merely routine business communications written by Lyman, and that under any circumstance their meanings were by no means transparent. Others saw evidence of criminal intent in these guarded messages. He wrote to Allen when his nephew was at Batavia on his way east on March 6:

"Nothing new. Take very particular care of all your papers and also the letter I wrote you. Don't leave any of them where they'll be seen by anybody."

Three days later he addressed Allen at Albany, advising him that S. Newell Brown, the confidential clerk working on many secret transactions, was en route to New York on the fast Telegraph stage with $14,000 in uncurrent money, which they had been unable to exchange for current in Buffalo. Lyman had directed Brown to dispose of all he could on the way to New York, and "what you cannot sell on the way, you must manage to the very best advantage; if you can't sell it so as it will answer, leave it in pledge for current, rather than let the notes lay over." Rathbun continued:

> Those notes of 17th endorsed D. E. E. [David E. Evans] must be taken up, let what will stand at the door. You know what to do and how to do it. It is no use for me to advise you how to manage without knowing anything of the circumstances. You must do the very best you can and if it's in your power to send anything home, send Newell back as soon as the Telegraph can take him, for we are and shall continue to be in hot water right up to our elbows.

Rathbun also told Allen to pay a note that Rathbun had drawn on Janes. Rathbun was not quite sure how Janes would like it. The note was in favor of Lyman and had been endorsed by Lyman and Peter B. Porter, Jr. This device of drawing a draft on someone at a distance was a common practice of the time, which was employed extensively by the United States Bank in interbranch bank dealings. It was a means of gaining time in payment of a debt, because the note had to be forwarded and went through many hands in the process. Rathbun also informed Allen that Lemuel White, the merchant-broker-agent, was "on the clean jump in New Jersey for money" and was considering applying for it in Philadelphia.

In this letter was one of the most hotly disputed statements: "Newell has a package of notes for you which *must* be used with the utmost caution." What was there about these notes that so set off Rathbun's anxieties?

Writing to Allen at New York the next day, he repeated much of what he had said in the previous letter on the chance that the earlier communication might have missed Allen at Albany. Its most suggestive parts from the standpoint of the charges against him were:

You must look out sharp for the paper endorsed D. E. E. That must be taken care of let what will become of the rest. . . . Newell has a package of notes for you, some of them certified. You must use them with the utmost caution. You know all about that business. "Be as wise as a serpent and as harmless as a dove."

In all this business you must do the very best you can. You know I have more out-door cares than any one had ever ought to be troubled with. . . . These are troublesome times; but hope to see better soon. There is no way now but go straight through from the mark.

He was worried about some of the Paterson Bank notes deposited with R. S. Williams, a New York broker, and told Allen that he must redeem the money and not let it go back to the bank: "If possible you must buy it off Williams with some of your certified paper, but you must look sharp how you show him or sell him your paper for it will be looked at by S. N. Brown, I presume."

His next day's letter, of March 11, to Allen, conveyed both hope and fear. He had received from Sherwood, his broker-agent, a proof sheet of the bank notes for the Granville Bank.

They are a very fine looking bill. I don't know how the thing will take with the community, or how we shall succeed in it; I do think rather favorable, and unless the legislature interferes I see no reason why we can't make it a very important matter. The charter (if good for any thing) is worth more than any one of the charters in this State. However, all this business is an experiment.

The letters I get from Mr. Redmond [cashier of the Peterson Bank] talk fair. I think much of his ability as a financier and I think he is right in regard to his views of my business and all the knowledge of me he has had from Mr. [Lemuel] White. That White is a giant; stick to him and have him stick to you and my business in the money affairs—as long as he can be of any use—and I'll attend to his affairs here. Keep everything right side up and in fair colors with Janes. We may have to make great use of him; therefore want him to have a favorable idea of things and that is to have a right idea. The more he knows of our business, the better he'll be satisfied with it. It's a big business.

His notes with the "eleven endorsers" at the New York Life Insurance and Trust Company were on his mind when he wrote, with evidence of increasing anxiety, the next day.

I want you to say one thing to Col. R. Steele [the New York broker with whom he had dealt for years]. I see in one of his letters he says I have reported such and such persons to the Trust Company as to the goodness of my paper, etc. Now that won't do for him to be referring people there, for if my credit is good there he is taking the very one to destroy it. Now that must be stopped if he has ever practiced it and you can get along with him in this way: Say to him, you know I have an object to accomplish which is of vast importance to me and by frequent reference to the Trust Company of the goodness of my paper it would be wholly and entirely frustrated. Therefore he must be extremely cautious about referring any one there for the goodness of my paper.

My fears that you'll not be able to manage that large amount 17th and 19th about crazes me. . . . My [ar]rears are so great that I can't think of anything else. You have no idea how such things worry me. It does seem as though it would completely unman me for every kind of business.

Having heard from Allen, he commended his nephew the next day for raising $6,000 at the Seneca County Bank at Waterloo, New York, but regretted that similar attempts to raise money in Batavia, Canandaigua, and Utica had failed and said that things looked "rather squally." His letter spoke of notes of which he had entries at his office in his home and that he would try to find time on the following day to check other entries in the records at the counting-house. When he wrote his next letter, March 14, he was "nearly used up by anxiety."

On March 15, he had more bad news for Allen. One of the drafts on the New York broker, Joseph Guavier, discounted at a Canadian bank, had been protested in February, but then had been paid. Now, however, another had turned up protested at Buffalo. Although he had "ransacked the town," he had been unable to find Canadian money and so had paid it with a $2,000 draft on Allen in New York, figuring that the draft would take many days to go back to the Canadian bank and then start on its way to New York. Rathbun was desperate with worry.

You must struggle along the best way you can using all the paper you can *prudently;* for one month to come is hard every day. It's all hard. Our whole life is hard. Hope we shall have an easier time in the next. There is no bac[king] out of it now. We must go straight through. . . . I have no time to write and can't read what I have written for I am half crazy and half tired out. . . . You know I'm under whip and spur every moment of my life. Can't write anything straight.

Three days later he had more bad news. The $2,000 Canadian draft had been intercepted at the Canadian side of the river and had gone directly to New York, "so that must have come down on you with a vengeance and much sooner than I expected. . . . These are the very hardest times we'll have here but don't be discouraged." Yet he somehow concluded, with little trace of irony, "We'll see brighter and brighter days, if we live through this."

His letter of March 20 bore still more bad news, for a draft of $1,382 drawn on Ebenezer F. Norton had been protested at the National Bank in New York. Note Rathbun's concern about the travels of prominent local men:

> If it's possible for you to make a raise, pay it for really there is no prospect of my doing anything here. You never knew money so scarce as it is here. This is probably the hardest month there ever will or can be in Buffalo. . . . I shall send you some notes by tomorrow's mail for you to carry over to Paterson to give Mr. Redmond. I should send them direct to him as they are some he sent for, but I dare not, as I suppose H. Pratt and Dr. Johnson are both in the city. I therefore thought I'd send them to you and you could tell when and how to give them to Mr. Redmond and in such a manner as he would not be showing them. . . . Look sharp at Pratt's movements. See if he goes to Philadelphia.

The letter mentioned that he did not know Lyman's views on their relations with Guavier and Steele, and it stated that Benjamin would see him soon, but implying that he did not see his brother every day. Apparently Allen was writing many of his letters direct to Lyman and receiving instructions from him as well as from Benjamin, although none of those letters have been preserved.

His next day's letter again referred to $52,587 in notes for Redmond to pay for Paterson Bank stock. He repeated his fears that because Pratt and Johnson were in New York, they might be called on to say what they know of the soundness of Rathbun's notes.

> This is too risky a business. You must look to the right and left before you let them [the notes] go out of your hands. When you think it's a fit and proper time, give them to Redmond yourself and tell him I don't like to have them put in the market, for it's an injury to my credit. Hope you'll manage this prudently.

Rathbun added to his arsenal of tricks and lies, yet another argument.

> Tell Mr. Redmond my friends are ready to endorse for my benefit to any extent, but they don't want their names hawked about Wall Street for it interferes too much with their own operations. You must use the same language with regard to my own name: That I fear the injury will be greater than the benefits arising from the banks. You must talk strong language to him and find out what use he's going to make of these notes before you give them to him.

Allen and Janes handled the New York business satisfactorily and the crisis was for now surmounted. When Rathbun wrote Allen on March 28, he was worrying about how he was going to be able to leave for New York himself and said that the Commercial Bank had refused to renew a draft on Guavier and that they had had to pay it with another draft on Janes.

He wrote Allen on April 1 that he had been engrossed in business at Niagara Falls, and that there was trouble because he could not keep track of all outstanding notes without an assistant. He showed particular concern about certain notes attracting attention.

> I have this moment ascertained that a $2,000 [note] given to Davenport, Wickliff and Company last winter, endorsed D. E. E., is due 1 April. Now what will be the result of this business I really don't know. I *fear it's protested* and that's a ruinous business. Those notes endorsed D. E. E. must be protected if possible in preference to others.

He urged Allen to make the rounds of the New York banks each day to discover whether there were any outstanding notes that had been overlooked: "This is a most terrible hard day for us here and everywhere. But don't give up the ship. Stick to it like a giant. There is no other way. We must go through, and straight through, there's no mistake."

Rathbun said, in this letter, that he was planning to start for New York on April 4. Events of that day and immediately succeeding days became very important later in legal proceedings.

Just before Rathbun boarded the stage for the East, Lyman gave him a wrapped package of notes, which he gave to Allen, as he had intended, shortly after arrival in New York. It was brought out later that Benjamin put the package in his pocket without examining it.

The next series of extant letters was written by Benjamin to Lyman. For Benjamin, they were harder to explain away, for it was impossible to contend seriously that Lyman had written to himself with the intention of harming his brother. Besides, they bore the mark of Benjamin's desperation.

The first of those was written from Batavia, which Benjamin reached on the night of April 4. He urged that Lyman get notes certified by Judge Rochester, which would be useful "in Philadelphia," and from Millard Fillmore, who had already "strongly endorsed" notes sent to Lewiston. He said to tell his wife, who doubtless was worried about his health, "that we have got along well."

He arrived in New York on the early morning of April 8, "nearly used up." With him was Perkins, the manager of the Rathbun stores who was to buy stock in the metropolis. In his statement later, Rathbun said that he had gone to New York to complete the Paterson and Granville bank transactions and to arrange to have notes engraved for the new Commercial Bank at Fort Erie. While in New York, he employed Blatchford and gave Janes a power of attorney to pay certain bills.

The New York affairs of the House of Rathbun were in another crisis, this letter indicated, even though Janes had taken hold "with a giant's arm." Notes due on April 7 were met only by $16,000, which Redmond secured at the last minute from the Merchants' Exchange Bank. But that and $23,000 more had to be paid back on April 9.

Gloomily describing the situation and the tightness of money, Rathbun told Lyman the next day that their nephew Allen was "getting rather tired. . . . He lacks perseverance. Janes is worth an army of him but it may not be policy to tell him what I say." He said that Allen was going to start home, and that Lyman was to "have everything in readiness to start him west, [for] soon as western banks understand the extent of pressure, they will [have] begun to curtail their discounts."

His next communications urged Lyman to make sure that copies were kept of all notes, for many were being discovered only when they were protested or about to be protested. Another note had a postscript written by Allen, the only one of his communications extant, which also urged that a better record be kept of notes.

Benjamin's letter of the twelveth was an important one, implying again criminal behavior. He had been in Paterson all day, and Allen and Janes had had to let $12,000 in notes remain overdue by a day.

> It really looks squally. I can't see how we are to get along at all. Must hope for the best and look out for the worst.
>
> Have you us'd the notes got of [Alanson] Palmer? And have you got the notes of Henry Kip [a prominent Buffalonian for whom Rathbun was doing some building]? If you have all or any on hand, can't others be got like them, and sent here for use?
>
> It is absolutely necessary to have some paper here by somebody else. There has been so much of my paper in the market, it's impossible to use a note with my name as signer, if there were a hundred endorsements on it.

He was also worried that some of their "business notes," those used to pay for store stocks, might be protested; this would be very serious. He urged, "Can't you get Coit, Kimberly and Company's note and give them a receipt that I'll provide for them and perhaps you can get me others. I suppose you get my idea. If you can get one, you can get more of the same date. Send me all the notes signed by other people."

These damningly ambiguous statements, hinting at fraud and forgery, were followed by another, in which he spoke of Noyes Darrow, whom he had asked to help Lyman during his absence: "Perhaps you better put something into his hands as security, and get two or three $2,000 notes and send; and if you can get two *you can get more.* Some of Thomas Day [another prominent Buffalonian] might be of use."

Amid this crisis, Benjamin wrote the next day to David Evans in Batavia, seeking his assistance in overcoming the glut of Rathbun notes. Unfortunately for Rathbun, his letter to Evans was saved by the Batavia financier.

> The enclosed three notes of $5,000 each, with multitude of endorsers, were got for a special purpose. But for certain reasons it is desirable to change the shape of the paper. Therefore, I wish you'd do me the favor to lay the enclosed three notes of $5,000 each (with many endorsers) in your private desk and sign the enclosed bank notes same date, same amount and payable at the same place. Enclose them by mail to me directed to care of H. Janes, Esq., No. 8 Liberty Street, New York, and before they arrive at maturity, I will get up and return your notes for those here enclosed.

Why I requested you to lay the enclosed notes in your private desk is that they were got for a special purpose and, if known by some of the endorsers that other use was made of them, it might create some feeling. I find the use I want to make of the paper requires it made by some other person and, not having time to make the change with this great number of endorsers and finding your individual name with my endorsement will answer me the same purpose, propose you sign the enclosed three notes and return to me by mail as soon as may be and you shall never have occasion to regret it.

Evans accepted the notes, each bearing the signatures of the "eleven endorsers," and mailed Rathbun his own notes for $15,000.

Benjamin's next letter to Lyman, written April 16, emphasized that "this has been a most horrible hard day." Conditions were so bad that "everybody says the panic of '32 was no comparison to this. I hope you send some checks and use them if you can take up some paper. You probably can get some real endorsements on these checks if necessary."

He also indicated that he "had arranged notes with the Trust Company," probably referring to the series with the "eleven endorsers" that had begun in 1835.

A letter two days later reported a terrible day when Redmond again saved them from disaster. The only note allowed to become overdue was a $1,000 draft on William B. Rochester and Company. Lyman must have written something to worry his brother, for Benjamin urged that "you must take some time to rest. You must not expose yourself too much for if you get sick, *all* goes by the board."

He wrote twice on April 18, first asking Lyman "would it not be possible to get some good notes for Janes?" and then concerning the handling of the purchases of land at Niagara Falls. The next day he again sent two letters, emphasizing the "tremendous hard times."

You must man every nerve and stand strong and firm as a giant. If you give out we are all gone. . . . We must twist and screw in every shape that's possible to get along for the present. . . . everybody is alarmed here about money but they don't know anything about what we have gone through. With firmness, I think we shall carry it through, although it looks rather dark at present.

Everything due on Buffalo contracts, he said, must be collected in money or notes, and attempts must be made to raise money in

Virginia and in Ohio, far enough inland for the banks to have escaped for a time the pressure of the current money market. He said that temporarily they were managing, barely, by day-to-day borrowings.

On April 21, a small memorandum was folded into his letter asking Lyman whether he could "get endorsements of A. P. and S. M.," referring to Palmer and Sylvester Mathews, a baker turned speculator. His final letter from New York, three days later, said that "I am half crazy with ten thousand calls"; and a postscript added that Noyes Darrow's notes and bonds had arrived on time.

In a few days Benjamin was back in Buffalo but more trouble was ahead in the next weeks. In his later statement, he explained that many notes fell due in New York in mid-May and that Lyman had failed to get funds there in time to avoid protests, although he (Benjamin) did not know why.

The May difficulty, coming on the heels of the troubles in March and April, shook his credit severely in Wall Street. Afterward, discount rates rose sharply, increases that his attorneys later claimed cost him $1,000,000.

> This [the New York protests of the May 20 notes] created quite an uneasiness with my brother, staggered Mr. Janes—created some timidity in the mind of my newly-appointed cashier of the Paterson Bank and, for a time, shook the confidence of my New York friends.
>
> I discovered that my brother was laboring under intense anxiety and appeared to be alarmed, fearing that so much paper being protested at once would shake the confidence of endorsers and he should be troubled to get them to continue their endorsements (as he said to me).
>
> He told me that among the papers protested were a number of notes endorsed by D. E. Evans, of Batavia, and he said he thought I had more influence with Mr. Evans than he had; he wished I would write to Mr. Evans and explain the facts which he said were that he had sent a messenger to New York with funds to enable Mr. Janes to provide for all that paper, but for some reason did not arrive in New York in time to save protest but that the paper would all be taken up without delay. I granted his request and followed his directions.

Lyman told him at the time, Benjamin said, that he would explain the situation to the Buffalo endorsers, which convinced Benjamin that Lyman had more influence with "these gentlemen" than even he himself had. Later, he said, Lyman reported that all were satisfied with his explanation.

Coincident with these financial worries, Rathbun was frequently traveling to Black Rock, Tonawanda, and Niagara Falls to check on the progress of the railroad, and to his factory in Buffalo to make sure that the cars were being built properly. At Niagara, he arranged to meet land payments and to oversee laying brick foundations for the new Niagara Hotel. He could have had no suspicion that for seventeen years these foundations would remain unfinished, a "brick mine" for vandals.

In mid-June, according to Rathbun, "a friend and highly respectable gentleman of this city" met him on the street and informed him that from indications he had from New York he "was afraid there was something going on wrong in my money matters which I knew nothing about." Although Rathbun did not identify this informant, it was probably General Potter, the lawyer and former district attorney, who had heard the rumors from Palmer.

If this news surprised Rathbun, his description of his response reaction was singularly mild. He said that he inquired of Lyman about it, but getting no clarification of the situation from his brother, he decided to go to New York himself to see what was afoot. He was too sure of Janes's integrity, he said, to suspect him of any wrongdoing.

Moreover, among the many memoranda of promissory notes in Rathbun's handwriting that were later introduced in evidence by the state was the record of the fact that on June 15 he had sent Janes at New York twelve $5,000 notes, dated four and six months from the eighteenth and twentieth of June. After these, Rathbun had written: "With the eleven endorsers, E. D. [Darrow] instead of H. M. [Henry Morris], all the others the same, payable at Manhattan Bank, New York."

These notes, it was pointed out, were like the series first begun in 1835 with twelve endorsers except that now they totaled $60,000 instead of $15,000 and the nearest renewal date of the original notes was April 15, 1836.

If he were very worried, Benjamin's two letters of June 20 to Lyman, mailed from Avon and Batavia on his way to New York, ignored the subject completely except for this otherwise cryptic sentence: "Colonel P. [Palmer] makes himself ridiculous by his pompous and ridiculous manner. See him however and tell him to keep quiet about my affairs of the 20th of May." He also advised Lyman to "look out very sharp for notes of protest for I am sure there will be some and I fear there will be many."

From New York on June 24 he advised Lyman that poor Janes had lost weight under the pressure of his worries. Janes had to pay $50,000 the following day and "he fears it's impossible to raise the money." It was then that he directed Lyman to pay General Porter $20,000 on the Niagara Falls contract before July 1, although how he expected his brother to accomplish that miracle was not explained.

Among the memoranda allegedly in Rathbun's handwriting and found later were some headed "Filled up and left with H. Janes while I was in New York 27th June, 1836." These listed twenty-four $5,000 notes, in sets of three, each with "eleven endorsers" and dated four and six months from June 22 and 23, all payable at the Manhattan Bank in New York. Another notation was: "My note endorsed D. E. E., four months from 23 June and ditto six months from ditto, $5,000 each, payable at Merchants' Bank, New York."

His letter of June 27 to Lyman did not mention these notes. It did express some slight fear of an old associate: "I suppose Palmer is here before this time. Can't find out yet that he has bought any paper. You'll look to him of course. See that he keeps his mouth shut if he has seen anything wrong."

Besides expressing regret that Brown had been unable to raise money in Pittsburgh, the letter had a vague reference to a debt on flour, which was destined to be among the many things to plague him shortly: "Your information in relation to the flour came just in time to save Janes from accepting it. Has been protested this day. I don't know what that fellow of Allgood means—get the flour and then try to get the money on the draft."

Rathbun during this time was doing other mysterious financing. Additional memoranda, identified as his scrawled, almost illegible script, revealed that $97,000 in notes of $2,000 to $5,000 face, all made either by David E. Evans and endorsed by Benjamin Rathbun or made by Rathbun and endorsed by Evans, had been issued between April and June 1836. Further there was listed $131,000 in notes endorsed by David E. Evans at Batavia followed by the notation: "Sent three to Mr. E. and kept twelve. H. James got them. 2nd May sent six more to Janes—same date and amount; sent two sets 14 May 1836, six months; one set 18th June, four months, to H. James, N.Y."

Still other memoranda mentioned three $5,000 notes signed by Lyman Rathbun on June 13 and 14 and endorsed by Darrow, Daniel Girder, Townsend, Coit and Company, and Thomas Day, and

$34,000 in eleven notes of May 5 endorsed by various persons, among them Evans, Burt, Girder, Wilkeson, Darrow, and Henry H. Sizer.

Later, when these memoranda were produced and when notes were turned in for payment, none of these endorsers acknowledged having signed the notes. Rathbun stood, therefore, accused of forgery.

Rathbun's statement did not touch on these confusing memoranda. It did explain, however, that when he got to New York in June and found so much of his paper afloat that he knew he would require a sizable loan to meet it. He consulted the lawyer, Richard Blatchford, who promised to obtain the loan if Rathbun could produce a satisfactory bond as guarantee.

Rathbun went from New York to Montreal to arrange details in connection with opening the Fort Erie Bank and explained in his statement that the three banks would facilitate his operations and "make the stock more productive." A loan of $500,000 obtained through Blatchford, plus the $300,000 he was confident he would raise right away through the sale of Niagara Falls property, persuaded him, he said, "that I could extricate my affairs from their embarrassed condition."

The day after he returned to Buffalo, July 9, he received a note from Evans in Batavia informing him that he was coming to Buffalo. On July 10, a greatly agitated Evans appeared at his office. Evans confronted Rathbun with inescapable evidence that one of the $5,000 notes was forged. Rathbun said the news "confounded" him. The note had traveled a wide circuit, which had delayed discovery of the fraud. William R. Gwin of Medina received it from his flour agent in New York City. Gwin was a longtime associate of Evans and Ellicott interests, and he presented the note to Evans for payment. Rathbun described his surprise.

This information from Mr. Evans was astounding to me. To what extent this business had been carried on was impossible to imagine. Now what to do—what course to take—or what was my duty to do —was a very important matter. Here was a struggle indescribable. None ever equalled it in the whole period of my life. I have had many, very many, hard and severe struggles in my business operations, but nothing ever presented itself in this shape.

Rathbun got $5,000 in cash from Lyman, without telling his brother (or so he said) what it was for, and gave it to Evans, taking back in return the forged note.

Evans was greatly relieved by Rathbun's readiness to correct the matter immediately. But he also told Rathbun that he had heard there were now other forged notes in Albany, and he was going to have to investigate that rumor on his way to Philadelphia and the South. He was planning to leave Batavia in three days and he suggested that Rathbun accompany him. He even agreed to advance $50,000 upon his arrival in New York, if that much were necessary to extricate Rathbun from temporary embarrassment. However, he insisted upon some security, which Rathbun furnished him the next day in the form of a mortgage for the whole amount.

Pleading the pressure of business in Buffalo, Rathbun did not accept the invitation to join Evans on the trip. He did nothing further on this delicate matter while he awaited word of Evans's findings.

Meanwhile, Rathbun wrote to Blatchford to complete the New York loan negotiations and hurry to Buffalo to wind up the transaction. But Blatchford replied from Albany that he had just learned that Evans was en route to New York and had decided to return to New York and come to Buffalo with Evans.

While Rathbun's statement does not elaborate this point, obviously the news that Blatchford and Evans had met must have been disquieting. The loan Blatchford was arranging would surely fall through if the matter of forgeries was brought into the discussions, and if Blatchford came to doubt Rathbun's honesty.

Blatchford wrote again from New York, this time informing Rathbun that Evans had advanced the agreed $50,000 to Janes for Rathbun's benefit, quieting some of his fears as he waited anxiously in Buffalo.

On July 29, Rathbun was in Niagara Falls getting ready for the ceremony to mark the arrival of the first railroad cars. From there, he dispatched by express mail an urgent note to Lyman in Buffalo. This was later used against him in court, because it contains more than subtle hints of the need to keep prominent people from exchanging information about Rathbun's affairs and, by doing so, enlightening themselves about the possibility of Rathbun's use of their names on his notes: "Mr. E. [Evans] and Mr. B. [Blatchford] coming from New York," he wrote, "and must be kept away from other people when they get here. Keep your mind free, so as to know what to do with them when they come in. I hope this will not excite any suspicion by coming express."

Rathbun's lawyers naturally claimed that this note reflected Rathbun's fear that there might be interference with the proposed loan.

The prosecutors contended that it expressed his fear that the forgeries might be exposed. How Rathbun expected Lyman to keep the two men, and particularly Evans, from communicating with others is hardly clear. It certainly seems evidence of his desperation.

Rathbun did not know, and may not have known even after the two men arrived in Buffalo, that Evans and Blatchford had hurried to Philadelphia to see Nicholas Biddle. Shrewd, powerful, and arrogant, Biddle had once defied the president of the United States, and he now ruled the Bank of the United States of Pennsylvania. Biddle was Blatchford's best client. Biddle showed them two more of Rathbun's notes held by the bank. Evans discovered his name on these, too. Now hot on the trail of bad paper, they began to suspect that many more notes held in New York City were also fraudulent.

The drama rapidly approached its conclusion, as Blatchford and others carefully set a trap for Rathbun. Blatchford arrived in Buffalo on July 30 and told him, Rathbun said, that the arrangements for the $500,000 New York loan were complete and that it could be consummated if the security were satisfactory. In response, Rathbun informed Blatchford of the names of some of those whom he expected to endorse his bond for the loan. On the morning of Sunday, July 31, Blatchford reported to him that he had seen some of them and was satisfied—if Rathbun could produce security. He did not tell Rathbun that he had discussed the forgeries with Pratt, the first time that hardfisted banker admitted knowing positively about them, but Rathbun could not avoid having been suspicious. Buffalo was too small for him not to know that Blatchford was staying as a guest at Pratt's home.

At the Sunday meeting Blatchford proposed that Rathbun make a statement of all his real estate and personal property that could be put up to secure the loan. That afternoon both Blatchford and Evans came to see him and Rathbun gave Evans the statement Blatchford had requested. Evans expressed, said Rathbun, "very great surprise at the extent and value of my estate and took it to show the endorsers."

Rathbun's description of these events judiciously omits what must have been extensive discussions of the forged notes afloat in the East. Someone, probably Blatchford, must have convinced him that he immediately had to provide a guarantee that the $15,000 owed on the notes with eleven endorsers would be paid. Consequently, Rathbun then executed a consent to the entry of a voluntary decree of judgment against himself. The next morning, just as the doors of the Chancery Court clerk's office were opened, Lewis F. Allen was on hand to file the judgment, the decree being docketed as of 9:00 A.M. at $30,000, double the face.

Rathbun probably guessed that excited meetings of the "eleven endorsers" were then in progress. Describing these to a friend, Col. Ira Blossom said that the endorsers ascertained on Monday, August 1, that $330,000 or even more of the forged $5,000 notes bearing their names were outstanding. These and similar estimates must have come from Blatchford or Evans. There was no one else who could have made the information available in Buffalo.

Evans by himself came to see Rathbun early on the morning of August 1. He brought with him a statement of Rathbun's debts to him and demanded that Rathbun consent to entry of an $80,000 voluntary judgment in Evans's favor. Unless this were done, he implied, he would interfere with the consummation of the proposed loan. Evans's demand embraced the $50,000 he had advanced Rathbun in July, the $15,000 he had sent him at New York in April, and $15,000 in additional notes he had given him at other times.

When Rathbun proved reluctant to endorse this procedure, Evans declared that he had talked with some of those Rathbun expected to guarantee his loan. They, Evans said, did not object to Evans having a first claim on the property for notes that he had advanced, because he had made the advances not for profit, but generously to accommodate Rathbun. Evans clinched his argument by producing a bond and power of attorney granted by one of those Rathbun expected to endorse the loan. Rathbun then executed the judgment and Evans hurried to file it in the court clerk's office, where it was docketed at 11:30 A.M. at double the face, or $160,000.

Evans came back later in the day with Blatchford and with Daniel Chandler, who was a Batavia lawyer and the district attorney of Genesee County, whom he introduced as his counsel. Although Rathbun had known the Batavia attorney, he did not realize then that he would soon wish Chandler had never existed.

Evans now informed Rathbun that the loan would be effected, if Rathbun would assign his entire estate as security to those who signed the bond—or this was, at least, Rathbun's interpretation of the proceedings, when he sought to prove there was a conspiracy to take control of all his assets. Evans certainly must have told Rathbun that the proposed guarantors knew of the forgeries and that they wanted the possibility of possessing full control over all his property to be certain that they would have enough money available to settle all claims, if that were necessary. Whether or not Blatchford endorsed

Evans's statements is not clear, for it appears that the lawyer said little. Obviously Rathbun thought that he did. He believed that both Evans and, in effect, Blatchford, too, had promised, Rathbun later wrote, that "the whole matter should be kept secret and indeed spoke of it—and regarded it—merely as a precautionary measure on my part to serve in the contingency of my not being able to settle my own affairs, that then those persons who were to become my security should have full power to settle it."

This may or may not have been the correct interpretation of the events of that momentous day. It is the interpretation that Rathbun advanced. It has never been officially refuted. It certainly omits what must have been much conversation about related matters, including both the forgeries and the fact that Hiram Pratt knew of three forged $5,000 notes with the names of the eleven endorsers, and indeed already held two of them in his strongbox.

Before the end of the protracted meeting, with Chandler's assistance, Blatchford prepared a lengthy assignment of all of Rathbun's real and personal estate to five men. He told Rathbun that the proposed assignment contained all the power and provisions needed to put it into immediate effect. Rathbun then signed it.

Destined to be forever unresolved is the question of whether Rathbun may have been deceived into signing this document with promises of an obviously nonexistent loan. (This is what he contended later.) Or was it simply the case that he was manipulated into signing as the only course in a hopeless situation? It is impossible to say which interpretation is true. The events of the next two days, however, strongly support Rathbun's contention. Three months later a committee of his creditors, after its investigation, stated, "[It] has not heard denial of the fact that Rathbun claims to have been forced into the assignment by false pretenses." Of course, these men, too, wanted a piece of Rathbun's property, and were jealous of those who now controlled it.

Rathbun must have plumbed the depths of despair when he affixed his signature. Even if he were still buoyed by the hope that he might get out of the morass without disaster, he was deliberately putting himself and all his property under the power of others.

Because it is apparent that the agitated Rathbun believed, or made himself believe, that the assignment would never be put into effect, his failure to read it carefully is understandable. Blatchford's formidable legal reputation, towering far above his Buffalo contemporaries, was probably sufficient assurance to his mind that the assignment would be complete and exactly what it was represented to be. Moreover, Rathbun must have hoped that Blatchford was still working in his interest. Unfortunately for Rathbun, the assignment left a great many legal difficulties unresolved.

Why Blatchford prepared a document with some obvious legal problems, leaving out powers that would make it workable, is a second mystery. That a thoroughly competent lawyer should have designed such a scheme suggested deliberation. It implied very probably Blatchford's collaboration with his Buffalo host, Pratt, and perhaps also with Evans, whose burning and justifiable anger at Rathbun was not concealed in the meetings.

As the assignment stood, the Rathbun estate would have been forced to sacrifice or abandon its equity in many of the best properties it held. Overseeing the vast wealth was a board of trustees, whose members could benefit greatly from their position. The deed of assignment appointed as trustees five men, several of whom had obviously discussed their service with Blatchford in advance. (The others claimed later that they did not know that they were to serve until after Rathbun had signed.) Because Rathbun had supposedly been obtaining the agreement of leading Buffalo citizens to sign the bond that Blatchford wanted, these men could not have been on Rathbun's original list. Whom he actually had nominated for the board was never announced.

The trustees were Pratt, Allen, Clary, Congressman Love, and Millard Fillmore. Of these, Love and Fillmore served only a few months before resigning, Fillmore because he succeeded Love in Congress, and Love because he could not afford to give the time required. Fillmore, however, continued his association in the lucrative post of counsel for the three remaining assignees. Rathbun had been closely associated with all of them and considered them his friends.

Hiram Pratt, Rathbun's rival in some things and associate in others, was by then president of the Bank of Buffalo, at which Rathbun himself had helped give him his start. A pious Christian, he was also president and treasurer of the philanthropic Sailors' and Boatmens' Friend Society and president of the Erie County Temperance Society. Although long protesting his friendship for Rathbun, Pratt was later proven to have known more about the forgeries than he first admitted, and to have benefited materially from Rathbun's downfall. Rightly or wrongly, Rathbun partisans looked on Pratt as Rathbun's persecutor and as the greatest beneficiary from his collapse.

Lewis F. Allen, the opportunist, whose singular part in many of the proceedings did not always do credit to his intelligence, was generally adjudged to be a smart businessman whose excellent contacts and assiduous cultivation of the right people were making him wealthy. He was the husband of Margaret Cleveland. Her nephew, Grover, long afterward lived with them while he was getting the education that laid a basis for the career that would extend to two terms in the White House.

Joseph Clary had been one of Rathbun's best friends when he was a bachelor living at the Eagle and had handled a lot of Rathbun's legal business. A decided conservative, he had profited little from the mad speculations that went on around him. He was an "office lawyer," whose chief business came from advising clients.

Like Pratt and Allen, Thomas Love was close enough to Rathbun to have been one of the original dozen endorsers of the 1835 series of notes. He was a friend and neighbor of Clary's on Franklin Street. He had been "first judge"—the senior judge—of the Court of Common Pleas, then Erie County district attorney and in 1836 western New York's representative in Congress. He was generally regarded as a thoughtful, patient, and widely respected man.

Millard Fillmore, the fifth trustee, had also been a strong supporter of Rathbun, writing letters endorsing his application for credit, and exhibiting constant friendship toward him. Then in his thirty-seventh year, and already a political power in New York State through his long association with Weed and his participation in the Anti-Masonic movement, Fillmore had served in Congress until he resigned to make more money, and had agreed to let Love succeed him. Then he succeeded Love. His energy and stable character made people feel that he would get somewhere in life. They would not have been surprised had he run for governor, but few as yet were able to envision him as a potential president.

To these men, Rathbun had signed over the right to control every cent he had in the world. He thought he knew them all, and that he would be able to continue to exercise his not inconsiderable charm upon them. A rude awakening lay ahead for him.

At Blatchford's suggestion, Rathbun bundled together his deeds, contracts, and other appropriate papers and took them to Pratt's house. Here, for the first time since he had placed his signature on the assignment, he met the trustees as a group. He then learned that Fillmore, and perhaps Love, had been recruited only under pressure from Pratt and Evans.

Present at this meeting with the assignees, who had been discussing the forgeries when Rathbun arrived, were Evans and Chandler. Because the day was nearly gone and the Niagara Falls sale was to begin the very next day, the group agreed to forego further discussion until after the sale. Rathbun acknowledged what they possibly already knew: that only if the sale were a success could he straighten out his affairs.

Rathbun declared, in his later statement, that this meeting broke up with the unanimous agreement that nothing would be done until after the Niagara Falls sale, which they were all to attend. Upon their return to Buffalo, he claimed, it was understood that the discussion of the terms of a loan would take place.

Rathbun's contention was that there was a want of frankness in all these proceedings. If he had understood that no loan was forthcoming, he claimed, he would have abandoned the Niagara Falls sale and obtained the best legal talent available for his defense. He only signed the agreement of assignment when he did, he said, because he was told it was the only way he could obtain the loan and not interfere with the impending land sale. There certainly could not have been any hint of possible criminal action at these meetings, although at the very least the lawyers Love and Fillmore must have recognized the questionable legality of the arrangement in which they were now involved. Rathbun, after all, appeared to be a felon, and the question could legitimately have been raised as to which other laws, beside forgery statutes, he might have broken. His ability to continue to represent himself in matters concerning his property, to say the least, was a complex question. Yet, thus far, there had been no serious discussion between Rathbun, the trustees, and the attorneys about the forgeries.

Early on the morning of August 2, the entire party except for Thomas Love went to Niagara Falls. Concealing his agitation, Rathbun pretended enthusiasm in greeting the Porters and other associates and talking to prospective buyers. Rathbun maintained remarkable poise, considering the strain he had been under and the uncertainties of the immediate situation. He laughed and joked with those at the sale. Little was apparently said about Rathbun's troubles by the Buffalo group, even when they ate together at the Niagara Falls Eagle, where they then spent the night. Pratt, however, talked privately with Rathbun about the forgeries, he later testified, and stated that Rathbun showed much "distress" over this subject.

Two brief letters Rathbun sent to Lyman that night, and found later, strongly support Rathbun's claim that he anticipated being able to go on with his business as before. He would certainly not have worried, as he indicated evidence of worrying in these letters to Lyman written at that time from the Falls, about hay for his horses and the payment of notes in New York if he had actually contemplated losing control.

A story, attributed to George R. Babcock, son-in-law and junior law partner of General Potter, indicates Rathbun's marvelous composure at Niagara. Babcock was sitting near Rathbun during supper on the night of August 2 and Rathbun remarked to him that he had not noticed him doing any bidding. Babcock explained that the acreage in which he was interested had not come up. Rathbun afterward took his arm, led him outside, and determined in privacy exactly what land Babcock wanted, and then assured him that he would have it offered the next day.

Rathbun, Evans, and the assignees had hardly reassembled on the morning of August 3 when Chandler announced that he was returning to Buffalo with Evans and Blatchford. Rathbun protested this move vigorously as a violation of the agreement, but the three insisted that they were going anyway. Rathbun finally got them to agree that they would all meet at Pratt's house in Buffalo at seven o'clock that night for further discussion.

Although it strains belief that Rathbun still expected to get the loan, in his later statement he insisted that he had told the entire group at this point that if the loan were not granted, he would halt all his business and close his doors. But he must have been suspicious that something was afoot.

In his statement, in fact, he said that before leaving the crowd of buyers at Niagara Falls, "some friends" had advised him not to return to Buffalo but to flee. Rathbun declared that this advice was given by friends who did not know the facts.

It was brought out later, however, that Rathbun's "friends" were Pratt and Clary, and that Pratt alone had the discussion with Rathbun in a carriage en route back to Buffalo. Pratt vehemently denied that he had suggested flight. He did admit remarking that Rathbun's "personal safety" was the first element to be considered. Pratt said that Rathbun, "in agony," had asked his advice after discovering that the story of his failure, and all the circumstances, including the forgeries surrounding it, by now were probably common knowledge.

Pratt's account was that they talked about the forgeries and that

Rathbun said that he had learned about them some time before, but that they were so extensive he did not feel he could simply call in the forged paper and make good the amounts of money covered by the notes. He said that he had made tremendous efforts daily just to keep going, reaching out for money to New Jersey, Pennsylvania, Connecticut, Rhode Island, Ohio, Virginia, and New York City. But even these efforts, Rathbun had said, had been insufficient, and that he had, therefore, to get control of banks. The Niagara Falls sale, Rathbun had told Pratt and Clary, was his last hope of catching up with the immense flood of forged notes.

In a carriage with Pratt and Clary, Rathbun returned to Buffalo. The carriage drove up Falls Street to the Buffalo Road, along the route on which Rathbun's workmen were completing laying the railroad tracks, over lanes made more dusty by the work in progress. At Tonawanda they were met by a messenger bearing word that the news was "out" in Buffalo that not only had Rathbun's empire collapsed, but also that Lyman himself was now under arrest.

It is less surprising now that the news leaked out by the afternoon of August 3, than that it had not become general knowledge even earlier. The filing of judgments totaling $190,000 against Buffalo's chief citizen on August 1 might well have made the clerk of the court suspicious, and eager to gossip. Moreover, without Rathbun's knowledge, the deed of assignment became a public record at 10:30 A.M. on August 2, when it was filed in the office of Horace Clark, clerk of Erie County. Why Clark kept it secret for a day, and at whose behest he was acting, is another puzzle. Pratt, for one, denied later that he had known the deed was going to be recorded.

Yet there must have been some agreement among the assignees on the recording of the deed, for it meant Rathbun's ruin. It seems improbable that one of the group would have acted independently on a vital matter that concerned them all. But, if they had decided that Rathbun must be broken, why the farce of the trip to Niagara?

Chandler probably filed the deed, for he, before the trip to the Falls, on August 2 "proved" the validity of the document before Hezekiah A. Salisbury, commissioner of deeds. Chandler provided the oath that affirmed that he saw Benjamin Rathbun sign it.

The assignment's meaning was too plain to have been accepted by the county clerk as just another record. A lengthy document, with sheet after sheet attached listing schedules of property and debts, it was self-explanatory. Indeed, it spelled out that whereas the party of the first part has been, for some time past, engaged in an extensive business and has become embarrassed in his pursuits and is indebted for large sums of money and is possessed of a large property; and whereas he is indebted to many persons who from peculiar confidence in his honor and integrity have lent him their credit, responsibility and money, which indebtedness he feels specially bound to protect and secure

Therefore, the document continues, Rathbun for the sum of $1

[has] sold, assigned, conveyed, transferred and set over, aliened, remised, granted and released and doth by these presents sell, assign, convey, transfer, set over, alien, remise, grant and release unto the said Pratt [etc.] . . . all of his estate, property and effects, lands, leases, houses, buildings, goods, merchandise, tools, horses, carriages, and harness, contracts and agreements, etc.

Thus the ownership of the House of Rathbun was formally and legally passed out of the hands of its founder.

From its encounter with the messenger at Tonawanda, the entire party hurried on, avoiding speaking with Rathbun, yet watching him. Pratt testified later that Rathbun was in great distress after hearing the news. It is easy to imagine the dejection that possessed him as the horses bore them closer and closer to the place where only a few hours before most people still had complete confidence in his honor and integrity.

He did not get a chance to go home, where his wife awaited him hoping for assurance that the rumors that filled the city were a mistake. Instead, at the door of the Rathbun countinghouse, there waited, apologetic but impressed with his serious responsibility, Sheriff Lester Brace, an old friend of Rathbun's who had employed the "Master Builder" to construct his own home. He had a warrant for Rathbun's arrest, which he proceeded to serve.

The warrant, issued by Mayor Samuel Wilkeson on a complaint sworn by his old friend Dr. Johnson, as head of the firm of Johnson, Hodge and Company, charged Rathbun with the crime of forgery. Johnson affirmed that his banking house had accepted a $14,000 note with an endorsement by Evans, which Evans now denied was his.

Rathbun did not argue. They walked the short distance to the jail past throngs of the curious who began to murmur and catcall when they saw Rathbun in custody. In the county jail, which he had designed and built just two years before, Rathbun was put in a cell eight feet by five feet. Its only fittings were a bunk covered with straw and a wooden pail.

It was not long before Sheriff Brace returned to hand another warrant through the cell door. This one was based on a complaint sworn by his good friend Hiram Pratt. Alone in his cell reading the warrant, Rathbun's cup of bitterness was full.

12

Convulsions and Reckonings

Outside the jail all was turmoil as the night of August 3, 1836, passed into history. Crowds gathered in the streets. Lamps and candles burned late in homes and financial offices. Taverns overflowed with men discussing the news. George P. Barker, the ambitious and suave district attorney who had long been the leading Jacksonian Democrat in the city, recognized his chance to make a name for himself and his party by smashing Rathbun, a symbol of the conservative business elite. In the courthouse, he was busy interviewing the assignees and all those he could reach who had been doing business with Rathbun. He was building a case for the grand jury.

Lying inert on his bunk in that cramped cell, Rathbun was forbidden by the sheriff to make a statement to the newspapers. He was not even allowed to communicate with Lyman, who was held in a nearby cell.

Rathbun learned that when Lyman had heard through an employee that the story had become public, he had sent two trusty men on horseback, one to carry the message to Benjamin, the other to get through to Rathbun Allen, who was then in Ohio. The point was to warn both of them to stay away from Buffalo.

Lyman had intended to take his saddle horse, which he often rode proudly at the head of parades, and gallop off to safety. But one look at the crowd-filled streets had convinced him that escape was impossible. He then hurried out the rear of the countinghouse, and down Pearl Street to his dwelling on Eagle Street near Main. His dutiful wife stoutly denied that he was home when the sheriff came. Courteously brushing her aside, however, Lester Brace soon found Lyman on the roof, cowering behind a chimney.

Mayor Wilkeson was one of the most conflicted that first night. He had acted without a second's hesitation in issuing warrants for the two Rathbuns and their nephew, Rathbun Allen. Wilkeson had summoned Pratt to his office, when that banker got back from Niagara, and directed that he sign the second complaint.

Yet, for all his gruff and businesslike demeanor, Wilkeson was a kindly soul. He had done what he had to do, but the news nonetheless came with stunning force. He was deeply torn as he did his duty. The mayor, who was also the local correspondent of the *New York Advertiser,* revealingly wrote to that publication that acting in this matter was, for him, a test of his manhood.

> The part which duty compelled me to act in this affair was most painful. . . . To commit my friend, whom I have known and esteemed for the past sixteen years as a kind and benevolent neighbor, a public-spirited citizen and a uniform friend to good order, to commit such a man as a felon would make you act the woman.

The extent of the forgery that was then unfolding amazed Wilkeson. Writing for the *New York Advertiser,* he detailed that many names had been forged and that the sums involved were staggering. David Evans's name alone was fraudulently attached to $250,000 in notes. An Ohio bank held $70,000 in bad paper. Investors soon scrambled to dump stocks in Ohio banks. Wilkeson's early information, though sketchy, provoked a general uneasiness throughout the nation's financial markets. Soon banks with which Rathbun had *no* connection would be forced to defend themselves against "runs" by panic-stricken depositors. In faithfully relating events, Wilkeson himself had helped spread fear.

Rathbun's failure and arrest caught Buffalo's newspaper editors unprepared. Their editorials were at first ambivalent. Most editors seemed to have difficulty maintaining balance between the duty to report the facts to the public and their loyalty to the House of Rathbun. Salisbury's *Commercial Advertiser,* particularly, was in a quandary. Had it not declared, just four days before the failure, that "it may truly be said" of Rathbun that " 'he touches nothing which he does not ornament and improve?' "

Indeed, the *Commercial Advertiser*'s daily edition on August 4 had a tiny story on the failure, which slid past that distasteful matter with astonishing lack of detail. Its weekly edition, issued a few days later, repeated all the stories that subsequently had appeared in the daily, but also carried just alongside earlier stories that had appeared before the failure. These praised Rathbun and presented details of his protean labors—on the Buffalo Exchange, the Niagara Falls Railroad, and on the land sales at the Falls—that were creating the bases for economic development of the Niagara Frontier.

Soon it would not matter greatly what the Buffalo papers printed. Everyone in western New York quickly learned the lurid details of Rathbun's fall as a consequence of rumors, which doubtless were embroidered by fancy. The matter was simply too important to daily life and too laden with larger meanings about the wages of ambition and the costs of success to be let alone.

Fast horses had immediately carried the news of Rathbun's arrest to other cities, where financiers and simple citizens gaped at the downfall of the "Girard of the West." Dispatches from Buffalo correspondents and from neighboring towns were quoted at length in newspapers outside the area. Businessmen who had been at or simply near Buffalo at the time of the crash were interviewed. The accounts were uniformly unfavorable to Rathbun, but they were also optimistic that Buffalo would survive the failure undamaged.

Buffalo businessmen were kept busy trying to make certain that their credit among distant associates would not be jeopardized. At the same time, they took the occasion to denounce the activities of the money brokers, whose machinations had been making victims of them as well as of Rathbun. Colonel Blossom, one of the "eleven endorsers," writing to an associate on August 4, echoed the prevailing judgment on both Rathbun and on the moneylenders: "The greatest loss which will fall upon us here, besides the disgrace of these acts of villany, will fall upon the brokers and they will lose heavily, but they will get but little sympathy for they have for years shaved the man most abominably."

Excepting Paterson, New Jersey, and Granville, Ohio, which were directly involved, New York City's financial markets felt the greatest shock. Rathbun's interest payments had been setting the pace for the national money market, and his downfall was devastating news.

The news reached New York City on Saturday, August 6, and it instantly created an upheaval among holders of loans on Buffalo security. The *New York Journal of Commerce*, in a long article headed "Great Failure at Buffalo," summarized the feeling.

The news of the failure of Benjamin Rathbun at Buffalo, which was received this morning, caused a very unusual sensation in Wall

Street. His affairs have for months past been the subject of much speculation and his notes, endorsed by ten or twelve of the best names of that city, have been crowded upon the market at the enormous discount of three or four per cent a month. They have served for the quotations of some of our neighbors in giving the condition of the money market.

The credit of everybody in Buffalo, of course, became deeply implicated and it was said repeatedly that, "if Rathbun failed, all Buffalo must fail."

Concluding hopefully that this pessimism may yet prove to be unwarranted, the newspaper said that Rathbun's valuations of two and one-half million for his property, as against one and one-half million of liabilities, gave ground for hope "that the affair will not in the end prove injurious to any one."

This article also contained an excellent summary of the tale of the $15,000 loan of 1835, which was to become, when Rathbun was tried, the heart of the state's case against him.

On a particular occasion he procured L. F. Allen and eleven others to endorse three of his notes for $5,000 each. The transaction was generally known in Buffalo. These notes, with the endorsements thereon, he multiplied at his pleasure and the forgeries passed unsuspected, as whenever a forged note was mentioned, it was taken for one of the well known and genuine notes. The forged paper was sold in Wall Street, in Canada, and wherever a market could be found for it.

This New York news story erroneously reported that Rathbun "acknowledged that he had forged the names of rich neighbors." Then and later, he steadfastly denied his guilt. The erroneous report of a confession, however, circulated in Buffalo.

Newspapers, far and wide, picked up the various elements of the story, seizing all the compelling human interest potential of the forgeries. But the stories deal even more with the fears that haunted the money markets that Rathbun's collapse was certain to precipitate a sharp financial contraction. Whether the hopefulness of many early predictions was genuine or instead a bold face adopted to confront an anticipated catastrophe cannot be known. No matter which was the case, there was plenty of evidence of concern.

The *Rochester Republican* commiserated with Buffalo over the failure. As a consequence of the testimony of a Rochester woman who had been in Buffalo during the first days of the crisis, the paper painted the picture of a community in shock. It stated that the event has "thrown a gloom over the entire city—the before busy throng was mute, gathered in anxious clusters in various parts of the city, wondering at the sudden downfall of its master spirit."

Certainly there was a great deal of fear in Buffalo. The fourth of August was marked by a gathering assemblage of Rathbun's employees, many of whom had come to the city from surrounding areas either to demand their pay, to find out what would happen to their jobs, or just out of curiosity. City officials grew more and more alarmed at this gathering crowd, which filled the streets in front of the Eagle and Rathbun's countinghouse. Their alarm increased when a handbill circulated, calling for a mass meeting of the workmen. A riot appeared probable. Agitated and angry, some in the crowd shouted for the plunder of the well-stocked Rathbun stores, the doors of which had been barred and the shutters fastened, to take their back pay in goods.

The assignees posted reassuring notices in an attempt to quell the crowd, which eventually numbered more than twelve hundred Rathbun employees. Many more than that packed the streets just for the excitement. When it became clear that the posters were failing to allay fears, some of the assignees circulated through the streets. They gave brief talks where the throngs were thickest, and told the workingmen to return to their homes and to be assured that they would ultimately be paid.

The angry mass of men refused to break up, and Mayor Wilkeson anticipated a riot. He called the assignees in and pointed out the disaster that could engulf the city if the assemblage became a mob and began burning and looting. He placed the responsibility squarely on the assignees to give even more concrete assurances that would induce the men to disperse voluntarily.

On August 5, when the crowds assembled for the mass meeting, the assignees as well as the city and county officials were on hand. This time, each of the assignees gave his word, to the later, bitter regret of all of them, that Rathbun's workers would be fully paid. Seconded by the officials, who emphasized the prominence and personal responsibility of the men who had given the pledge, the assurances worked magically. The workers left quietly and the danger of civil strife passed.

The notice of the roster of assignees, which was first posted on August 4, was dated August 2. If this date really represented the time of the group's composition, it was written before the group went to Niagara and would prove that the downfall of Rathbun had been agreed upon before that expedition. The document paraphrased the deed of assignment and set up the procedure and priorities for payment of debts. The first (or "preferred") creditors, who were to be paid after the costs of the trust itself were met, were the clerks, mechanics, and laborers and all the individual purveyors in the counties of Erie, Niagara, and nearby Chautauqua to whom Rathbun was indebted for personal work, building materials, horses, or other personal property. Evans with his $80,000 judgment, Allen with the $15,000 judgment, Pratt with his judgment, and all the holders of the small engraved notes signed by B. Rathbun, which had been circulating like money, were also considered preferred creditors.

The notice called upon all persons having or controlling Rathbun property to account for it to the trustees and directed the immediate suspension of all payments on debts, execution of contracts, and similar commitments until the trustees granted further authority. It urged patience, and invoked the reputation for probity of the assignees as proof that justice would be done everyone involved.

But would justice be done Rathbun himself? He had reason to wonder. For Rathbun, those first few days in jail were fearful and confused. Disgraced, humbled as he had never been in his adult life, he vacillated between periods of violent despair and moments when he demanded to be admitted to bail in order to salvage what he could of his collapsed empire. Abandoned by nearly all his former friends, he could not even find a lawyer among those attorneys with whom he had worked in the past. Those he had known best were now either against him or afraid to defend him. His choice was limited to newcomers to the bar who were hungry for a case that promised to put them in the limelight.

While Rathbun was in this agitated state, John C. Spencer came to see him on behalf of the assignees. One of the best-known lawyers in New York State, Spencer knew Rathbun well. He had long been associated with controversial cases; for example, he had been the first special prosecutor appointed at the Morgan trials. Why Spencer was enlisted is not clear, though his imposing reputation may provide an explanation.

What Spencer said to Rathbun is lost, but he certainly appears to have been persuasive. Before Spencer left him, Rathbun had executed a supplementary assignment and a power of attorney that gave the assignees all the powers they lacked in the original assignment.

These were buttressed by a voluntary judgment he made against himself for $2,000,000.

The action was the most generous of Rathbun's life. He must have hoped that it would enable the trustees to preserve the maximum value of his properties for the creditors. He could have made a condition that he be freed first to manage the property. He could have refused outright on the ground that he had granted the original assignment under false pretenses. Instead, he gave away his trump card without conditions and with no certainty that he would benefit at all.

While Benjamin was trying to get bail and permission to consult with Lyman, Rathbun Allen was taken into custody in Ohio. On August 13, the young nephew was brought back in irons and lodged in the jail with his uncles.

Although the community was outraged at the three prisoners, men who widely were believed to have violated their trust, feelings about their wives and children were quite different. The two Mrs. Rathbuns had sustained a terrible shock for which they had been totally unprepared. Writing in the conventional terms applied to women of property, the *New York American* remarked in a Buffalo dispatch: "The wife of B. Rathbun is held in universal regard. In her praise every tongue is eloquent, and for her every heart in this city, bleeds. Lyman Rathbun, also, has an estimable wife who is overwhelmed in affliction."

A false report about Benjamin's wife, however, was widely disseminated. It was that she "was unable to bear the shock a revelation of his proceedings produced, and is now laboring under mental alienation." Alice Rathbun was made of sterner stuff, however, and soon increased the number of boarders in her house to raise the money to keep her family going and to provide a decent fare in jail for Rathbun. Henry Hawkins stayed with her to help out in all the heavy chores around the boarding house. Lyman's wife also took in boarders for the same purposes.

Lyman Rathbun Howlett, the younger nephew who had been a confidential messenger in the countinghouse (and who surely knew much about his uncles' complex affairs), surprised all by disappearing only a few days after his uncles were jailed. Before then, Howlett had been assumed to have been merely a giddy, handsome boy who knew nothing of the business. A halfhearted search failed to reveal his whereabouts. It was later discovered that Howlett himself had been engaged in casual forgeries in his uncles' behalf.

An employee of Henry H. Sizer's brokerage house soon recalled that Howlett had come to that office once to renew notes having seven endorsers. While he was presenting one, a Sizer clerk discovered that it lacked an endorsement. Howlett took the note and a packet he carried to a writing desk for a minute, did some writing, and came back with a signed note. The clerk suspected nothing, for the boy explained that he happened to have a fully endorsed note with him. In retrospect, they were certain that he had boldly forged the signature under their very eyes.

Under the supplementary assignment, the assignees had the legal authority to resume the work they had halted when they found that the original document gave them no authority to do anything. They abandoned, however, the great bulk of Rathbun projects. Only a few activities, such as the stagecoaches and the construction of the Niagara Falls Railroad, were permitted to continue.

The assignment valued Rathbun's real estate at $2,237,150 and his personal property at $854,000. Against the real estate, he acknowledged encumbrances of $530,900 and against the entire estate additional obligations of $177,000. His valuations were suspect at the time, with contracts abandoned and work stopped. The general deflation touched off by his failure and by Jackson's specie circular made his valuations even more questionable.

His valuations were far too high in other respects. He valued, for instance, the block comprising the Niagara Falls Eagle, the new stores, and the basement of the huge hotel at $160,000, less $7,000 owed. But in its unfinished state, the basement was nothing but a lined hole worth less than the vacant land.

Stocks in retail stores in Buffalo and Niagara he valued at $120,000. Perhaps they would have brought that figure if sold at retail, over the counter. But, thrown as they were soon on the auction block in huge lots in a falling market, they could produce only a fraction of the retail price.

The valuable property near the canal where his docks, warehouses, and workshops were had cost him $100,000 to acquire from William Peacock and family. He valued it, with his improvements, at $150,000. But the entire transaction had been purely verbal, and the original owners now declared that, under the agreement, the property was forfeit. It took a long legal battle by the assignees to reverse the Peacock's determination.

Rathbun considered his shares in the Paterson and Granville banks to total $177,000, but both banks succumbed to the failure and subsequent depression. Helping to kill the one in Granville was the rapid return for redemption of $50,000 of its essentially valueless currency, which had been loaned to Rathbun with the understanding that he would so spread it around the nation that the notes would come back only slowly. The Buffalo assignees were not a party to this agreement. They sent the notes back in bulk, still in their original wrappers, with a demand for specie, which, of course, could not be honored.

With all, as August wore on, a Buffalo correspondent on the *New York Journal of Commerce* was hopeful that all Rathbun's debts could be paid, because of the vast potential of Rathbun's properties at Niagara Falls: "The Niagara Falls property will, some day or other, be worth an immense sum of money. There is no doubt in my mind that a million in money might be made over what Rathbun has to pay the Porters and at which sum, with Rathbun's expenditures since added, I doubt not the assignees would sell it."

The assignees would have been delighted to sell Rathbun's great speculation for what he had paid. But who would buy? The promoter was discredited and jailed. The title was complicated by the new ownership and by the question of whether or not Rathbun had fulfilled his contract with the Porters. Thus, for all its potential value, the entire Niagara Falls estate was in limbo.

Moreover, unquestionably the assignees were short of money. They found, or received in payment of small debts, only $31,000 in cash in the first few months of their stewardship, yet they had to pay out the nearly $42,000 due the laborers, clerks, and others for personal services. They had no money to finance new operations or even meet the overhead on old ones.

Within a few days of the failure, Buffalo was filled with holders of Rathbun's notes or their representatives. All wished to learn firsthand what was going on, but no one could tell them. Confronted with the difficult task of trying to piece together an empire that had existed most coherently only in the head of a genius, the assignees found it necessary to move very slowly to straighten things out.

"Protests," the notarized declarations that notes had not been paid to those due them, were pouring into Buffalo. The notes themselves were being rejected as forgeries by those whose names were endorsed on their backs. There was also a backlog of protests, some dating from before the collapse of Rathbun's empire. Harlow Case, the deputy postmaster, was compelled to deny publicly that he had mishandled Rathbun protests before the failure. His denial, however, contained the naive admission that, to save himself work, he had been putting the protests into Rathbun's mailbox instead of the mailboxes of endorsees, as the rules required. Rathbun had been willing to accept them. Case's statement provided an unanticipated solution to one of the more puzzling aspects of the affair: why the forgeries had remained undetected for so long.

The new protests now no longer went into the Rathbun mailbox. Instead, they went directly to those whose names they bore. Thomas Farnum, who worked with Orlando Allen in an exchange and brokerage business, related later that Lyman Rathbun had borrowed $10,000 from the firm on the security of Benjamin's notes, all of them endorsed by solid citizens. They were payable at a bank on different days, but had never been presented for payment, because Lyman always paid or renewed them a day or two before they were due. After the failure, Ebenezer Johnson called on Farnum to show him a note that his firm held bearing a forged Orlando Allen endorsement. Johnson asked whether or not they would pay. In reply, Farnum took a $500 note from his safe with a Johnson, Hodge and Company endorsement, which Johnson denied having seen before. Farnum added that more than $200,000 in forged endorsements of his firm's notes turned up in New York, Boston, Philadelphia, and Cincinnati, but that they had never paid a cent on them.

The same thing was taking place everywhere. Every note issued by Rathbun, as well as many unrelated notes of persons whose names were forged on the Rathbun notes, now fell into question. Wholesale repudiation followed, for good notes could not be distinguished from bad ones. Finances were hopelessly snarled, because there was no way of distinguishing the valid from the spurious. It simply proved impossible to gauge with any accuracy the extent of the forgeries. Estimates ran as high as $7,000,000 in these virtually unnegotiable notes.

Some Rathbun notes, such as those given as bonds in connection with land purchases and some of those belonging to persons specifically mentioned in the assignment as lenders, did gain recognition. Among those considered still extant were notes given to William Bird for land at Black Rock. Also paid were notes of Benjamin to Lyman Rathbun, payable at the Bank of Buffalo and endorsed "B. Humphrey of Batavia," who was probably their brother-in-law, the tavernkeeper husband of Jeanette Content Rathbun.

When the jailed Rathbun heard that the assignees had decided to liquidate all the assets of his estate, he became frantic. He did everything that he and his volunteer legal advisers could do to get admitted to bail. If only he could get out, he believed, he could change this policy and the trustees could be guided in how to salvage the maximum value of his properties. His business sense told him that their approach was certain to destroy much of its value.

Their inventory very roughly completed, the assignees announced that an auction of Rathbun's personal property would begin on September 12.

This inventory was the cause of widespread marvel. It seemed beyond belief that one man could assemble so much in so little time. The personal property, which was inventoried in such general terms that it was obvious the trustees had only a vague idea of what it comprised, ranged over a wide selection of industrial and commercial goods. The list included a million feet of milled pine and hardwood, plus great quantities of joists, beams, and scantlings for construction; materials and metal stocks in his warehouses and at his blacksmith, tin, paint, carpenter, and other shops; tools for blacksmiths, carpenters, joiners, coach makers, and railroad laborers; stocks of dry goods, groceries, thousands of barrels of salt, corn, coal, and other staples; nearly two million bricks, and great stocks of cut stone and several thousand bushels of lime and mortar.

His stage line was offered with thirty to forty four-horse stage-coaches with teams, "comprising two hundred of the finest horses of any stage establishment in the United States" and mail routes running over five or six main roads. Also for sale were ten to fifteen pairs of matched horses, twenty to thirty span of carriage and wagon horses, forty to fifty lumber wagons, two canal boats, two splendid omnibuses, and many carriages, light wagons, and small stagecoaches. His shares in bank, railroad, and other stocks were also offered for sale.

To that point unknown in detail to the general public, his real estate, with its valuable buildings and lands in Buffalo and at Niagara, left readers amazed. The property owned outright in Buffalo was listed in thirty-one separate lots; his Buffalo land contracts in eight lots; his Buffalo leases in nine lots; his property at Niagara in ten lots and two contracts.

The trustees' announcement of their plans to sell his personal property signaled Rathbun to issue a statement to his creditors from his prison cell on August 31. The statement called a meeting of creditors for the morning of September 12, the day the sale would start. He proposed that they organize to protect their interests by blocking wholesale destruction of the value of the property he had assigned.

He used new figures in this statement, but they still gave a positive balance. Much of the statement seemed a flight of fantasy, though its purpose certainly seemed noble. He now estimated that the estate was worth $2,581,000 and that his debts totaled only $1,800,000, so that if the property were rightly handled there would be ample money to pay everyone. (Whether his calculation of debts included all the forged notes, he failed to state. There was the clear implication, however, that it did.) He argued that creditors in the second class, some twenty-four persons and firms to which he had admitted owing money in his original assignment, could correct the defects of the assignment by taking over the obligations of the first class (mechanics, laborers, and clerks). He appeared to indicate that, if this were done, the assignees would resign and the creditors' association could take over the trust. Then he himself would resign his residuary interest in the estate.

> Although I believe that my property is more than sufficient to satisfy my creditors, I yet have no wish to reserve any share for myself. All that I now desire so far as the property is concerned is that every creditor of mine should be paid the utmost cent to which he is entitled. Whatever may be my fate or future condition in life— whether I be convicted or acquitted of the charges preferred against me, to know that by me no one has been injured—that all my liabilities have been faithfully discharged—will in every situation furnish me with infinite comfort and consolation.

This appeal brought the formation of a creditors' committee, chiefly representative of New York City groups, which stepped forward with money to pay bail on the theory that Rathbun's personal guidance would enable them to salvage more from the wreckage than could be effected without him. Rathbun, however, was again denied bail.

Later, a local committee, chiefly composed of creditors, was organized to see that the funds were handled properly, that fair payments went to creditors, and that Mrs. Rathbun's dower right was protected. (This last, generous objective was apparently included after the direct appeal of Senator Tracy, who was acting as her attorney.)

Henry Roop, president of the Granville Bank, presided over these creditors, and the eccentric twenty-nine-year-old lawyer, LeGrand Marvin, who made himself famous as a litigant in later years, was elected chairman. Alexander A. Evstaphieve, son of the Russian minister to the United States and a broker at Buffalo, was the secretary. The group appointed a subcommittee to organize creditors, its membership including Orlando Allen, partner of Farnum and Pratt's brother-in-law; Capt. Stephen Champlin, one of Commodore Perry's officers who had settled in Buffalo, and Philip P. Kissam, a broker.

Late in the year this Buffalo creditors' association published a plan for settlement of the estate. The pamphlet discussed the entire situation, reviewing the clouded titles to Rathbun property, and proposed an arrangement like that Rathbun himself had suggested. It reported that Rathbun was quite willing to relinquish his theoretical residual rights but that he had, apparently somewhat to their surprise, attached conditions to his acquiescence.

Before he would approve the plan, Rathbun insisted on certain terms: that Mrs. Rathbun be assured of $15,000 in lieu of her dower rights; that the association agree to pay all the small-currency-type Rathbun notes in the hands of shopkeepers; that Horace Janes be paid $200 to recompense him for a trip to Buffalo; and that Lyman Rathbun get $11,671.03 and that Rathbun Allen get $650, presumably amounts that Rathbun owed these relatives. Added to the rapidly deteriorating, general economic situation, these conditions doubtlessly helped lead to the failure of the whole plan.

Meanwhile, in September most of the assignees sold most of the personal property for about $178,730, much of which was in notes of two months' to two years' duration. They planned to sell the remainder at the same time that they sold the estate.

The September sales, with their big attendance, led the *Albany Daily Advertiser* to conjecture that the demands of creditors might be met in full. But by the end of October, when rumors began to circulate about the actual receipts of the sales, the *New York Evening Post* was speculating whether even fifty cents on the dollar would ultimately be paid.

Perhaps Rathbun expected something like this. He had been in business too long not to know that immense offerings could demoralize any market, and despite a conspiracy of silence by its newspapers, the Buffalo market was fast going downhill. To be sure, Rathbun's numerous visitors, many of them expecting momentarily to see the great man freed to take up the reins of his empire, kept him apprised of life in Buffalo. In their eyes all seemed like it might yet be put right easily. Rathbun was too acute, however, not to have recognized that his failure had brought a general weakening of the city's entire economic structure.

As the surprise of the failure wore off, people went on with their regular pursuits where they could. But the Rathbun affair was still the most important subject of conversation, and curiosity seekers ambled about Buffalo and Niagara Falls to gawk at the buildings Rathbun had erected. They stood outside the jail, hoping for a glimpse of the notorious criminal. Mrs. Rathbun's daily visits always brought a momentary hush in the talk of the assembled crowd as she passed, carrying food to her husband.

The opening of the American Hotel was not delayed, for it had been practically finished. Palmer leased it for nine years to Preston Hodges. The hotel opened with a fanfare that completely mocked the plight of the man who had designed, financed, and built it. Rathbun might even have been near enough to hear the music and noise of the opening from the window of his cell. In sharp contrast to his lodgings, it was said that the hotel's $50,000 worth of appointments made it "more richly furnished than any other in the United States."

With Rathbun's workmen idle, however, construction locally nearly ceased. A few of those whose construction projects were almost finished gave new contracts to other builders and were thus able to have their structures completed. But the work on both the new hotel at Niagara Falls and on the great Exchange Building came to a halt. Along Main Street in Buffalo, sightseers stared at the piles of rubble that remained on the site of the Exchange to mark the spot where Rathbun had demolished buildings to make room for the new, far grander one. Would the Exchange ever be completed? No one dared to guess.[1]

The sale of lots at Niagara Falls was halted, because of the confused contractual situation, at the close of the second day after a total of $120,000 worth had been purchased. Presumably the down payments on those lots were returned to the bidders, for the money certainly did not appear in the assignees' accounting.

The humble folk, the mechanics, laborers, and workmen who

1. In fact, the Exchange would never be completed. After Rathbun's fall, and the long depression of 1837–43 that followed in its wake, a chastened mood took hold in local business and civic circles. In the context of this mood, the epic scale of Rathbun's projections for the Exchange now appeared much too costly and aesthetically extravagant. The nearest the postdepression city came to realizing the idea of a centrally located structure where commercial relations might in various ways be systematized and where market information would be gathered and disseminated was the modest Merchants Exchange Building. A small and simply designed two-story brick building at the waterfront, it housed the Buffalo Board of Trade and was opened in 1844.

had been on the Rathbun payroll milled about the city, unemployed, disgruntled, hoping that their jobs would be restored. With their money soon spent, they accosted well-dressed citizens on the streets and appealed to them for work, and they pleaded with merchants for credit. The stores that bore the Rathbun name over their doors remained closed until successful bidders at the auctions carted off their stocks. Only the stage lines and the city omnibuses, each vehicle bearing the Rathbun name, remained in operation.

Newspapers gradually became more certain. The *Commercial Advertiser,* which was still restrained and carefully avoided ad hominem remarks, wrote that Rathbun's work had been fine, but added nonetheless that if he had not done it, others would have. It added, too, "In the execution of his plans, Mr. Rathbun was gradually monopolizing many branches of industry so as to destroy the mechanic whose means were unequal to the contest." Rathbun's monopoly, this sage editorial concluded, had forced prices up; now competition was bringing them down again back to healthy and competitive levels.

This complete and probably deliberate current misunderstanding of the economic forces then at work not only confused the public at the time but also blurred later efforts to come to an understanding of the vast damage the Rathbun failure had done to Buffalo. Withdrawal of Rathbun's projects and stores from the Buffalo market obviously depressed trade, and thus decreased rather than increased competition. The falling prices, only indirectly reported by the *Advertiser,* resulted from a lack of buying power and a drop in demand. Some of the weaker merchants had begun to fail. Even those who possessed money and had little debt began to live cautiously.

The devious interrelationships of credit in one way or another had involved every substantial business in the mess. With suits pending against them, businessmen found it next to impossible to raise new credit while they were repudiating notes presented for collection. Merchants and banks quickly reorganized their procedures, and now attempted to eliminate the loose practices that had brought them into trouble. Moreover, they began refusing to accept the small bills from dubious, nonlocal banks, long illegal in the state, which had been in general use in the city. Removal of these bills from the market immediately brought a shortage of currency for ordinary use, just when falling prices made the bills necessary.

As the inner workings of Buffalo's economy began to wind down, worthy civic projects had to be shelved. The University of Western New York faced an uncertain future when it opened in November. It advertised its excellent services and cheap tuition, but had no money to keep going. The endowment that had been pledged seemed harder to raise as the days went by. Palmer and the others who each promised $15,000 to endow a professor's chair now found it impossible to pay. Rathbun's pledge of $1,000 was merely listed as one of his many debts. The new university, ballyhooed as a frontier Oxford, evaporated in a month. Higher education, in the form of a modest medical college, would not come to Buffalo for another decade.[2]

Buffalo did retain its motley, boomtown clatter. There were remnants of the frontier amid the life of middle-class commerce. Immigrants, especially Germans, arrived with every canal boat. The population, already diverse, continued to swell. The fashionably dressed wives of Buffalo's first families continued to walk the same unpaved, sidewalkless streets as the remnants of the local Indian peoples who lived at the fringes of society. Above the streets, however, the dust had not yet settled from Rathbun's fall. In the recesses of second-floor offices, bookkeepers worked overtime to straighten, as best they could, the tangled finances of their firms. In his cell, Rathbun awaited trial.

2. In 1846, now as the University of Buffalo, the institution was revitalized, but only as a medical school. The comprehensive university that Palmer, Rathbun, and others had hoped to create lay many years in the future. Only in 1907 did the University of Buffalo create a liberal arts college and open its doors to undergraduate applicants.

13

The Wheels of Justice

While Rathbun and his creditors worried about how to get the most value out of his property, by August 22 District Attorney Barker methodically compiled enough evidence in the matter to summon a grand jury.

Four days and many witnesses later the grand jury found true bills on numerous counts against Benjamin Rathbun, Lyman Rathbun, and Rathbun Allen as principals and accessories in a gigantic forgery conspiracy. The basis for these first charges was not the hundreds of notes already protested, but notes allegedly found in Benjamin's possession when he was arrested. They involved the signatures of the forwarder John B. Macy; his brother, Samuel H. Macy, a broker; Johnson, Hodge and Company, bankers and brokers; Thomas Day, financier; and the firm of Potter and Babcock, lawyers.

Another grand jury considered further charges, and found additional true bills against the three men on September 21. The indictments that day were based on, among others, forgery of the names of ten of the eleven endorsers on the famous $15,000 loan of 1835. Henry P. Darrow's name was also on that note. Why Darrow appeared as endorser instead of Henry Morris on many notes was never explained.

Other indictments were found against Benjamin and one or both of his associates by succeeding grand juries in December 1836, and July 1837. They represented hundreds of counts, although they embraced charges of forgery of less than twenty-five different persons and firms.

These juries would not pass a contemporary test for conflict of interest. Gen. Sylvester Mathews, for instance, was the foreman of the grand jury that found a true bill, among others, on the use of his own name. Orlando Allen, one of those whom Rathbun owed money and a member of the creditors' committee, was foreman of the December 8 grand jury. Lewis F. Allen, one of the eleven endorsers, was a member of the 1837 grand jury. Moreover, several jurymen were either related to those victimized or were closely associated with them in business.

Rathbun's creditors generally were more interested in recovering their money than in his prosecution, and to this end they wanted him out of jail and seeing to his affairs. The New York committee, headed by the brokers Henry P. Tallmadge and John Paine, employed Salem Dutcher, a well-known Albany lawyer, to get Rathbun out on bail. Appeal after appeal failed. Finally, after endless arguments and against the strong opposition of the district attorney, Circuit Court Judge Addison Gardiner decided to admit Rathbun to bail on September 24, 1836. Dutcher was supported in his appeal by Henry K. Smith and Thomas T. Sherwood, who along with Evert M. Van Buren now made up Rathbun's volunteer legal team.

Judge Gardiner set bail at the enormous figure of $60,000 and bonds for that amount were filed by six men, five of them creditors. The bondsmen were Pierre A. Barker, Samuel H. Macy, James McKay, Thomas T. Sherwood, and Tallmadge and Paine.

The principal object of Rathbun's release, the *Buffalo Journal* hastened to assure an angry public, was "the great need of his [Rathbun's] assistance in arranging his most extensive business and for a more speedy allotment to his creditors."

Breathing the air of freedom for the first time in two months, Rathbun immediately began to assist the committee in creating a plan to salvage as much as possible from the ruins. He did not realize that a Genesee County grand jury was meeting in Batavia at the direction of District Attorney Chandler, Evans's erstwhile counsel, and that Evans was testifying. When that grand jury adjourned, it had indicted Rathbun on three counts.

In consequence, he had been free only a week when, on October 1, he was again arrested, this time on the Genesee County charges. He was taken to Batavia for arraignment, and then, again, committed to his former cell in the Erie County jail without bail to await trial at the March 1837 term in Genesee County. The unexpected move completely stymied the plan of the New York committee.

Meanwhile residents of western New York were increasingly angry and agitated over the failure and the subsequent disclosures, and there was now a widespread demand for immediate punishment of Rathbun and his associates. People favorable to him were now few and far between. His supporters were chiefly his former teamsters, artisans, and mechanics, who had convinced themselves that their misfortunes, after his downfall, were due to a cabal of his jealous competitors.

Despite this increasingly adverse public sentiment, Rathbun Allen was eventually admitted to bail, set at $14,000, in early October by James Stryker, the senior judge of the Court of Common Pleas, on the application of his attorney, Horatio J. Stow. The next day Judge Stryker also decided to admit Lyman to $20,000 bail. The seven men who put up Allen's bail and the ten who served as sureties for Lyman were an oddly assorted lot composed of lawyers, brokers, shopkeepers, and merchants. They were far from the imposing names the Rathbuns could have commanded a few months earlier. But they do illustrate the complex and inbred nature of local business affairs and friendships, and the peculiar ethics that guided relations between the Rathbuns and some of the prominent men of their social and business circle. Lyman's lawyer was Henry K. Smith, who also was one of the guarantors of his bail. Smith was a son-in-law of Sheldon Thompson, one of the "eleven endorsers," and his wife was a niece of James L. Barton, who had become one of Rathbun's most implacable enemies.

Less than two months after leaving jail, Lyman disappeared suddenly from Buffalo. Whether Benjamin knew this was to happen cannot be said. What is known is that Lyman had come to the jail a few times to visit Benjamin and that they had spoken extensively. A tremendous outcry was heard over Lyman's disappearance in early December. No one admitted knowing anything about it. Benjamin expressed complete surprise. Lyman's wife declared that she had no suspicion that her husband was planning to leave the court's jurisdiction. The district attorney had the court quash Rathbun Allen's bail immediately, and that young man went back to a cell.

Lyman's disappearance caused consternation among his sureties. They foresaw being forced to pay out $20,000 on account of the Rathbuns, besides the financial losses they had already incurred. An investigation was immediately launched and a manhunt instituted. Posters offering $2,000 reward for his apprehension were prepared by Lyman's bondsmen. Six agents were employed and $2,000 was expended within a few months in a vain effort to capture him. The widely disseminated posters gave the only extant description of the man. He was five feet, three inches tall, of florid complexion, with a sharp nose and gray eyes. His hair was nearly dark. He "stoops a little walking, steps lightly"; he spoke in a low voice and hesitantly and "salt rheum diseases his head below the hair on his forehead, and makes him have a scurvy appearance."

The search found evidence that Lyman had been in Louisville, Kentucky, where, by a remarkable coincidence, Lemuel White happened to be stopping. White learned that Lyman had been there and got Louisville police to seize his nine trunks, found in possession of a Captain Ferris. A former New York adventurer and an officer in the army of the new Republic of Texas, Ferris was identified as Lyman's traveling companion during some of the time since his flight from Buffalo. White obtained a Kentucky court order to sell the trunks at auction for the benefit of Lyman's sureties. But no explanation was ever made as to how Lyman, who had fled on horseback from Buffalo, managed to carry all that baggage with him.

Their agents' reports enabled the sureties next to state confidently that they had trailed Lyman to New Orleans, where he then disappeared. Further searching enabled them to report later, however, that he had been located finally in the Republic of Texas. When they applied to the federal government for an extradition order, they discovered that no extradition treaty had yet been negotiated with Texas.

Henry K. Smith was elected Erie County district attorney in November 1836, despite his association with the Rathbun defense, and one of his first duties on assuming office was to appear before Judge Gardiner and ask that Lyman's bond, which he himself had endorsed, be forfeited.

The jurist, possibly moved by the sad plight of the imperturbable, articulate attorney, and doubtless sympathetic because a serious effort to apprehend Lyman was being made by the bondsmen, consented to continue the bond instead. But by June 1837, when the bondsmen reported that Lyman was still in Texas, their own condition was desperate. The economy was in crisis. Credit was drying up and debts were being called in. They had to ask the court to reduce the bond. It was cut to $1,500 but now even this looked frighteningly large. They declared that they would have been far better able to pay $3,000 six months earlier than they were to pay $1,500 that dark June.

Amid the early efforts to find Lyman, Rathbun Allen escaped from jail, and he, too, disappeared. At 6:00 P.M. on Christmas Eve, 1836, when the jailers were feeling kindly disposed toward their pris-

oners, Allen apparently disguised himself and walked out under the
nose of a newly appointed underturnkey. Sheriff Brace got the
county to offer a $1,000 reward and posters were disseminated
throughout the East. These described Allen as "about 23," five feet,
nine inches tall, with a florid complexion and prominent nose and
chin. He had full black eyes and "a gentlemanly appearance."

The disappearances of Benjamin's associates were fortuitous.
Coupled with the absence of some other witnesses, they won him
several deferments of his trials. Each time his trial was called up, his
lawyers expressed willingness to let him go on trial only as an accessory to crimes committed by the two others, who had disappeared.
The state, however, would not agree to that, but neither could it
produce Lyman and the nephew.

Rathbun's lawyers found that the state had information that
made his defense more difficult, but kept it from the public until the
trials. Acting for the assignees in going through Rathbun's business
records immediately after his arrest, Clary, Love, and Dyre Tillinghast had discovered in a vault in the countinghouse many letters
and memoranda in Rathbun's handwriting. These letters, some of
which have already been quoted in connection with the developments
preceding his failure, immeasurably strengthened the case against
Rathbun.

Moreover, although it was kept from admission at the trials by a
technicality, additional damning evidence had also been found by the
three men in Rathbun's desk at his home. This consisted of six notes
of credit, which bore on their backs the same eleven endorsements as
those that had been widely forged. The face of these notes was un-
dated and unsigned, but otherwise they were identical to many in
circulation. In his statement, Rathbun explained away these curious
pieces of paper by saying they had been prepared by Lyman and sent
to him. He put them aside, he said, because he felt that there were
already too many notes on the market with the same endorsements.
He denied knowing they were spurious.

The direction of popular sentiment, however, had begun to work
against the force of this damning evidence. The delays in Rathbun's
trial, in fact, were having an entirely unexpected effect upon public
opinion, which appeared to be shifting from its collective certainty of
Rathbun's guilt to a more moderate position. Rage at his duplicity
was turning to suspicion of his prosecutors, the assignees, and those
who had filed complaints against him. Behind this lay not new evidence, but anxieties about the local economy. Buffalo's commerce

was worsening by the day. Rathbun's collapse with its aftermath of unemployment, declining mercantile activity, and impaired credit had brought the city's development to a sickening halt.

In September, the *Commercial Advertiser* could still try to whip up confidence by beating a familiar drum. It emphasized that other people were continuing construction of the buildings that the failure had left incomplete (a statement only partly true). The paper also claimed that new construction would earn at least ten percent annually on its investment. A month later the publicity was getting cruder and apparently more desperate, too. Now stories were being printed, for example, recalling cases where someone in 1833 had made a hundred percent when he sold a certain piece of land at $5 a foot. For the same land in October 1836, the owner had refused $150,000, for he knew that it "would bring that under the hammer even in hard times." Another tall tale: a piece of land on Seneca Street that two years earlier had sold for $1,200 now brought $12,000 on a resale. "Everything is stable" and is going along well, the editor wrote, though had this really been true perhaps such emphasis would have been unnecessary.

By December, the situation had become so bad that the same newspaper was trying to explain why Buffalo's economy was, in fact, contracting faster than the deteriorating national economy. Existing Buffalo banks were inadequate to meet local needs, it claimed, because fully $1,900,000 had been withdrawn from circulation in the city in a very short period. The paper's explanation of this figure was that $400,000 had been lost by the withdrawal of the United States Branch Bank and partial payment of the debts owed it; that Rathbun's failure had cost the city $600,000, much of it in unfinished buildings; that $300,000 had been taken away because of the law abolishing small notes; and that $400,000 in circulation had been cut off from the Buffalo banks through the influence of the Jackson specie order.

But Buffalo's situation was a specific instance, if an extreme one, of a general problem. Throughout the country, finances were in a dire state. The national business recession set off by the collapse of speculation in western lands—and in no small part, too, by the collapse of Rathbun's empire, which certainly exerted a psychological blow to investors—had deepened in the fall and winter. By spring 1837, the nation was amid a full-fledged depression, the first large-scale economic contraction in America's history. Values were falling, and money was becoming scarcer. Every bank note was suspect.

Banks were collapsing. Newspapers were beginning to be filled with notices of forced sales, foreclosures, and failures. Many needed to sell, but few wished to buy. Few could afford to.

Accurately sensing that this dire situation might work in his favor because he had always been associated with prosperity and opportunity, Rathbun and his advisers decided to capitalize on the growing sense of desperation. In his cell Rathbun spent most of January 1837 working and reworking a statement to present his case in the best possible light. He completed the statement by February, and in the next few weeks some of his associates attempted to get newspaper editors to run Rathbun's test. They all refused, perhaps fearing they would be seen as taking a position on a matter before the courts.

Finally, to get it before the public in its entirety, it was run as a paid advertisement, which appeared in the *Buffalo Commercial Advertiser* on February 21, 1837. It was reprinted, unchanged, in the weekly *Patriot and Commercial Advertiser* of March 1. The statement ran five and one-half columns of the small print ordinarily reserved for advertising notices.

The statement, one of the most interesting documents associated with Rathbun, reveals the pride of a self-made man, ticking off his acquisitions and enamored with the image of his huge empire, as it had existed before his fall. He confidently asserted that if he had been let out of prison on bail, he could have straightened out his finances so that the empire could have been left intact, or, if necessary, liquidated at a loss to no one.

Addressed to the public, the statement opened with an evasion that implicitly contradicted Rathbun's heroic view of himself as the master of a vast business empire. In effect, he disavowed knowledge of and hence blame for the affair that had led to his arrest, by saying that his business was largely controlled by others. Thus, he said,

> [t]he great extend and variety of my late business operations; the notoriety of my failure and the charges against myself and others, as well as the imputations upon persons whose names appear on my paper unite many powerful reasons requiring of me a public explanation which has ever been my intention since the failure; but for want of that knowledge myself of the transactions most important to those immediately interested, this public explanation has been deferred, hoping further information would be obtained. But as the prospect lessens of procuring such further information, and fearing it will not be obtained in time to meet the *wishes* and protect

the *interest* of those most to be affected—I proceed to lay before the public, such facts as have come to my knowledge relating to the financial transactions of my late business concerns.

My knowledge of this subject is very limited—having obtained most of it since the failure, from those who had the entire control and management of the financial department. The interviews for obtaining much information have been limited; and answers to my questions have been given with apparent reluctance and caution. Consequently, I could not advantageously press the inquiry, and often desisted for a time, hoping to remove the apparent restraint. But, as I did not avow the object of my inquiry, that cautious reluctance increased, until circumstances occurred which wholly precluded my getting any further information at present on the subject.

This complex, vague, and ultimately evasive way of saying that he had tried unsuccessfully to pump his brother, and that his brother's disappearance closed the door to further information, characterizes the entire document. Simple thoughts are hidden in circumlocutions and prolixities. Even the closest reading will not reveal possible answers to important questions.

Rathbun portrays himself as a busy man of affairs, so occupied with the acquisition of new properties and construction contracts that he had no time for petty business details, bookkeeping, and records. His complete confidence in his brother's abilities is stressed and reiterated. Discrepancies between this picture and the letters he knew the state possessed are ignored except for the statement that he wrote business memos and correspondence only at his brother's dictation. Each of the major pieces of evidence that the state planned to use against him was explained, somewhere or other, in this long statement.

When the statement was written, Rathbun probably could assume that his brother was safe beyond the reach of the law and that his nephew was presumably in a place of safety. He was on secure ground, therefore, in laying the entire responsibility upon the shoulders of Lyman and Rathbun Allen. He must have been aware of the maxim that the principal is responsible for the acts of his agents, but he also could put his hopes into creating sympathy for his plight.

He declared in unequivocal terms that his brother had admitted his guilt to him. The forgeries, he said, began on a small scale to take care of a pressing situation, but soon had gotten out of control because of the pressure generated by the "enormous shaves" of the moneylenders.

Relating how he had entrusted Lyman with all the management of his finances, he declared that "I furnished him my signature in blank on notes, drafts, and checks, in all the variety of forms as endorser and drawer, and in addition to which he had a full power of attorney to sign my name and transact all manner of business for me." So much did Lyman have his confidence, he said, that he never knew, until after the failure, the full extent of his liabilities. Even now, he said, he lacked the entire story. But he affirmed his opinion that Lyman had meant no harm.

This statement declared flatly that he was deceived into signing the assignment of his property, a contention that seems substantiated by the circumstances and facts of that event. He makes no direct accusations, however, against particular persons.

The *Commercial Advertiser* accompanied its publication of Rathbun's statement by a sardonic editorial, for which it would be quickly taken to task. Remarking that the statement was in Rathbun's handwriting and "bore the marks of being his own composition," the editor claimed that it had been received a few days earlier and was given to the compositors without an opportunity for extended study. "Every reader should decide for himself as to the degree of credit which should attach to its statements. It is very ingeniously drawn up and is, probably, the best case that could be made in the writer's behalf."

The next day the editor was confronted with a letter from Evert Van Buren, one of Rathbun's firmest legal defenders, which the editor printed with reluctance, he said, because he suspected that it would further prejudice Rathbun's case. In view of the accusations against Rathbun which the *Commercial Advertiser* was carrying regularly, however, it seems hardly probable that the editor expressed the true reason for his reluctance.

Van Buren strongly criticized the newspaper's statement, which had accompanied the Rathbun advertisement, that claimed that it had no right, after accepting it for publication, to impugn it. The message implicit in the editor's remarks was that Rathbun's statement was a self-serving tissue of lies, unworthy of close inspection. The law, Van Buren declaimed, holds a man innocent until he has been proven guilty. He wrote:

The statement was made by Mr. Rathbun as an act of justice to the numerous and respectable individuals whose names have been forged upon his paper and who have frequently solicited it. It was made by him after mature reflection and advice from several sources and without the remote idea of affecting his "case." He did indeed hope that the Truth would have a tendency to vindicate his character from the assaults which rumor and conjecture have for the past six months so assiduously made.

Though most Buffalo editors had been afraid to publish Rathbun's statement for reasons of their own, it created quite a sensation elsewhere. Almost all the major newspapers reported it and quoted sections. The *New York Commercial* ran practically the full text. The Van Buren, Ohio, *Times* went so far as to describe it as "a true and fair statement," a questionable evaluation, for the Ohio paper was hardly in a position to pass upon its truth or falsity at that time.

The statement did indeed benefit Rathbun. It seems so clear and candid that many who had been convinced of his guilt now experienced doubt for the first time. They remembered that he had not tried to flee even though he had had the opportunity. Although one could dispute the morality of shifting the responsibility to men who could not be reached for questioning or punishment, he had tried to explain the major evidence against him. In contrast to his relatives, who had refused to explain themselves, he had stood his ground and apparently manfully awaited the judgment of his peers.

That judgment lay immediately ahead. Handcuffed to his friend, Sheriff Brace, Rathbun was taken from the Buffalo jail on March 27, 1837. He was loaded aboard one of the stagecoaches that still bore his name, and then driven to Batavia for arraignment before the March term of the Genesee County Court of Oyer and Terminer. It was well understood that now there would be no postponement of this trial.

The trip was tedious and uncomfortable. Prisoner, officials, and driver were exhausted by a slow, jolting journey over the road, which ice and snow had made almost impassable. It required seventeen excruciating hours to make the less than forty-mile trip. Throughout, Rathbun remained bound to the sheriff in fear that even at this late moment, he might find a way of imitating Lyman and the nephew. He was lodged in a room that had been reserved at Batavia's Eagle Tavern.

Witnesses, newspaper correspondents, representatives of financial agencies, and curious citizens from all over western New York crowded the village. So many people were jammed at the tavern's door to glimpse the notorious criminal that Sheriff Brace had to rush him around to a side entrance to get into the building.

His case was called the following day before Judge Gardiner, the

Rochester jurist who covered the whole Eighth Circuit. Sheriff Brace, at the Court's direction, formally turned the prisoner over to the custody of Genesee County Sheriff Townsend.

Chandler, who had been Blatchford's sharp-eyed assistant in preparing the defective assignment, now appeared in his public character as Genesee County district attorney and representative of the people. Assisting him was John B. Skinner, a promising and brilliant thirty-eight-year-old lawyer. Skinner's service in this case helped boost him to a judicial post within the next few years.

Black-bearded and thin-lipped Henry K. Smith was then serving as Erie County district attorney, but he continued as Rathbun's chief counsel. (This he did even though Lyman had never paid him before disappearing.) T. T. Sherwood, Buffalo's dramatic trial lawyer whose endless tricks annoyed colleagues and confounded judges, and Evert Van Buren, a specialist at composing briefs, made up the remainder of Rathbun's Buffalo legal team. The newspaper descriptions of these gentlemen were characteristic of the polemical politics and partisanship of the day. No matter what they were before, they were now accused alternately of contradictory moral and ideological offenses—of being hated followers of Martin Van Buren, hirelings of big banks, or apostate Whigs.

Rathbun was arraigned on a three-count indictment. He was charged with having forged notes with intent to defraud, with having in his possession notes that he knew to be forged but which he intended to pass, and with having "uttered" notes knowing them to be forged. Twelve jurymen were picked. Contrary to current opinion, which held that it would be difficult to impanel a jury because nearly everyone had a fixed position on Rathbun's culpability, the twelve were chosen in record time. Only one potential juror had been excused, and he by mutual consent of both counsels.

Chandler outlined the state's case, making it clear that the case revolved around the three $5,000 notes that Rathbun had mailed Evans from New York on April 13, 1836, and which he had asked Evans to keep secret and to exchange for three of Evans's own notes of the same amount. Rathbun's explanation for this transaction, it will be recalled, was that the three notes had been obtained for another purpose and that the endorsers might have been offended had they heard of their new use. Evans had done as Rathbun asked, keeping the three notes that were now alleged to be forged.

The notes that Evans had retained were entered in evidence. They each read:

$5,000   Buffalo, 15 April 1836

Four months after date I promise to pay to the order of Lewis F. Allen, Hiram Pratt, Sheldon Thompson, Ira A. Blossom, Joseph Clary, John W. Clark, Joseph Dart, Jr., Charles Townsend, Henry Morris, Thomas C. Love and Ebenezer Johnson, five thousand dollars at the Manhattan bank in the City of New York for value rece'd.

B. Rathbun.

Each note was endorsed on its reverse side with what purported to be the signatures of the eleven men named on the face.

Evans, the chief witness for the state, testified that Rathbun had visited him in Batavia on April 5, 1836, and had then gone on to New York. On April 19, he said, he received Rathbun's letter of April 13 asking him to change the notes. While this was a surprise, he had done as Rathbun requested, sending him three $5,000 notes of his own and retaining those with the "eleven endorsers" as security. Rathbun cashed Evans's notes with John Ward, a New York broker, and Evans got the notes back canceled after he had redeemed them from Ward.

Lewis F. Allen testified that his name on the notes was not his signature, although a good imitation. He went further and testified that Pratt's also was not genuine. (Pratt was ill and unable to attend.) Allen detailed the history of the three notes, first procured on April 8, 1835, and periodically renewed, for the last time on April 15, 1836. He admitted that the renewal process was casual. Ordinarily Rathbun sent him the notes; he signed his own name and attached a memorandum to the effect that "this is all right" and forwarded the notes to the ten other endorsers for their signatures.

Allen declared that Pratt had come to him late in June 1836 and told him both that another set of notes was in circulation in New York and that the Rathbuns may have tricked them into signing the extra set. Allen said that he had stoutly defended the Rathbuns, denying that possibility, and had gone immediately to discuss the matter with Lyman. Under questioning by the defense, he admitted that he had only written an enquiry to Lyman, and he was put in the position of accepting as plausible the possibility that the endorsers had been deceived into signing a second set of notes, even though he was adamant that he himself had not signed a duplicate set.

Further questioning upset other details of Allen's story. He admitted that he, not Rathbun, may have prepared the first set of notes but he maintained that the renewal sets were prepared by Rathbun and brought to him by Hawkins. He had had no dealings with Lyman on the transaction and denied ever having signed any of the series in blank, although some of the others testified that they might well have done so.

General Heman B. Potter, Lyman's former militia commander, testified that Clark and Pratt's signatures were not genuine. (Clark was in New York and unable to attend.) Under questioning, Potter bolstered the main defense contention that Lyman handled all the details of the Rathbun empire and that Benjamin "never received nor paid out" even when he had kept the Eagle. Potter further testified that most of Benjamin's time in the year before his failure was spent working away from Buffalo, arranging the omnibus line at Niagara and supervising the Cattaraugus sawmills and the Lockport quarries.

Over vigorous defense objections, the prosecution entered in evidence the thirty-two Rathbun letters and memoranda uncovered after the crash. It was forbidden, however, to enter into evidence the "six pieces of paper" in the form of endorsed but unfilled promissory notes found by Clary in Rathbun's desk.

Morris, Love, Blossom, Dart, and Townsend denied having signed more than the one series of Rathbun notes. Clary stated that he had signed two $1,000 and four $50 Rathbun notes in November and April besides the $5,000 series. Dr. Johnson contended that he had signed only the one set.

Using the context of the letters, the prosecution attacked the defense contention that Lyman did all the business. The letters were the major sensation of the trial, because their existence had not been widely known before that time. The prosecution emphasized their numerous ambiguities, which strongly suggested that Benjamin was aware of the forgeries, but no single document clearly proved this.

The state's chief witness was Hiram Pratt, who finally arrived under subpoena. He testified that he had signed only twelve notes in all (four sets of three $5,000 notes each). Pratt's examination brought out that he had received a letter from John Ward, of the New York brokerage firm of John Ward and Company, sometime after June 20, informing him that the Ward firm had $15,000 in Rathbun notes dated June 18 with Pratt's endorsement and asking him to accept two of the $5,000 notes for stock in the Niagara City Association. Pratt testified that he was astonished by this news. He said that he had replied to Ward that the only $15,000 in notes he remembered having endorsed were in the hands of the New York Life Insurance and Trust Company. Still he was not completely sure, he admitted, that the Ward notes were forgeries until after Blatchford's arrival on July 30. In the interim he had accepted two of the Ward notes in exchange for stock. He did not emphasize that he had made Rathbun provide for payment of these notes by giving them preferential treatment in the assignment.

After Pratt's testimony, the defense demanded dismissal of the indictment on technical grounds. It claimed that the prosecution had not proven that Rathbun had committed forgery as defined in the statutes, because there was property behind the notes. The defense stated as well that the only proof against him was the letter to Evans and that this letter proved that Evans knew that the notes were being diverted from their original purpose. The last argument was to challenge Genesee County jurisdiction on the ground that the offense, if any, was committed where the letter was mailed.

Judge Gardiner ruled that the first and second counts of the indictment were invalid and that the trial should continue on the third count only, which charged Rathbun with "uttering" forged paper with intent to defraud.

Henry K. Smith, his sharp eyes piercing the jury, began the defense contending that the great amount of publicity given the case had prejudiced his client's trial. He argued that the testimony of endorsers was affected by their own self-interest. A guilty verdict would help them recover monies in separate civil actions against Rathbun. He would prove, moreover, that under any circumstance Rathbun knew nothing of the details of his business.

The defense called an imposing list of witnesses, headed by Barker, and including many of the leading brokers and of Rathbun's own employees and confidential agents. Several defense witnesses testified that they had seen young Howlett imitate signatures. DeLong, Rathbun's general "outside agent," testified that he had seen Rathbun receive the packet of notes on April 4 just before he left for New York. The defense contended that Rathbun had not examined the packet, but accepted it and later took three of the notes it contained to send to Evans.

Every defense witness attested to Rathbun's good reputation. They described his orderly methods of business, but all stated that Lyman alone handled the details of the daily business affairs. A few, like Barker, admitted that they had heard rumors of the Rathbun bankruptcy years before in Otsego County, but that they had seen no reason to let these rumors affect their judgment of a man they knew to be honest and ethical.

Recalled by the defense, General Potter said that Palmer had written him from New York about the quantity of Rathbun paper afloat and that he had spoken to Rathbun about it. He said that the report was followed by a widespread rumor in Buffalo that Rathbun's credit was drying up, but that even so no one had any reason to suspect forgery.

When all the evidence had been presented, Sherwood summarized for the defense in a seven-hour address to the jury. He blasted the prosecution, and charged that its witnesses were actuated by pecuniary motives. Skinner closed for the prosecution with a plea, on the evidence of forgery, for the full penalty.

In a learned charge to the jury, Judge Gardiner clarified the question that had been raised about the motives of witnesses. In England, he said, the witnesses could not have testified and still have recovered monies under civil action, but New York law permitted them to do so.

Fifteen hours after the jury retired to deliberate, its foreman reported to the court that they could not agree. The newspapers said later that the jury stood nine to three for acquittal when it stopped balloting. Judge Gardiner thereupon discharged the jury and ordered Rathbun freed on $5,000 bail and returned to the custody of Erie County to be brought back for retrial at a later date.

Although the trial had not exactly vindicated Rathbun, it cheered his supporters. Rathbun had successfully taken a blast from the state's heaviest artillery. They believed that his chances for acquittal at a later trial were much enhanced.

14

The Wind Shifts

For a time Rathbun's trial distracted supporters and opponents from the strain of the general economic collapse. Jobless workers hoped that he might resume business activities and bring prosperity with him. On the other hand, his bitterest opponents could take some comfort in explaining away the depression by the actions of one dishonest man. Winter, a normally slack season, concealed the seriousness of the crash. As spring returned, it became harder to maintain that all would be well. Credit had dried up everywhere. In New York, financiers screamed for the repeal of the specie circular. Merchants hoped that the new president, Martin Van Buren, would be better served by his political instincts than Andrew Jackson had been.

To many anxious citizens, the solution seemed simple. All the trouble stemmed from Jacksonian tinkering with the Bank of the United States and with the system of credit that had sustained sales of western lands. If there were only more banks issuing more credit, all would be well. To make this point, two well-attended meetings were held in Buffalo shortly before Rathbun's trial. Resolutions were passed reflecting the popular belief that an immediate enlargement of the banking system was vital to the survival of the nation and of Buffalo. Resolutions, however, could not stop the force of the financial contraction.

In his cheerless cell in the Erie County jail, Rathbun was temporarily forgotten as disaster after disaster rocked the nation's financial structure.

The City Bank was the first in Buffalo to wobble. On March 6, 1837, it had suspended specie payments after one brokerage firm had taken $29,000 out of its vaults over the course of a few hectic days. Soon the other banks suspended payments. Then, on May 6, the state banking examiners, doubting the solvency of local banks, procured an injunction that ordered all three of them to cease all their operations immediately.

Four days later, New York City banks, all gasping under the pressure of unending demand for specie, suspended payments. On May 12, at Biddle's orders, the great Bank of the United States of Pennsylvania, its vaults supposedly filled with gold, suspended payments. Throughout the country, banks stopped paying specie, and the nation's financial machinery ground to a halt. The United States had fallen into the abyss of a depression.

Western New York's busiest people now were the lawyers surrounded by clamoring, debt-ridden clients. Friend turned against friend, and neighbor against neighbor, to demand the payment of debts and to raise the cash to pay their own debts and prevent the seizure of their property. Land contracts were voided for nonpayment, second and third mortgages, which burdened most property, were foreclosed, and, in their hurry to get cash and hold on to it, borrowers forced prices down and down.

Peter West, Buffalo's elderly town crier, was kept busy calling out auction announcements. Newspaper columns were filled with sale and foreclosure notices. Failures were the order of the day. Benjamin Fitch, the snuff-pinching auctioneer who kept the pockets of his blue marseilles coat loaded with the sharp tobacco concoction, was almost daily intoning, "Going, going, gone" over the stocks of retail stores that once had been brilliant successes but had failed as the economy contracted.

General David Burt, another of Lyman's old commanding officers and another whose name had been forged on many Rathbun notes, became the steadiest buyer at these bargain sales, snapping up quantities of all kinds of goods for resale in his gable-roofed Main Street store. Burt, who claimed that Rathbun owed him $31,000, repudiated the many forged notes in his name and kept enough assets liquid to remain among the few who could buy.

At the sale of the stock of the defunct Dexter and Masten wholesale dry goods store, boxes of what were described as "notions" were offered. Sewing goods had been scarce in Buffalo, and, without examining the boxes, Burt became caught up in the excitement of the bidding. Burt carried his $1,400 worth of purchases to his wagon, hauled them to his second-floor storeroom on the block and tackle that always hung conveniently over the street from a projecting roof timber, and discovered that he had bought enough hooks and eyes to supply Buffalo well into the next century. When Burt died many years later, these boxes were still in his warehouse.

Burt was the exception rather than the rule. Most of Buffalo's prestigious gentlemen of property were touched by the depression. Just a year before, Alanson Palmer bought the American Hotel from Rathbun and was building a palatial house. By the end of March 1837, however, the land broker announced bankruptcy in the *Commercial Advertiser* with a singular notice:

> Come and Get your pay
> Money I have none
> But such as I have
> I give unto thee

The good nature that served Palmer well in boom times kept him afloat for a time. He reasoned that if his debts did not exceed $250,000, the creditors would be satisfied within five years. Like others, however, Palmer did not reckon how far down the economy would sink before hitting bottom.

Dr. Ebenezer Johnson, the former mayor, tried to keep up appearances at receptions at his two-story brick Italianate villa called "the cottage." But around the house that Rathbun built for him, a former that carried him to fame in New York. Sheriff's sales menaced everyone: Robert Bush, Isaac Smith, John B. Macy, Guy E. Goodrich, Sylvester Mathews, Thomas Day, Daniel Girder, Ebenezer F. Norton, Samuel H. Macy, and others—the roll was endless as the days passed.

Many of Rathbun's properties were sold at auction late in 1837. In February 1838, Postmaster Dibble, who still held the $40,000 mortgage on the Eagle Tavern, sued in chancery court, and the Eagle was auctioned off at a sale in its own taproom to Isaac Harrington for only $52,525. This was about one-third the value Rathbun had placed upon it in his assignment.

During these confusing days, the Rathbun creditors fought among themselves for preference. One of Augustus Porter's letters candidly tells of this.

> The power of the assignees is very limited and I fear the whole property, so far as Rathbun had any interest, will be expended in the settlement except however the personal property, the avails of

which may probably pay off the first class of creditors. We intend to take immediate steps to foreclose on mortgages and provide all proper legal steps to secure ourselves and unembarrass the property.

To a large extent, especially at Niagara Falls, that is what happened. The Porters got their lands back and so did many of the others who had sold to Rathbun. DeVeaux, the storekeeper with an unbounded admiration of Rathbun's genius, bought most of the former Rathbun lands north of Niagara Falls village for a pittance, relative to what Rathbun had contracted to pay. Before DeVeaux' death, those lands had made him one of the richest men in the region.

Writing to Blatchford, who was then handling the affairs of the Bank of the United States, General Porter pleaded for an extension of the $300,000 debt that William B. Rochester and Company owed that institution, and recapitulated the serious situation that faced Niagara Frontier financing.

The first great reverse we had to overcome was the extraordinary failure of Benjamin Rathbun whose extensive dealings were deeply connected with and tainted a large proportion of the pecuniary operations of the people of Buffalo. By this failure our company not only sustained a direct loss of some $25,000 to $30,000 in his spurious paper then in our hands, but a still more severe one by the injuries inflicted on the debtors and to our operations generally and on the members individually, several of whom, Mr. Burt and Mr. Evans, sustained heavy private losses thereby.

Though the three Buffalo banks were eventually restored to partial functioning by the removal of the injunction, only Hiram Pratt, among their leaders, weathered the storm reasonably well financially. This was doubtless a factor in his choice as mayor by the new city council in 1838. But, at the same time, to a growing number of the disheartened and dispossessed, Pratt was becoming a symbol of the disaster, the man who had destroyed Rathbun and with him Buffalo's prosperity.

This development was largely due to an entirely new element injected into this scene of recrimination and wide-scale disaster. It was the appearance of the first issue of a tabloid newspaper, *The Buffalonian,* on Christmas Day 1837.

The new paper was edited by an unknown, who signed himself "George Arlington," but was later identified as Thomas L. Nichols, a twenty-two-year-old native of New Hampshire. The young man had wandered into Buffalo earlier in the year and had become the local correspondent of Bennett's *New York Herald,* as well as a reporter for the *Commercial Advertiser.*

Trained in the emerging school of journalistic sensationalism, Nichols saw a chance to capitalize the burning discontent hard times had brought to Buffalo's people. Overnight he became a vituperative exponent of Rathbun, perhaps because Nichols recognized that there was a vast reserve of sympathy among the sort of ordinary working folk whose livelihoods had depended on the Master Builder. That Rathbun was an innocent man and a victim of disloyal friends who had conspired to destroy him to seize the property he had accumulated, was the line Nichols took editorially: "I became acquainted with the facts of the [Rathbun] case and found that a clique of sharpers had entered into a deliberate and treacherous conspiracy to crush him and divide among themselves an estate over 2½ millions; and they have done it."

Nichols visited Rathbun in prison and was "struck with his noble appearance" and with his "calm endurance" over twenty-six months in jail. "I insisted that he get bail; his friends were incited to execution and he soon walked the streets and got kind greetings from those whose treachery and ingratitude made them ashamed."

Nichols presented the case in the most simplified moral absolutes: Rathbun and his supporters were splendid men; his prosecutors and opponents were scoundrels, cheats, drunkards, and libertines. Though the Rathbun case provided the day-by-day grist for his mill, he dug up every other available scandal reflecting on the local elite—except when it related to his heroes.

His paper became the talk of Buffalo. His editorials, directly and by word of mouth, nurtured the doubts about Rathbun's guilt. He appealed to those who wanted to believe that Rathbun was innocent and that freeing him would restore prosperity. As a matter of fact, Nichols's writings so helped to becloud the issues that they could never be clear again. A school of sentiment now developed that engagingly pictured the erstwhile rascal Rathbun as a martyred hero, the way in which some local folklore would remember him throughout the remainder of the century.

Nichols's targets for abuse were the assignees and the prominent public men who spoke as if there were no doubt about Rathbun's guilt. They all proved themselves to be thin-skinned where this novel journalism was concerned. Nichols records that an attempt to tar and feather him was thwarted by pure chance. In another act of intimidation, a group of men wrecked the small printing office where the *Buffalonian* was issued. Prominent people were found to be responsible. Henry P. Darrow, a leader of the First Presbyterian Church and the brother of Rathbun's former friend, Noyes, was one of those convicted. James Low, also found guilty, later gave an affidavit implicating a dozen leading citizens in the outrage. With strong language and harsh accusations, Nichols continued to provoke his elite targets. For Hiram Pratt, he employed his choicest invective.

> Did he pity Mrs. Rathbun when day by day her heart was breaking —when he was driving her brain to madness and dispair [*sic*], by his infernal malice against a man who had been his greatest benefactor? A craven, black-hearted hypocrite, were it not for this we might relent and pity him.

Betrayal and envy were the watchwords of Pratt's life, according to Nichols. He leveled one charge after another against Pratt. Pratt had always shown base ingratitude to his adopted father, Dr. Cyrenius Chapin. Pratt had once "peddled salts and senna in a little drug store" on Main Street where he had been set up by friends, but he returned their favor to him by endeavoring to "prosecute and scandalize" them. His base character had led him to try to cheat his brother's widow and orphans out of land they rightfully owned. He had settled the estate of another brother and got the property himself. He had used these ill-gotten funds to open an exchange office where he practiced usury and extortion. As a forwarder, he had cheated his partners out of their share.

Nichols now had established the context for Rathbun's problems in Pratt's pathologic personality. Pratt, he said, had flattered Rathbun so persistently that he won his support, and that Rathbun's influence then resulted in his selection as cashier of the Bank of Buffalo. But Pratt then violated an agreement to give Rathbun the use of his credit at Geneva, New York. He injured Rathbun "because he hated and envied him." He endorsed Rathbun's paper and later declared that it was forged. He knew his name had been used illegally, but had countenanced it, for it allowed him to scheme to control Rathbun's estate. He had secured Rathbun's assignment, and then "in violation of a solemn promise" had a man record the assignment.

Pratt, Nichols charged, went to Niagara Falls with Rathbun, but had left a man in Buffalo to circulate rumors that would frighten

Rathbun into staying away while plotting went on in the city against him. Then he had advised Rathbun to flee, and later had tried to get him to plead guilty. Pratt then had pressed Mrs. Rathbun to persuade her husband to plead guilty. Also, Pratt had induced young Howlett to run away, because he knew the truth about Pratt's notes, and then assisted Rathbun Allen to escape from prison. Pratt had cheated the Rathbun creditors.

There was much more of this, including the charge that Pratt had plotted to oust Goodrich as president of the Bank of Buffalo to get his place. Finally, Nichols stated that Pratt had removed Stephen G. Austin as counsel for the bank and had appointed Stow, Rathbun Allen's lawyer, to the place, and had then paid Austin $9,000 to $10,000 "to prevent disclosure of corruptions which might have sent him (Pratt) to prison." If a tenth of these charges lodged somewhere in the public mind, it alone could damage a man's reputation.

Nichols made others suffer similarly. David Burt, who was pictured on one occasion as giving a party in his Niagara Square mansion and pretentiously wearing his brigadier general's uniform while he sat on a sofa urging liquor on his guests, also received rough treatment. Burt is a man, Nichols said,

> without one single great, or noble, or generous quality; disgraced by acts of petty meanness which every decent man must despise; a bear in his manners; and a loafer in his habits and conversation. He holds his present place in society, solely by reason of the wealth acquired by a life of meanness.

Clary, "who sat on Rathbun's golden throne," Nichols charged to be one of those who urged Rathbun to go on expanding his business, although Rathbun had wanted to stop a year earlier. Now Clary was using Pratt, Evans, Allen, and Love for his own ends, and they were all trying to keep the Rathbun property and pay no dividends. He accused Clary, along with Fillmore and Pratt, of getting wealthy administering Rathbun's property.

Nichols seemed to be deliberately courting a martyr's role. He reported that Henry W. Rogers, who had succeeded Henry K. Smith as district attorney, tried three times to get him indicted. If this was Nichols's wish, it was eventually granted. A grand jury was empaneled, which indicted him for libels on Pratt, General Porter, Horatio Stow, and others.

In a self-revealing book, *Journal in Jail,* Nichols in 1840 recounted his trial, conviction, and punishment for the Stow libel. He was tried at the June term in 1839 before Court of Common Pleas Judge James Stryker, whom Nichols described as "a man notorious for his debauched habits and pecuniary unscrupulousness." Nichols claimed that to get Stryker to preside, "certain persons" paid for his return from Washington and for his board in Buffalo during the trial.

Rathbun's lawyer, the voluble and tricky Sherwood, did his best to defend Nichols, but the evidence of libel was beyond questioning. District Attorney Rogers assisted by John Skinner, who had helped prosecute Rathbun in Genesee County, won a conviction on a charge of malicious libel.

Nichols praised Rathbun in direct proportion to his damnation of the members of the local elite. "There are few men of this age whose fate and genius are so remarkable as those of Benjamin Rathbun," Nichols wrote eulogistically. His motives, Nichols declared, were good —to save his brother and nephews from disgrace, to save those working for him, to protect his creditors and the city "of which he is the architect; for Rathbun made all of Buffalo that is worth looking at." He spoke bitterly of the "treachery of the scoundrels who fawned on him"; Rathbun was the most honest man of the group. "These men demoralized Buffalo. No city has such a low tone in moral sentiment or in terms of honor and principles of justice so little regarded."

Indignation meetings were held in behalf of the convicted Nichols, one of them at the Court House, where both Sherwood and Evert Van Buren gave inflammatory speeches. Those present hissed Pratt and demanded his recall as mayor and the resignation of his henchmen. A benefit performance by a theatrical company raised enough money to pay Nichols's fine and get him out of jail near the end of his term. But even Nichols eventually was found to have his own price. With engaging candor, he admitted in the closing chapter of his book that the "clique" offered him a bribe of $750 in cash and the quashing of suits against the *Buffalonian* if he would leave town—and he accepted the offer! He justified himself on the ground that they had framed evidence against him and that they would have prosecuted his friends if he had remained.

With public sentiment aroused by the *Buffalonian* and leading citizens arguing publicly and bitterly about Rathbun, it was now evident that no local jury would convict Rathbun unless the evidence was overwhelming. Rogers, the new district attorney, decided to rid the books of unprovable charges. At the July 1837 grand jury session, Rogers got authority to *nolle prosse* nine of the 1836 indictments and one obtained much later. Four indictments were continued for trial at the January 1838 term. The court also commissioned two Texans to interrogate Lyman officially, if they could find him, in behalf of the defense.

Rathbun was free throughout this period. The assignees had not acted to dispossess Mrs. Rathbun from the family home. There, preparing for a later career as a hotel keeper that he could not then have anticipated, Rathbun helped his wife take care of her many boarders. Moses Rathbun and his third wife were likewise keeping their Oak Street home filled with boarders, sometimes as many as thirty at a time. Maria, Lyman's wife, was renting rooms in her Eagle Street house. Later, the well-educated Maria turned her front parlor into a classroom and became a full-time teacher.

Rathbun himself occasionally strolled through the streets, and was recognized by most people. Indeed he had obtained a new local celebrity. But despite much kindly encouragement, people with money feared to trust him. Moreover, with the indictments in two counties hanging over him, he could do nothing toward reestablishing his career.

15

The Penalty

Incessant and emotional, public dissatisfaction at the endless legal technicalities that had delayed Rathbun's trial forced authorities in the summer of 1838 to the realization that either the case must be brought to trial immediately, or the indictments must be quashed. Time had worked in Rathbun's behalf. The *Buffalonian* had also done its work. It had helped cause tensions among Rathbun's foes, so that they no longer presented a solid front.

Rathbun and his lawyers had managed to give the public impression that they were ready for trial, if only the missing witnesses, principally Lyman and Rathbun Allen, could be found and brought back to testify. Because this appeared to be impossible, they were on safe ground. It was known that Lyman was in Texas somewhere. The younger man had disappeared, though rumors had him somewhere in the South, most likely, it was said, New Orleans. They had been working every trick in the lawyer's repertoire to delay trial and, so far, had won postponements at every session of court in both Erie and Genesee counties.

Writing to a correspondent in March, Colonel Blossom described what happened at the Batavia Oyer and Terminer to which he had been summoned as a witness: "[Rathbun] by dint of hard swearing again got the trial postponed. According to his own declaration his rights would be endangered should he go to trial without the testimony of his brother Lyman who he had recently ascertained is in Texas."

Early in July, Rathbun's lawyers applied to the Batavia court for the appointment of a new commissioner to take testimony from Lyman. Rathbun's application declared that Chandler as district attorney had made no attempt to get this testimony, and he cited the fact that the court in Erie County had delayed trial for that purpose. The court agreed to a further delay and authorized John Birdsall, a Texas jurist, to take testimony from Lyman.

Meanwhile, on July 2, 1838, Rathbun's case was again called before the Erie County Court of Oyer and Terminer with Judge Nathan Dayton of Lockport presiding. Dayton, who had succeeded Judge Gardiner that February, was an enigma to the Rathbun lawyers. They suspected that he was opposed to them, even though he had granted earlier postponements in both counties.

District Attorney Rogers, whom Nichols had described as being of "mediocre abilities," having "inordinate vanity," and being "dogmatic and overbearing but servile to superiors," headed the prosecution. Appearing with him (and clearly indicating by his presence the political importance now attached to finishing the Rathbun case with a conviction) was the famous Samuel Beardsley, one-time neighbor and friend of the Rathbuns in Otsego County and now New York State attorney general. Beardsley personally represented Gov. William L. Marcy. The same Buffalo lawyers, Smith, Van Buren, and Sherwood, who had appeared in Rathbun's behalf at Batavia, made up his counsel now.

Smith's appeal to have the case delayed again was now buttressed by a letter from Lyman to Benjamin and other letters from Lyman to Benjamin's counsel. Posted from an undisclosed location in Texas on May 29, 1838, the one to Benjamin suggested that Lyman retained an enduring, strong attachment to his brother. Lyman said in the letter that a courier had brought him word that a man was waiting to take his testimony, and that he was now on his way to speak to the man.

> I immediately started although as I was situated it was a very difficult time for me to leave, but believing the urgent necessity of the case nothing short of death would stop me from doing my duty; and, depend on it, the balance of the part I am to act in this business shall be attended to as prompt as if you were personally present to keep giving it a job. I shall go ahead.

Lyman related that he had had to forego valuable land operations, and that he had been riding in rainstorms and swimming in swollen creeks to get to the emissary. He had caught a bad cold and had a "blind headache," but that he would ride on the many miles that would be necessary to give his testimony. He promised to "write again soon" and signed himself "yours for ever."

Though it was not emphasized at the time, his remark about acting a part suggests, if we wish to read it in a literal way, that his earlier actions, including his flight from Buffalo, were part of a prepared drama, or at the least, a drama in which the players instinctively knew their parts.

Evert Van Buren advised the court that he was filing two letters that he had received from Lyman. One, dated May 2, said that he (Lyman) reviewed some of the issues that were key to the Batavia trial. Of the notes with eleven endorsers, the most important, he wrote:

> Should it appear on trial that the endorsements on said notes are not genuine, I know B. Rathbun was entirely ignorant of their being anything wrong with the notes, for I handed the notes to him myself when he left for New York Monday 4th April as genuine endorsements. Supposing myself they were so; and told him what I suppose the fact to be that they were a set endorsed for the purpose of renewing others [of the] same amount. [I] referred him to the circumstances of sending two sets to Albany (by my request) to overtake Mr. Love and get his endorsements as he was to be absent for some time.

The other letter, dated May 28, the same day as his personal note to Benjamin, informed Van Buren that Lyman had that day for the first time learned of the interrogatories that Judge Birdsall had been commissioned to administer to him and that he was leaving immediately to make the long, arduous trip to answer them.

After listening to these communications and supporting arguments, Judge Dayton ruled that sufficient time had probably already elapsed to obtain the interrogatories and that the case should go to trial.

The trial proceeded on one of the indictments still standing. It was based on alleged forgeries of the names of Martin Daley and General Mathews as endorsers of three notes of $2,000 each that Rathbun had used in January 1836 as collateral for advances on a contract to build stores for Joy and Webster, the forwarding firm. Rathbun had had a number of other Daley notes, obtained either through the C. Taintor brokerage firm or from Daley himself, for whom he had been building a new home in Pearl Street.

With public feeling so polarized, it proved difficult to assemble an impartial jury. After protracted efforts, the jury box was filled, and the trial proceeded with many of the same witnesses and evidence that had been presented at Batavia a year and a half before.

One sharp difference, however, was soon apparent. Judge Dayton was not the mild jurist that Judge Gardiner had been. Cross-examining a witness too vehemently, Defense Attorney Sherwood discovered this to his inconvenience. He was suddenly brought before the bench on a charge of contempt, and was sentenced to two days in jail. This precluded his presence at the trial's conclusion.

After all the fireworks, to the chagrin of the prosecution, the jury on July 6 returned a verdict of acquittal. Rathbun's lawyers and supporters held an impromptu celebration in the courthouse square to show their jubilation.

But Rathbun himself could not participate. Not until September 10 could he could give $5,000 bail on one of the remaining indictments. The bond was being furnished by Buchanan, the loyal house painter who had put up bail for Rathbun Allen. Another $5,000 on a second indictment was furnished by Samuel Haines, the carpenter. Rathbun's artisan friends alone seem to have remained constant.

The great break in the Rathbun case had occurred before this, although it was not recognized at the time. Under pressure from New York State authorities, who were responding to tips they had received, Louisiana authorities had picked up Rathbun Allen in New Orleans. Governor Marcy issued an order for his extradition, which Louisiana honored. Allen, who would languish two months in the summer heat of a New Orleans jail, was finally bundled aboard a ship in irons, taken first to New York and then to Buffalo, chained to his captor, a man named Burr.

Pro-Rathbun feeling was so strong in Buffalo by then that Burr, after depositing his prisoner in the jail, found himself on the street in the center of a threatening mob, the target of rotten eggs and other unsavory missiles. Burr had to flee across the square and into the Eagle Tavern. The crowd would have followed him there had not a constable raced up and rescued him. Horatio Stow had managed to retain his appointment as Allen's lawyer. It is probable that this was managed through Orange Allen, the youth's father and Rathbun's brother-in-law, who, according to Nichols, had turned against Benjamin with a deadly hate for getting his son into such desperate trouble.

Nichols declared that Allen was being held incommunicado in the jail, and permitted to see only Stow, his father, and District Attorney Rogers. He claimed that although Stow had often said publicly that Allen would never be convicted on any of the many indictments standing against him, he and Rogers so terrified the mild-mannered clerk, who was then only twenty-four years old, that he finally agreed to turn state's evidence in return for future immunity.

As Rathbun's appearance before the bar of Genesee County approached, Nichols opened the floodgates of the vituperation that was soon destined to take him to jail for libel. Not only was he slashing with his violent verbal attacks at all the state's prospective witnesses but he also began to pound Judge Dayton. His first approach was in the form of an open letter to the jurist, asking for his resignation. Perhaps Nichols and Rathbun's lawyers thought this might be effective. But it is hard to believe that anyone could expect the judge to read with equanimity that he possessed "matchless prejudice" and that he was "treated with contempt by the bar." These were actually mild charges compared with what Nichols had in store for him.

According to Nichols, Rathbun Allen was hustled to Batavia secretly and at night, in a closed carriage. His presence created an entirely new situation when Rathbun's case, the third count of the original Genesee County indictment, was called on September 26.

Tall, commanding Attorney General Beardsley not only was present but also had prevailed upon District Attorney Isaac A. Verplanck to let him run the prosecution. Verplanck and Chandler assisted him. Rathbun's Buffalo lawyers were the same men as before, although they had again added a Batavia attorney for the trial.

The trial was in turmoil much of the time, Judge Dayton rejecting objections by Rathbun's vocal lawyers and occasionally threatening to jail them for contempt.

Rathbun Allen, as a prosecution witness, testified that he had lived with Benjamin Rathbun from 1832 until 1836, and that he had served first as clerk in the dry goods store and then for two years handled only financial matters. In fact, it appeared that no one could have been closer to Benjamin except Lyman. He declared that he was in New York in April 1836 with Rathbun and that his uncle had three or four sets of notes, all identical, one of which was to go to the New York Life Insurance and Trust Company to renew the notes that company held. His uncle told him, Allen testified, to sign Evans's name on eight or twelve pieces of paper taken from his trunk. Rathbun Allen said that he had done this, and he also admitted that one of the forged notes shown him in court was one that he himself remembered signing. After he executed these forgeries, Allen testified, his uncle had said that "the other notes, if used, must be used very carefully."

Doubtless by prearrangement, at the conclusion of this damning testimony, Allen was released on $4,000 bail furnished by his father and was back in Buffalo, to all intents and purposes a free man again.

The defense's introduction of the interrogatories, taken by Lyman under oath in Texas, came as an anticlimax to Allen's admissions. Lyman carefully absolved Benjamin of all knowledge of the forgeries. At the same time, he avoided admitting his own guilt. In many sections, his answers seemed to be almost exact quotations from parts of Benjamin's extended public statement of February 1837.

> I was the financial agent of B. Rathbun. . . . His pecuniary arrangements necessary to carry on his general business in 1834–35 and 1836 and up to the time of the failure were transacted by me and under my special control. B. Rathbun had no management, or special control of his financial affairs. Notes, checks and drafts were signed and endorsed by B. Rathbun in all the variety of shapes necessary for use, and were left with me for all the purposes I had occasion to use in conducting the financial operations of the concern in all the variety of forms necessary in so extensive an establishment.

Lyman declared that Benjamin left for New York on April 4, 1836, and took two sets of notes with eleven endorsers (three $5,000 notes in each set), endorsed with the names of the eleven including Morris. He said that he had given one set to Benjamin on April 2 to use in renewing the Trust Company loan, putting this in his trunk with other papers. The second set he had given his brother on Monday, April 4, while he was busy talking with Robert Bush.

> I put a wrapper around them and told him to leave the notes with D. E. Evans or other responsible person for Mr. Janes, the New York agent, wrote me pressing notes for notes made by someone other than Benjamin Rathbun. I told Benjamin Rathbun to be careful where [they were] used. He took the notes in an envelope without opening it and put them in his pocketbook.
>
> In November or December 1835, after T. C. Love had left for Congress, I got Benjamin Rathbun to fill six notes of $5,000 each for eleven endorsers and send them to Love for him to endorse and return. He did so and sent them to Love in Albany care of A. H. Tracy [then state senator] and they were endorsed by Love and

returned to Rathbun. He turned them over to me and asked me to get others endorsed whenever needed. He never saw the notes afterward till I handed them to him in April.

Referring to the sets of allegedly forged notes that Benjamin had had, under cross-examination Lyman stated: "I supposed them [the signatures of the endorsers] to be genuine and delivered them to Benjamin Rathbun as genuine. If any of them were not, it was not possible for him to know it."

Lyman denied categorically that Benjamin had given him general instructions on finances from time to time. He also denied any knowledge of a definite arrangement for securing the endorsements.

These generally unsatisfactory interrogatories, with their evasions and denials, fell short of substantiating Rathbun's defense, especially when they were seen in relation to Rathbun Allen's direct testimony.

The climax was slow in building. James L. Barton, who as a justice of the peace acted as Buffalo's police magistrate, was one of the witnesses. He was strongly antagonistic to Rathbun. Even before the first trial, Barton had told many people, at least according to Nichols, that Rathbun was a "damned villain who ought to be hung."

Now the argumentative Evert Van Buren grappled with Barton. He evoked long-slumbering echoes of the Morgan case. He called attention to Barton's willingness to testify in the Rathbun affair, and compared it to his refusal to appear when fellow Masons were on trial. Later in the day, outside the courthouse, near the Eagle Tavern in Batavia, the two men met and Barton struck Van Buren with his fist. District Attorney Rogers swung at Van Buren too, calling him a "damned rascal." Van Buren fended them off with his cane, finally breaking it over Rogers's head. That Van Buren, who was known to have recently been ill, was attacked by two men was more ammunition for Nichols.

In this tense atmosphere, Attorney General Beardsley summarized the state's strong case. Sherwood spoke for Rathbun for five full hours. His summary was bitter and vituperative. He wove into it remarks about the bias of Judge Dayton. He referred to the "Jesuitical Hiram Pratt and that knave Lewis F. Allen." He presented from every angle the defense contention that Rathbun was being prosecuted to conceal the fact that others wished to divide his property among themselves. Smith spoke, too, and set out the case that no forgeries had occurred at all. He declared that the "endorsers had 15,000 good reasons" for swearing that Rathbun's notes, which, he said, they themselves had endorsed, were forged.

The jury did not deliberate very long. When it returned to the courtroom, its verdict was guilty.

Immediately after the jury's report, on October 3, Judge Dayton sentenced Rathbun to the maximum term permissible under the verdict: five years at hard labor in Auburn Prison.

Rathbun's lawyers entered notice of appeal, but Judge Dayton refused to entertain a request for bail and directed that Rathbun be taken to the prison.

He had a few minutes with his wife in the jail before he left Batavia that same day. Mrs. Rathbun was composed and firm. She was accompanied by her friends, two respectable ladies who had never been in a jail before.

Genesee County Sheriff Wilder was more courteous than Rathbun's old associate, the bluff Lester Brace, had been. He and his son drove Rathbun to Auburn, unshackled, in a private carriage. When they got there, he let Rathbun stop briefly at the American Hotel to speak to some friends. Only then did he turn him over to officials at the prison.

A brief autobiographical profile was taken when he entered. It established the former "Master Builder and Architect" as: forty-seven years old; a native of Windham, Connecticut; a merchant by occupation; light in complexion; five feet, six and one-quarter inches tall. The heavy stone walls now swallowed him up, and he became as faceless as the official profile that was retained in the files of the state penal authority. Moreover, he became voiceless. Auburn was then being operated under an experimental and oppressive system that absolutely forbade prisoners speaking except to answer an overseer.

The night Rathbun left for prison, Evans entertained the whole prosecution staff at a dinner, which became a raucous celebration. Most of those attending, according to Nichols's social note on the affair, got drunk. Later, in the Eagle Tavern bar, Evans paid for his revelry by being on the losing end of a fist fight with former Genesee County Sheriff Townsend. Evans, who had casually told his own friends that he would have been glad to pay a $50,000 bribe to see Rathbun convicted, now accused the former lawman of having bribed jurors at the first trial in Batavia. Townsend retaliated by blacking Evans's eyes, knocking him down, and kicking him.

The conviction shocked Rathbun and his friends. They had been confident, after the Buffalo acquittal, that he would never be convicted and that the remaining charges against him would have to be dropped. Until Rathbun Allen appeared at the trial, they had never contemplated the possibility that the young man might testify against his uncle.

His lawyers continued their attempts to get the case reviewed, but Rathbun, with the composure that had always characterized him, adjusted himself as best he could to prison life.

An unnamed Buffalo resident saw Rathbun in Auburn Prison in December of that year, according to a story in the *Commercial Advertiser*. He was dressed in soiled, coarse prison clothing, and his small but dignified frame was observed bent over a table shaping breech blocks for joiners' planes, the job to which he had been assigned. He worked dexterously, the story said, never raising his eyes from the task. His face was covered with a week's beard above which his high forehead projected like marble.

Alice Rathbun lived for several years in their Buffalo home with their moody son, Loomis. Loomis, raised in wealth and success, adjusted poorly to the family's reversal of fortune. Shunned by the sons and daughters of the "best families," Loomis grew morose. He looked for new friends among tavern roughs, and found solace in drink. This new trial added to Alice's worries about money and to her anguish while waiting for Benjamin's release. Acquaintances made a point to keep up their normal social contact for a time, but Alice made no more effort to welcome them. Gradually the visits dwindled.

The state supreme court finally agreed to review Rathbun's case, but the review made no difference. The decision was that the conviction was proper and that the sentence was legal.

The defense's last recourse, therefore, was an appeal to the governor, William H. Seward, of Auburn, the former leader of the Anti-Masonic movement and Whig associate of Weed who commenced in office in 1839. Rathbun's friends were not sure that he would get fair treatment from Seward, who had close friends and political allies among those most intent on seeing Rathbun in prison.

To overcome these influences, the application for gubernatorial review and the appeal for executive clemency were buttressed by a petition with several thousand signatures, among them many of the most prominent names in Buffalo and in the state. Because the state supreme court had already reviewed the case, the appeal was not based on the claim that the conviction was unjust on the evidence, but that the absence of Rathbun witnesses, especially Lyman, had precluded full presentation of his defense.

Seward let this application lie on his desk as long as he could. Finally, on May 27, 1840, he issued a long executive message reviewing the case and explaining his rejection of the petition. Much of the message was merely a paraphrase of the prosecution's summary. Seward's narrative of Rathbun's descent into disgrace read like the version of the affair that would over the years become, for those who rejected Nichols's version, the full truth of the matter.

> In carrying on this extensive business, the practice of forgeries was adopted, at first in a very small way, to save the protest of some important paper. Afterward his cashier, Lyman Rathbun, emboldened by success, resorted to similar proceedings as often as he became straitened for funds, making sometimes false checks and sometimes false endorsements. Sometimes quite an amount of spurious paper accumulated in the brokers' offices, and at other periods all was taken up. The necessity for forged paper increased so much that Lyman Rathbun and Rathbun Allen, the prisoner's nephew and clerk, were initiated and were all busily employed in making, selling and negotiating forged paper.
>
> The extent of these forgeries is not known, but it is notorious that the names of thirty-five persons and firms were habitually used as drawers and endorsers, and that it was impossible for the prisoner himself to distinguish between his genuine and spurious paper, without reference to private marks in his books. It is now well understood that the amount of forged paper remaining unpaid when the prisoner was arrested exceeded one and one-half millions of dollars. Including what was issued for the various purposes of renewal, postponement and payment, the whole amount forged must have been more than twice that sum. It is believed that these forgeries surpassed in boldness and perseverance all similar offenses in this and every other country.

Seward expressed doubt whether the prisoner had given exclusive management of his finances to his brother or that the forgeries were done without his knowledge. For Seward, Rathbun's own admissions were inconsistent with his innocence. He told a witness, Seward recalled, that he discovered the forgeries, but was so extended that he had to continue them. Seward then cited Rathbun Allen's testimony, and Benjamin Rathbun's own records proved he kept copies of the spurious notes to offer proof that Rathbun himself "was for a long period, if not from the commencement, the master spirit in the conduct of the forgeries as well as the only party benefited by them."

The case Seward presented was conclusive and damning. Moreover, he wrote, Rathbun still had six indictments against him, which needed to be prosecuted if he were freed from prison. Clearly Seward believed that if the state went to the time and expense of trying Rathbun on those indictments, he would simply end up in a cell at Auburn, anyway.

Seward's rejection was discouraging, but Rathbun's friends were persistent. They were back again before the governor in 1842, this time with an application for a pardon. The application was documented with every possible bit of information that could be obtained, as well as with character testimonials from persons in all walks of life. It was signed by thousands of responsible citizens of Buffalo and Batavia, and it bore the endorsements of fifty members of the state legislatuie.

Undaunted by this show of influence and authority, on May 5, 1842, Governor Seward rejected this second appeal, supporting his position with reference to his 1840 message and to the fact that no new information had emerged since that time to change his earlier decision. William C. Bouck was next elected governor, succeeding Seward in 1843. New appeals were now directed to him, almost up to the time that Rathbun's sentence expired. But he, too, refused to act. Rathbun remained in Auburn prison, uncomplainingly doing the daily tasks assigned to him. Auburn wardens and guards considered him a model prisoner, because of his pleasant personality and his obedience. Furthermore, he distinguished himself through his unending work with the prison sick, which, according to a contemporary *New York Herald* writer, "gained him many friends and a popularity never before experienced by an individual in his position." Even the most hardened criminals were said to respect him. It was almost as if incarceration was a kind of release. Freed finally of the vast obligations his passion for success had thrust on him, he found some relief in the anonymity, the routine, and the constraint of prison life.

As the end of his sentence neared, there was widespread speculation as to what Rathbun would do. Although the indictments still remained outstanding, there was a general conviction that they would —and should—not be pressed.

Buffalo newspapers continued to reflect an amazingly persistent undercurrent of hope, among artisans and laborers in particular, that Rathbun's return might bring back the predepression boom. Exactly how this magic could be effected by a former felon with a series of untried indictments against him they failed to say.

The *Hartford* (Connecticut) *Courant*, however, had a more realistic local correspondent who wrote near the end of Rathbun's term, "None think he will give a new impulse to the prosperity of the place. The truth is there is little or no diversity of sentiment in regard to the effect of his operations." This writer interpreted local sentiment among the city's business and civic elites to be that Rathbun had wreaked an incalculable injury to the city, and that he had been a selfish monopolist and reckless speculator, who set in motion the forces that overwhelmed and crushed the city's business. When he fell, it was said, the explosion caused wreckage and desolation from which it had taken years to recover.

Two rumors gained wide currency. One was that based on his prison experience Rathbun would become a physician and quietly practice medicine. Another was that he planned to move to Wisconsin and settle on a farm at Jefferson Prairie. The fact is that Rathbun did not know what to do except to return to Alice. She awaited his release in her boardinghouse. No longer in their extensive Main Street mansion, she had removed to a cheaper, unglamorous Exchange Street building, where she cooked and cleaned for boarders alongside what hired help she could afford to employ.

When he was freed on October 3, 1843, five years to the day from the time of his commitment, he boarded a train on the new railroads, which that very year finally linked Buffalo to the East, and returned to his family. He was uncertain of the future, and though healthy and fit, he looked older than his fifty-two years. Much of the fire and confidence of his younger days that had carried him into middle age had been burned away in prison.

16

The Return

The Buffalo to which Rathbun returned late in 1843 had changed considerably. People still grumbled about "hard times," but they had accommodated themselves to the new conditions, and they were going on with their lives as though money had always been difficult to obtain.

The city was larger, and new residential sections extended into many areas that had been vacant and even wild land. There were many new, and especially foreign, faces on the streets. Despite the economic contraction, many German immigrants had arrived in the late 1830s. Faces familiar to Rathbun were older, and some of his peers had passed away while he was enduring the living death of prison.

Physically the central business district appeared much the same except that the once-new buildings of the 1834–36 boom times looked more drab and dirty, and the older buildings had become shabbier. The depression curtailed not only care of existing structures but also construction of costlier ones. The only new commercial structures were jerry-built one-and two-story stores. Rathbun might well have surmised that he could have done a better job as a builder. All the banks were now gone, including the Commercial Bank and the Bank of Buffalo.

Fewer Indians were seen on the streets, for the Senecas had been dispossessed finally from their local reservation just north of the city, and whites were planning new land developments there. Stores were busy. Prices on clothing and almost everything else were low by pre-depression standards, but shoppers dressed more shabbily than they had in halcyon days. The smoke and noise of the coal-fired railroad trains added a new element to the business district, soiling the clothes of passing shoppers and frightening horses.

The canal was carrying more freight and passengers to and from the Great Lakes. The harbor was full of boats, partly as a consequence of the invention of grain elevators, which had greatly speeded wheat handling. Now grain transshipment and storage were on their way to becoming Buffalo's main business. The city was poised to become for a time the world's busiest grain port. Stagecoaches were fewer, having, in the 1840s and 1850s, been partly supplanted by railroads, but many of those still operating were recognizable by color and design as former Rathbun vehicles, though Rathbun's personal logo on their doors had been painted over long ago.

Rathbun was able to slip back quietly into these old-new scenes almost unnoticed. Although the newspapers had been printing items about his release for some time, relatively few people recognized him on the street. No one had any notion what he planned to do. Certainly no grand celebration marked his homecoming, even though a legend to that effect would enjoy a place in local folklore for many years. Not until the day after his return did it became generally known that he was free. When the word spread that he was back, many of his old supporters and employees did call upon him to pay their respects.

One fanciful story, written by an English traveler in 1849 and repeated as recently as 1930 in the United States, claimed that a civic holiday was declared upon his return, and that workers and professional people throughout the city contributed one day's pay to his financial rehabilitation. Yet there was much soul searching in progress, particularly among those who had most bitterly prosecuted him. An unspoken resolve took form to forget the past and let the outstanding indictments go by default. The feeling was general that Rathbun had paid the debt he owed society.

The simplicity of his return was emphasized in one of the few stories of that event, which appeared in the *Buffalo Gazette:* "Benjamin Rathbun returned to this city on Tuesday night and was yesterday visited by many of our citizens. He appeared to be in excellent health and spirits; in fact, we never saw him look so well as he now appears."

Rathbun Allen, who had never been prosecuted on the charges against him, was working as a clerk in a Buffalo firm and was boarding with his grandfather, Moses. Soon after Benjamin's return, he had a long talk with his nephew. He forgave Allen for having given the testimony that sent him to jail. To prove his sincerity, he welcomed Allen back as a boarder in his home.

About the same time, Lyman died in Texas. It was many months before Maria learned that she had been widowed. She had been very circumspect about their relationship during his years of exile. Though she had heard occasionally from Lyman, she never discussed him publicly. But after his death she permitted the Buffalo city directories to list her as "widow of Lyman."

A Texas memoir, Eph M. Daggett's *The Recollections of the War of the Moderators and the Regulators,* contains the only known record of Lyman's last years. Daggett, whose chief interest was in the warring factions that flourished in Shelby County before Texas gained statehood, describes incidentally some of the odd characters whom the author had met there in April 1837. One of these odd characters, imperfectly recalled, was a man known locally as "Brewster," who operated a ferry across the Sabine River at Brewster's Bluff. After they became acquainted, this man admitted to Daggett that he was "Simon Rathburn," as Daggett records it, the "great forger" of Buffalo.

"Simon," obviously Lyman, told Daggett that he had escaped from Buffalo by riding fast horses until they were exhausted, then procuring fresh ones and continuing unquestioned on his way, because of the credibility of his story that he was pursuing a man. He carried much money with him. Although this story cannot explain the presence of Lyman's nine huge trunks in Louisville, it may have been partly true. Lyman had help in his hurried escape from someone, but we shall never know who it was.

Lyman's first stop, according to Daggett, had been Grand Gulf, Mississippi, where a sister lived with a common law husband, a jeweler for whom she had abandoned her lawful husband in Buffalo. The sister took pity on Lyman, although neither he nor Benjamin had communicated with her after her adulterous escapade. The sister's new husband helped him select a partner, and Lyman and the partner crossed the Red River near Nachitoches, Louisiana, and then the Sabine at Myrich's Ferry. The partner helped him evade pursuers and built up a tale that Lyman, now "Brewster," was merely being pursued for a murder he had committed, a perfectly legitimate reason for being in the Texas of that time. Lyman bought headrights on the Sabine at Brewster's Bluff and located there.

Lyman acknowledged the forgeries to Daggett. Lyman stated that the Buffalo forgeries were only revealed because a Lake Erie steamboat was delayed by fog, which prevented him and Benjamin from mailing out the drafts that would have closed out the business of the forgeries without anyone being the wiser. But when it was found out, he quoted Lyman as having said, genuine endorsers of their notes, who stood to lose nothing even when their names had been forged, became frightened and denied their own signatures. This was, of course, all very dubious. It suggests that Lyman spent much of his last years inventing exonerating and self-serving myths about his role in the affair, perhaps to ease his conscience as he thought of his brother doing time in prison.

✎✲◉᷀

All of Benjamin's properties had been sold while he was in prison. Clary had handled the settlement of the huge estate. The terrific strain of this massive task was said to have so exhausted the lawyer that it caused his death in 1842, only a short time after his work was finally approved by the chancery court.

The assignees discovered early in the liquidation that they had made a significant miscalculation when they agreed under the pressure of impending riot to pay the workmen in full. They had, of course, done what was just, albeit reluctantly. But together with their own very substantial charges for salaries, lawyers' fees, and their sacrifice of the great bulk of all the real properties without recovering any of Rathbun's equity, that expense left only enough to pay half of what was owed to preferred creditors. Nothing at all was left over to pay to others.

Some of these debts that could not be paid were enormous. Horace Janes claimed nearly $400,000; the Paterson Bank had judgments exceeding $108,000; Joshua B. Wood and Theodore P. Bogart, New York brokers, had obtained judgments of nearly $600,000. Even Rathbun's father-in-law, Thaddeus Loomis, claimed nearly $1,500, quite possibly a relic of the even more distant Otsego County debacle.

The almost universal repudiation of the signed endorsements on Rathbun notes meant that relatively few were paid in part, let alone in full. Some holders of repudiated notes went bankrupt, others managed to keep in business with great difficulty, and still others absorbed their losses and kept silent. For years, however, lawyers continued to have a banquet as they took on cases stemming from the great failure.

Passage of a federal bankruptcy law in 1842 helped wipe out the tangle of debts made worthless by the failure and depression.

Merchants and debtors who had been hamstrung by the old obligations were able to slough off those millstones and get a fresh start.

But nothing in the way of legal relief helped a number of the other prominent men. Clary was not the only figure who had disappeared completely from the Buffalo scene. Hiram Pratt, who played his devious role in Rathbun's downfall, died in 1840. Pratt himself had been greatly hurt by the economic contraction. He had controlled hundreds of thousands of dollars, but left an estate of $75,000. Some $5,000 of this sum was in unpaid accounts for Rathbun goods that he had purchased from the assignees. Pratt's brother-in-law, Orlando Allen, who had also suffered in the cataclysm, succeeded him as president of the Bank of Buffalo, but his best efforts could not keep the bank from foundering in 1841.

Ebenezer Johnson, damaged by the failure and the depression, had removed to Tennessee where he was vainly trying, in the few years of life that remained to him, to recoup his fortunes in the iron business. Dr. John W. Clark, who had been one of the richest of the "eleven endorsers," was broken financially and relied on the bounty of friends. Alanson Palmer, once the buoyant multimillionaire, and for many the living symbol of boom times, was now to be seen on the streets in shabby clothes. Hopelessly insolvent, the beaten Palmer was headed for the poorhouse and then the insane asylum, where he died many years later. He was admitted to the Poor House by a city poor master who had once been a Palmer employee.

Judge Rochester survived the financial cataclysm, but he burned to death off North Carolina during an 1838 shipping tragedy. General Porter, who had moved to his new mansion at Niagara Falls opposite the crumbling foundations of Rathbun's great hotel, died there in 1844. Benjamin Barton, Jr., Dr. Cyrenius Chapin, and many other of the early settlers were in their graves.

But most of those whom Rathbun had known still lived, some as wealthy as, or even wealthier, than they had been. Others were damaged by the depression but not greatly so. Sheldon Thompson, who served as mayor in 1840, was rich and dealing in upper Great Lakes real estate. Lewis F. Allen was adding to his wealth. Thomas C. Love was the Surrogate, and as such, in a good position for wheeling and dealing. Millard Fillmore, who had been prominent in Congress as a Clay Whig, had returned to Buffalo to campaign for the governorship. Joseph Dart, Jr., was growing wealthier on the proceeds of grain storage and shipment, and he was honored throughout the world as the builder of the first automated grain elevator.

Barker, the district attorney whose invective had rasped on Rathbun's untoughened sensibilities in the early days of the failure, had become attorney general of the state, partly because of the prominence he had gained in the case. Bela Coe retired to live in quiet elegance on the proceeds of his investments. Coe resided in the stately home Pratt had built for himself before his death. William A. Moseley, a close friend of the Coes, served as a state senator and congressman, and was destined later to succeed Bela briefly as the widowed Mrs. Coe's second husband. Rathbun's stage agent, Edward L. Stevenson, prospered as a livery proprietor, partly because he came into possession at a low cost of many of the horses and coaches Rathbun had owned. Isaac T. Hathaway, Rathbun's other stage agent, was for a time superintendent of the Niagara Falls Railroad, but eventually had been reduced to the job of constable. Albert S. Merrill, one of Rathbun's chief foremen, was receiver for the defunct City Bank.

Though Rathbun never displayed any vindictiveness, he would have been only human to be pleased at news he heard about his one-time associate, David Evans, the man who sent him to jail. Even while the Batavia magnate was testifying against him in his first trial, Evans was undergoing an ordeal himself. While auditing its books to wind up its affairs, agents for the Dutch capitalists of the Holland Company had found him unable to give a satisfactory accounting. They discovered that Evans's personal investments, speculations, and operations were so involved with those of the company that they could not be disentangled. His forced resignation as agent was received in July 1837, and a month later he had to pledge his stocks, lands, and bonds to the company to pay an estimated $316,000 claim. Two years later, with prices and values still falling, Evans was forced to assign all his property to three trustees. This act precipitated another two years of arguments and suits. Eventually all the assigned properties were sold and the trustees were released without a serious loss to anyone, adding honor to Evans's name, but leaving him much poorer.

ᏋᎦᎤᏏ

The few years immediately after Rathbun's release were difficult for him. Without money and civil rights, and with no personal influence in Buffalo, he found that he had many vocal supporters but few real friends. He and Alice lived in greatly reduced circumstances, maintaining themselves by renting rooms. When he ventured out infrequently, he remained the properly dressed, stiff, and thin figure people always remembered, but, it was said, his face seemed harder and his affability more strained than in the old days.

Having failed to get Governor Bouck to lift the prison stigma from Rathbun, a few of his supporters were preparing new appeals for a full pardon, with restoration of civil rights, to Governor Silas Wright, who had been victorious over the Whig candidate, Rathbun's former assignee, Millard Fillmore. Inevitably, by this time Rathbun was becoming discouraged at the prospect that he would not be able to resume a place in society.

As if all this were not bad enough, Benjamin's home life could hardly be said to be pleasant. Alice continued hopeful of a better day ahead, but the work of the boardinghouse was tiring for the aging woman. Now as well, constantly reproaching them, was Loomis, their greatest failure. The son's moral lapses and personal eccentricities were by this time the mark of his adult character. His carousing and drinking had made him notorious. To Mrs. Rathbun's growing agony, Loomis openly charged his father with ruining his life. In his drunken frenzies, Loomis upbraided Rathbun with the prison record, which, he said, had wrecked his own future and made him an outcast among his contemporaries.

Rathbun was at first shocked by these outbursts. He threatened to forbid Loomis to stay in the house. But Mrs. Rathbun intervened, and Benjamin then tried to forgive his son at least until the next and more violent scene. Finally, while he let Loomis live with them when the young man wished, Benjamin completely abandoned trying to influence him.

During all these years, Rathbun had kept in touch with two of his first cousins in New York City. Robert C. and Aaron H. Rathbone, as they spelled their surname, were the sons of Aaron, the twin brother of Moses. The two brothers were well-to-do financially and socially. They had recently left the grocery business their father had founded decades before, and gone into the brokerage and insurance business in Wall Street.

Through their connections, they learned of an opening for their cousin in another field. Rathbun's New York cousins urged him to leave Buffalo, and generously promised to help him get a fresh start in New York. By that time, the decision was easy. Benjamin was sure that Buffalo offered him nothing further. Even if his civil rights were restored, he could never live down his past in western New York.

In 1845, Rathbun went to New York City where he was soon joined by his wife and son and by Rathbun Allen. Henry Hawkins, the loyal friend and employee, who had not found much to do with himself after the collapse of his friend's empire, came, too. Bolstered by his cousins' confidence and kindness, Benjamin began to regain some of his self-confidence. Moreover, word came that the efforts of his Buffalo friends finally paid off. Governor Wright had restored his civil rights, and thus made it possible for him to return to business.

His cousins convinced him that New York needed additional hotel accommodations, and that he should start a new hotel, a job for which he was thoroughly fitted, and where his name perhaps still might carry some prestige. If he could create a luxury hotel, as he had long ago in Buffalo, he might be able to attract the city's best trade.

Through acquaintances of his cousins, Benjamin proceeded methodically with his plans. On Broadway, at Courtland Street, he found some old buildings that he believed could be readily adapted to hotel purposes. Two of them, from 155 to 165 Broadway, could easily be linked and would do for a start.

He rented the main five-story building at 163–165 Broadway from Dr. Parmely, a wealthy Bond Street dentist. The adjoining building, 155 to 161 Broadway, which for years had been conducted as a fashionable boardinghouse, was ideally suited for hotel purposes.

At relatively small expense for repainting and furbishing, "Rathbun's Hotel" was opened on April 1, 1846. The main entrance led to reading and lounging rooms. Parlors for ladies and a dining hall were on the second floor, and the sleeping rooms were above. Rathbun Allen was the desk clerk, and Hawkins assumed his familiar post as steward.

Even though lower Manhattan was losing some of its charm and becoming commercial and congested, Rathbun's Hotel was received with fanfare by New York's knowing public. Upstate newspapers printed notices of the opening, and the name attracted upstate travelers who remembered the old Eagle of the 1820s.

The new hotel did well in the first few years. Its outlook was so promising in 1847 that Rathbun leased the adjoining building at 3 Courtland Street, and linked it to the Broadway buildings by a long corridor. The addition gave the hotel three hundred sleeping rooms, making it one of the city's largest at the time.

In these first years in New York City, Rathbun's attracted a respectable, elite trade. Its dining room became a place where it was good form to dine and entertain. Wealthy travelers found the hotel a proper spot to stay. Social columns of the New York newspapers chronicled the marriages and catered receptions held in its parlors, a testimony to the talents of Hawkins. A popular travel guide had this to say of the hotel in 1848:

New and magnificent furniture; style and fitting and furnishing different from others; its enterprising proprietor is constantly engaged in addition and improvements, and it is now at the mark of perfection. The public are acquainted with Mr. Rathbun's capacity for keeping a first class hotel.

Rathbun spent all his time trying to make the hotel a success, using all the skills his experience had taught him. But his age made the work that much harder. Because New York expenses were high, the profits never came up to expectations.

Tragedy dogged the Rathbuns in New York. Loomis, more isolated and resentful than ever, became a binge drinker. He was deep in an alcoholic dementia when he slashed his throat before the horrified eyes of his mother. When she tried to prevent him from using the razor again, Loomis lashed out at her. She lay near death for days. Rathbun committed Loomis to the asylum on Blackwell's Island, where he died within four years. During this same period, Rathbun Allen, whose testimony convicted his uncle, fell to the Broadway pavement from a fourth-story window, an apparent suicide.

The hotel itself faltered. Rathbun had once known how to make money as an innkeeper, but the rules for boom times in a frontier town did not travel well to New York where he held no monopoly. Luxury appointments and lavish entertaining promised a good return, but only if the hotel could be kept full. The hotel fell into decline and became shabby at a time when smart new shops were becoming established in his neighborhood. By 1851, almost penniless and without a home, he eased himself out of the hotel partnership. There was one final anguished moment when Henry Hawkins, Rathbun's longest and most loyal friend, also had to leave. Hawkins went to San Francisco where he would become the only black employee at the U.S. Mint. Rathbun went on to manage a series of New York City hotels, each more modest than the last.

In 1860, Rathbun received word from Batavia that his father, nearly ninety, had died. After Benjamin left Buffalo, Moses and his third wife and their daughter had lived for a time in Batavia. There the daughter married a distant cousin, G. W. Rathbone. When the young couple removed to Watertown, New York, they took her parents with them. After his wife died in 1857, Moses returned to Batavia to spend his last years. The old man's restless life was finally over.

Benjamin's last job, obtained when he was seventy years old, was to operate the Broadway Hotel, a small, four-story structure at the southwest corner of West 42d Street, which he took over on August 20, 1861. He conducted this hotel competently but without distinction. During the time he ran it, the place was never rated among the city's noted hotels. The building was old, and the location did not attract the elite trade Rathbun long ago had been so adept at serving. Work as he might, he was too old to see to all the details he had taken care of at the Eagle years before. He kept on the job night and day for eight solid years, with the increasingly frail Alice overseeing the housekeeping part of the hotel.

Near the end of the 1860s Rathbun began corresponding with an associate of much earlier days in Buffalo, David E. Merrill, who was himself now an elderly resident of Toledo. Merrill had been proprietor of the Steamboat Hotel near the docks when Rathbun owned the Eagle, which was then at the height of its fame. In his retirement he had become interested in Toledo's history, and he wrote to ask Rathbun for information about the city's earliest times.

This voice from so distant a part of his past brought back touching memories for Rathbun. The few Buffalonians he had seen in later years were young travelers. To them he was merely a relic of times about which oral tradition occasionally spoke. The older ones generally avoided him, and most of his strong public supporters had been in their graves for years.

Merrill had not been one of Rathbun's intimates. He was unsuccessful at the Steamboat, at a time when Rathbun was rising toward the peak of his career. But his first letter moved Rathbun.

The few letters Rathbun wrote to Merrill suggest a tired old man longing for friendship and for the opportunity to call up his memories, even though his past was both troubled and filled with tragedy. He expressed appreciation upon receipt of pictures of Merrill's family. Rathbun brushed aside a request for pictures of his wife and himself, and then, in his last letter, the man who often seemed such a vague and ambiguous image to those who first came into contact with him admitted that they never had any taken. No photographic likenesses of Rathbun, in fact, are now known to exist.

In the first letter to Merrill he described his early days in Toledo. His next letter, obviously written after Merrill had sent him a newspaper article he had published that contained Rathbun's reminiscences of early Toledo, expressed annoyance that the information had been published. Moreover, Rathbun contended that the account had contained errors (which were long afterward perpetuated in histories of early Toledo). But he ended nonetheless on a friendly note. "If that publication of old events was interesting to you or any other friend, I am satisfied, although I have no special desire to appear in public print." He wrote this on his eightieth birthday and added that "I am well and healthy for which I cannot be sufficiently grateful."

Alice's health, however, finally failed. When she died in 1871, Rathbun wrote to Merrill what was probably the most unguarded letter of his life.

> We have lived together almost sixty years—with the strongest affection for each other that ever existed between two for so long a time—strengthening with time—no one can have but a faint idea of my suffering. Others have lived and have been separated. But few have lived together so long as we have and none could have a stronger affection. It seems harder to be left alone at this advanced age than in earlier life. . . . We lived for each other and now it seems I have no one to live for—neither child nor grandchild.

Her death finally made him seriously consider retiring. Eight months later he sold his furniture at the hotel and moved to a cousin's farm at Fort Washington. For the first time since his return from prison he was not consumingly busy. His reflections now took on the language of a eulogy. Reminding Merrill that he was eighty-two years old, he pointed out that his life spanned every president of the Republic. He could remember accounts of George Washington's death as though the event were yesterday. He was a passenger on the first North American vessel moved by steam. But never given to overstatement, let alone to self-revelation, he wrote Merrill, by way of summary, "I have lived in a very eventful period." Eight weeks later, Rathbun was dead.

The *New York Tribune* carried a report of the funeral. The services were "very affecting and sad." "[The] kind words of the clergyman evidently brought to the minds of every listener the strange, eventful history of the departed." Those who filed past the casket were said to have remarked that in death Rathbun "wore a peaceful expression." Victorian convention demanded this comment. But when applied to Benjamin Rathbun, whose life had been once so propelled by an ambition he himself gave no evidence of understanding, and in consequence had been so marked by protracted crisis, perhaps in this case the observation really did have meaning.

17

"Half a Century Too Soon"

Rathbun's death evoked a number of reminiscences and efforts at searching for larger meanings. The *Tribune*, the only New York newspaper where slumbering memories had been jogged by his obituary notice, carried a long summary and interpretation of his life on its editorial page. This was widely quoted verbatim by newspaper editors throughout the country, most of whom themselves were now too young to recall the years of Rathbun's notoriety.

Although containing some factual errors, the *Tribune*'s editorial struck the right notes:

> There died, yesterday at Fort Washington, a man who six and thirty years ago was notorious throughout the land as the one man whose forgeries, up to that period, had never in the history of crime been surpassed in magnitude of amount, or skill of conception and execution. . . . They rose to millions and, for several years, were carried on with a celerity, persuasion and success that were amazing; nor in that particular specialty of crime has a successor reached the aggregate of enormity attained by him.

Recounting his start in Buffalo, the extension of his business into stage coaching, building and land speculation, the editorial continued:

> For the first time in the history of the State a fever of speculation broke out which for universality and wildness has never been approached by any other city in the Union. Rathbun was in everything; nothing daunted him; his example was so infectious that the gravest

and most timorous money grabbers were drawn into the vortex and in a night made fabulous fortunes on paper.

After briefly describing his trial, conviction, and punishment, the *Tribune* concluded:

The private life of this remarkable man was from his early manhood singularly irreproachable. He was modest to a fault, strictly temperate, never smoked or chewed, never gambled, kept no equipage, had no acquaintance with disreputable people, avoided public places, indulged in no extravagances but devoted himself assiduously to his business. He had few acquaintances, fewer friends, no companions. To the past, he never alluded. He realized to the full the results of his acts and meekly accepted the situation. Silently, patiently, uncomplainingly, he plodded on his weary, cheerless way until finally at the ripe old age of 82, himself and his crimes almost forgotten, he gently faded away.

This editorial provoked instant criticism, proof that the Master Builder's life and the meanings that could be made of it would continue to evoke sharp feelings. A letter to the *Tribune* signed by "R" (perhaps the cousin with whom Rathbun had lived) declared that the writer had Rathbun's solemn word that he had never committed a forgery in his life and that neither that crime nor any other was ever perpetrated with his knowledge or consent. Rathbun made Herculean efforts, the letter said, to retire the forged paper, and his efforts became part of the "network of circumstantial evidence" that brought about his conviction. Two previous trials in Buffalo, based on other paper, resulted in his acquittal because, the writer declared incorrectly, the paper was genuine.

"R" said that Rathbun had always maintained that he was convicted because of a conspiracy, and that he had intended sometime to write a complete statement to prove it. "He was the victim of the frauds of other people and nine-tenths of those in Buffalo years ago believed that." He said that soon after Rathbun began operating his first hotel in New York, Rathbun was subpoenaed as a prosecution witness to prove the genuineness of a $5,000 note, which was alleged by the defense, representing a deceased endorser, to have been forged. But, it was related, when the defendant in that process learned that Rathbun could testify, now that his civil rights had been restored, he immediately paid the note in full, knowing his case could not stand up in court to the light of the truth Rathbun could cast on it. Said "R" of Rathbun's crimes:

> The truth is that a large number of these endorsers, the magnitude of the amounts covered and the influence of the parties, made the conviction of Mr. Rathbun a matter of necessity. Every one of his genuine endorsers set up the pretense that their names were forged which like the cry of mad dog affected all the paper afloat, both genuine and spurious, and it was this that gave Benjamin Rathbun the name of the "greatest forger the world ever saw."

In Buffalo, only one newspaper, the *Express*, contributed anything consequential on the death of the man who had been one of the city's greatest early figures.

> He is described as "the man of the time," "the builder of Buffalo," "the ruling power of her destiny," etc., and it might perhaps be added her betrayer as well, for it was he who committed the crime of forgery, involving in its results a score or more of her best and wealthiest business men and an amount of money in excess of two millions of dollars.

After summarizing his career, the *Express* paid the ritual nod to the view that *hubris* holds the key to explaining Rathbun. Rathbun's life seemed self-evidently to be an object lesson for a culture needing to set out some moral boundaries around men's ambitions, even as it lauded that ambition in the competitive marketplace. The *Express* also seemed perplexed by the difference between the upright public character and the private scheming of ambitious men such as Rathbun.

> We cannot but note how true to nature is the story of his life. There are no distortions or discrepancies, nothing marvelous or inconceivable; and yet there is a justice righteously poetic, a truth stranger than fiction. A man possessed of wonderful energy and ambition meets, as he deserves, with almost unbounded success; he helps himself and his followers. But allowing his ambition to rule him, unaided by counsel of higher virtue, he makes one fatal mistake; and the vanities of his position and the admiration of his weaker associates being in the scale against a seemingly small lapse of conscience, he makes the easy transit from error to crime and commits a felony. Although men were foolish in their adulation, they were just in their censure and forty years ago convicted and punished him.

The depleted ranks of his Buffalo contemporaries sprang to life when news of his death appeared, and a struggle now took place to understand that life. A long letter, signed "K" and printed in the Buffalo *Courier,* praised Rathbun as a gentleman and a kind and obliging neighbor. But "K," too, would have inner and outer man at odds. The letter, which indicated a close acquaintance with the Rathbun affair, declared that never at any time was it proven that Rathbun did the actual forging. Rathbun was not convicted at the first trial because there was no evidence that he executed the forgeries. But, "K" continued, the subsequent trial proved that he had inspired the whole scheme. "K" even recalled Rathbun's difficulty in Otsego County so many years before, and believed it suggested Benjamin had long been inclined to crime, but was a master at concealing his true self.

Also coming forward with a viewpoint was Lewis F. Allen, the last survivor of the "eleven endorsers" and one of the two living assignees (the other of whom, former President Fillmore, said nothing publicly). Allen now wrote a series of letters. These defended Allen and his associates against implications that it was they somehow who had been corrupt. He declared that Evans and Pratt did not know of the forgeries and would have been as guilty as Rathbun if they had. In this he conveniently neglected to mention the matter of the agreement among the assignees, to which he was party, to hush up the forgeries. Nor was his recollection of certain other details in accord with contemporary accounts.

Allen's outburst was followed by one signed "Old Genesee," which declared that if Rathbun were not guilty, some of the most respected men of Buffalo were perjurers, which the writer refused to believe. He recalled Evans's loan to support Rathbun's paper just a short time before the failure as proof that Evans did not know.

Another "K" letter now criticized Allen, and Allen's reply accused the writer of a refusal to grant that the endorsers, too, had suffered from the situation. They were harassed, persecuted, and three died prematurely, he said. Other letters, such as one from a man who identified himself as a former clerk in one of the Rathbun stores, rallied to Rathbun's defense. These writers absolved him of many of the charges, one going so far as to dredge up again the Otsego County debacle, in which, it was said, Rathbun was completely innocent of wrongdoing. The fault for this was laid at Lyman's door! Obviously the writer did not know, or had forgotten, that Lyman was then too young to have been responsible.

The facts, therefore, remained in dispute long years after, and among some people they never lost their power to upset and to anger.

Rathbun's contribution to the built environment of the Niagara Frontier was much less ambiguous than the facts and meanings of his life. Streets he laid out, buildings he erected, even his grander schemes for development, including the waterpower and town at Niagara, all were fundamentally sound. Structures still standing into the twentieth century—and now at least one on the eve of the twenty-first[1]—attest to the quality of his construction, even though many of the best buildings he erected quickly disappeared after the 1890s to make way for the more spacious commercial structures made possible through modern construction techniques.

The Eagle, where he began his Buffalo career, went downhill rapidly as a popular hotel, because of the competition of the adjoining American Hotel, itself Rathbun's largest finished construction project. The Eagle survived the great fire that gutted the American in March of 1850, and afterward its lower floors were turned into stores. Its end came ignominiously when it was blown up on January 25, 1865, in a desperate attempt to halt another conflagration that destroyed the rebuilt American and leveled a whole Main Street block. Mrs. Isaac Harrington, widow of the man to whom Rathbun had first sold the Eagle and who had brought it back after the failure, still owned the old building when it vanished in a giant flash of gunpowder.

The great Niagara Falls Hotel that Rathbun projected and for which he had erected the foundations and part of the first floor was finally completed by a new company in 1853–54. Named the "International," it was the best hotel at the scenic resort and famous with travelers throughout the world, until it burned in 1918. The Niagara Falls Eagle had served as an annex to the International until it too was consumed by flame, and the larger hotel was extended to cover the site.

In Buffalo, the great Exchange that Rathbun projected was never built. Unfortunately, because he had leveled nearly all the buildings on the block just before his failure, the land was unoccupied for a long time. The buildings that were ultimately erected on the site were poorer than those he had razed. The Eagle Street Theater burned to the ground in June 1852, right after the famed Lola Montez appeared on its stage. The great monument to Commodore Perry,

---

1. The Title Guarantee Company. See chap. 9, n. 1, above.

which Rathbun had sponsored, was not raised for nearly a century, when it was finally erected on a smaller scale and in a different place. Many of the great mansions Rathbun built were long in use, a tribute to their designer and builder, until changing times and newer tastes doomed them to demolition.

Buffalo spread and spread, overrunning and absorbing its one-time competitor, Black Rock, in 1853. At the time of Rathbun's death, its population exceeded 120,000. Despite this growth and the realization later of many of Rathbun's projects, land prices in many sections of the city would never again compare with those reached during the boom years of 1835–36. Locally, at least, there would never again be an orgy of speculation of the type inspired by Rathbun and his peers.

Caught up intimately in questions of guilt and innocence, blame and exoneration, few of Rathbun's critics had enough perspective to recognize him as a product of his times who had made an impression and a contribution far beyond most of his contemporaries, but was limited by the values and models of the times in living up to his own best ideals. Most were too consumed by partisan feeling when it came to Rathbun. Samuel DeVeaux, the Niagara Falls merchant who greatly benefited from Rathbun's foresight, however, was the author of one of the best contemporary appraisals, written while Rathbun was in prison. He said that Rathbun was a farsighted businessman who saw the practical outlines of the future more clearly than his associates, but did not seem fully to know how to arrive at that future.

Although he used different words, local historian Samuel M. Welch, writing his recollections in the 1890s, articulately confirmed DeVeaux' estimate of Rathbun, not as a seer so much as a farsighted, practical and cunning entrepreneur: "Through the magnitude and boldness of his operations, he became the central figure round which people revolved. The truth is, he was not a visionary man; his schemes were based on prophetic wisdom; but he lived just half a century too soon."

Bibliography
Index

Bibliography
ROGER WHITMAN

$\bigcirc$nly sources that provided substantial information are listed below. Documents, books, and other materials examined that were merely of incidental utility have been excluded. Among the books omitted are numerous family genealogies; the extensive literature on the Morgan case; complete runs of the directories of Buffalo, Brooklyn, and New York City; most of the Niagara Falls guidebooks; local histories for Windham County, Connecticut; the city of Toledo, and Lucas, Sandusky, Ottawa and Licking counties, Ohio; the city of Paterson, New Jersey; the city of Erie, Pennsylvania; and Cayuga, Chenango, Cortland, Madison, Oneida, Orleans, Otsego, Seneca, and Steuben counties, New York.

Unpublished Records

Buffalo Historical Society:* Rathbun Papers; Ira A. Blossom Papers; St. Paul's Church records; Erie County Papers; scrapbooks; Farnum Notebooks; Peter B. Porter Papers; Augustus Porter Papers; early Niagara County Assessment Rolls; Notes on early Buffalonians by Dr. F. H. Severance; Buffalo Obituary and Marriage Indexes; Rathbun Statement to Creditors, Aug. 31, 1836; sketch of Henry Hawkins by John Lord Love; typescript of part of Eph. M. Daggett MSS.; miscellaneous papers and records of Buffalo and Niagara Falls Railroad, Bank of Niagara, and Niagara City Association; newspaper indexes.

Buffalo Public Library: Scrapbooks.

Canandaigua Historical Society: Index to death records.

County Clerks' Offices (deeds, mortgages, and miscellaneous records) and

---

* Now known as the Buffalo and Erie County Historical Society.

the Surrogate's records of Erie, Niagara, Ontario, Genesee, Monroe, Seneca, Cayuga, Otsego, and New York counties.

Court Records of Erie, Niagara, Ontario, and Otsego Counties.

Library of Congress: Nicholas Biddle Papers; Francis Granger Papers.

National Archives: Census records 1790–1850; post office mail route books for western New York, 1818–40; congressional and executive documents relating to postal contracts, 16th to 25th congresses.

New York Historical Society: W. John Quinn Collection of Research and Pictures of New York City Hotels, 1800–99.

Maps

Peter B. Porter's Map and Land Book in Buffalo Historical Society; early New York State maps in the Library of Congress; early locality maps in the County Clerks' offices in Erie, Niagara, and Genesee counties.

Newspapers

Complete files of early Buffalo, Batavia, Boston, Canandaigua, Cooperstown, New York City, Philadelphia, and Rochester newspapers examined in collections of: Buffalo Historical Society; Buffalo Public Library; Canandaigua Public Library; Congressional Library; New York Historical Society; New York State Historical Association; and Rochester Public Library.

Books

Adams, Edward Dean. *Niagara Power,* vol. 1 (Niagara Falls, 1927).

American Almanac, The. 1834–40 (Boston, 1834–40).

Atkins, Barton. *Modern Antiquities* (Buffalo, 1898).

Allen, T. F., *Gazetteer of New York* (Philadelphia, 1836).

Auburn Historical Society. *Collections,* vol. 7, 1889 (Auburn, 1889).

Bagg, Moses M. *The Pioneers of Utica* (Utica, 1877).

Bailey, W. T., *Richfield Springs and Vicinity* (N.Y., 1874).

Baker, George E. (ed.). *Seward's Works,* vol. 2 (Boston, 1884).

Barber, John W., and Howe, Henry S. *Historical Collections of the State of New York* (N.Y., 1841).

Beardsley, Levi. *Reminiscences* (N.Y., 1852).

Becker, Philip (comp.). *Statistics Relating to the Government of the City of Buffalo* (Buffalo, 1896).

Beers, F. W. (ed.). *Gazetteer and Biographical Record of Genesee County, N.Y.* (Syracuse, 1890).

Black Rock (Village of). *A Concise View of Black Rock Including a Map and Schedule of Property Belonging to the Niagara City Association* (Black Rock, 1836).

Black Rock Harbor Co. *Documents Relating to the Western Termination of the Erie Canal* (Black Rock, 1822).

Boston History Co., comp. *Landmarks of Monroe County, N.Y.* (Boston, 1895).

Brown, William. *A Four Years Residence in the U.S. and Canada* (Leeds, 1849).

Buffalo Courier. *Buffalo Old and New—A Supplement to the Buffalo Courier* (Nov. 11, 1906).

Buffalo Express. *Fifth Annual Festival of the Old Settlers* (Buffalo, 1866).

Buffalo Historical Society. *Publications*, vols. 1–34, (Buffalo, 1879–1947).

Cayuga County Historical Society. *Collections*, vol. 6 (Auburn, 1887).

Chancery Court. *Hiram Pratt, Joseph Clary and Lewis F. Allen, Complainants* vs. *Benjamin Rathbun and His Creditors, Defendants* (Mar. 3, 1837).

Conover, George S. *History of Ontario County, N.Y.* (Syracuse, 1893).

Cooley, John C. *Rathbone Genealogy* (Syracuse, 1898).

Cotterall, Ralph C. H. *Second National Bank of the U.S.* (Chicago, 1903).

DeVeaux, S. *Falls of Niagara or Tourist's Guide to This Wonder of Nature* (Buffalo, 1839).

Traveler's Own Guide to Saratoga Springs, etc. (Buffalo, 1841)
———. (Buffalo, 1844).

Disturnell, John. *The Travelers Guide Through the State of N.Y.* (N.Y., 1836).

Gazetteer of the State of N.Y. (Albany 1842).

Doty, Lockwood R. (ed.). *History of the Genesee Country* (Chicago, 1922).

Earle, Alice M. *Stage Coach and Tavern Days* (London, 1900).

Evstaphieve, A. A. (secretary), etc. *Plan of Association of Creditors of B. Rathbun* (Buffalo, 1836).

Faxon, C. *The Buffalo Almanac for 1834* (Buffalo, 1834).

Fitzpatrick, John C. (ed.). *Autobiography of Martin Van Buren*. In American Historical Association, *Annual Report, 1918* (Washington D.C., 1920).

Foster, James F. *Republic Metalware Co. 1836–1909* (Buffalo, 1909).

French, J. H., *Gazetteer of the State of N.Y.* (Syracuse, 1860).

Fulton, Deoch F. (ed.). *New York to Niagara, 1836—The Journal of Thomas S. Woodcock* (N.Y., 1936).

Gordon, T. F. *Gazetteer of N.Y.* (Philadelphia, 1836).

Granger, J. Albert. *History of Canandaigua* (Canandaigua, 1876).

Hall, Capt. Basil. *Travels in North America*, vol. 1 (Philadelphia, 1829).

Hall, Henry. *History of Auburn, Cayuga County* (Auburn, 1859).

(Heacock, R. B.). *An Exposition of Some of the Frauds Practiced upon the Indians* (Buffalo, 1839).

Hill, Henry Wayland. *Municipality of Buffalo, N.Y.* (N.Y., 1923).

Hinckley, A. *The Travelers Illustrated Pocket Guide and Hotel Directory* (N.Y., 1848).

Holmes, Oliver W. *The Turnpike Era* (in vol. 5 of History of State of N.Y., ed. A. C. Flick)(N.Y., 1934).

Ingraham, Joseph Wentworth. *Manual for the Use of Visitors to the Falls of Niagara* (Buffalo, 1834).

Johnson, Crisfield. *Centennial History of Erie County, N.Y.* (Buffalo, 1876).

Ketchum, William. *An Authentic and Comprehensive History of Buffalo* (Buffalo, 1864–65).

Letchworth, William P. *Samuel F. Pratt* (Buffalo, 1874).

Lord, John C. *Memoirs*, comp. by order of the Church Sessions (Buffalo, 1878).

McIntosh, W. H. *History of Ontario County, N.Y.* (Philadelphia, 1877).

Milliken, Charles F. *History of Ontario County, N.Y.* (N.Y., 1911).

Nichols, T. L. *Forty Years of American Life* (London, 1874).

Journal in Jail (Buffalo, 1840).

Vindication of the So-Called Clique (Buffalo, 1839).

No author. *History of Niagara County, N.Y.* (N.Y., 1878).

No author. *Souvenir History* (Lockport, 1902).

O'Callaghan, E. B. *Documentary History of the State of N.Y.* (Albany, 1849–51).

Old Settlers of Buffalo. *The Old Settlers Festival* (Buffalo, 1867).

Orr, J. W. illustrator. *Pictorial Guide to the Falls of Niagara* (Buffalo, 1842).

Parsons, Horatio A. *A Guide to Travelers Visiting the Falls of Niagara* (Buffalo, 1835).

Steele's Book of Niagara Falls, eighth ed. (Buffalo, 1840).

Peck, William Farley. *History of Rochester and Monroe County* (N.Y., 1908).

Poore, Ben. Perley. *The Political Register and Congressional Directory* (Boston, 1878).

Schlesinger, Arthur M., Jr. *The Age of Jackson* (Boston, 1945).

Seaver, William. *A Historical Sketch of the Village of Batavia* (Batavia, 1849).

Seward, Frederick W., ed. *Autobiography of William H. Seward* (N.Y., 1877).

Smith, H. Perry. *History of Buffalo and Erie County* (Syracuse, 1884).

Spafford, Horatio Gates. *A Gazetteer of the State of N.Y.* (Albany, 1813).

Gazetteer of the State of N.Y. (Albany, 1824).

Stokes, I. N. Phelps. *Iconography of Manhattan Island* (N.Y., 1928).

Thomas, C. F. S. *The Manufacturing Interests of the City of Buffalo* (Buffalo, 1866).

Turner, Orasmus. *History of the Pioneer Settlement of Phelps and Gorhams Purchase and Morris' Reserve* (Rochester, 1852).

Vandewater, Robert J. *The Tourist for 1834* (N.Y., 1834).

Van Durzee Bros. *Semi Centennial Review of Buffalo* (Buffalo, n.d.).

Wakeman, W. S. *Batavia, N.Y., in Pictures* (Batavia, 1902).

Ward, Dr. Henry K. *Annals of Richfield* (Richfield Springs, N.Y., 1898).

Weed, Harriet A. (ed.) *Autobiography of Thurlow Weed* (Boston, 1883).

Weed, Thurlow. *Stage Coach Traveling 46 Years Ago* (Albany, 1870).

Welch, Samuel M. *Home History: Recollections of Buffalo* (Buffalo, 1891).

Williams, Clara T. *Joseph Ellicott and Stories of the Holland Purchase* (N.Y., 1931).

Williamson, Jefferson. *The American Hotel* (N.Y., 1930).

Wilmer, Merton M. *History of the Niagara Frontier* (Chicago, 1931).

Wilson, James Harrison. *Life of Charles A. Dana* (N.Y., 1907).

Index